The Geneva Protocol

by

DAVID HUNTER MILLER

New York
THE MACMILLAN COMPANY
1925

PRINTED IN THE UNITED STATES OF AMERICA.

FOREWORD

The sources and history of the Protocol of Geneva of course go far back of its date, October 2, 1924. I have not attempted to trace them except in so far as they have a direct bearing on my legal study of the Document itself.

The form of the Protocol of Geneva is certainly not yet finally written; consideration of its legal aspects is perhaps therefore all the more desirable at this time.

The Protocol of Geneva is one chapter in the history of the League of Nations, the history of international relations of our time.

D. H. M.

New York City, December, 1924.

CONTENTS.

vii

ANNEXES.

The Geneva Protocol

The Geneva Protocol

CHAPTER I.

THE PROTOCOL OF GENEVA.

The Covenant of the League of Nations[a] lays down the principle that national armaments should be reduced to the lowest point consistent with national safety and the enforcement by common action of international obligations.

Thus, in the Covenant, the problem of disarmament[b] and the problem of security are viewed as correlative problems. Their study has gone on in the League of Nations since its organization. During this same period there has been widespread and increasing public interest in the matter.

The theory of the Treaties of Peace was that the disarmament of Germany and her allies was preliminary to a general reduction of armaments the world over.[c] Except as the result of the Washington Conference, and by that to only a very limited extent, there has been almost no reduction or limitation of armaments by

---

a. Article 8. The text of the Covenant is Annex A, p. 117.

b. Those who criticize the use of the word "disarmament" as meaning a reduction or limitation of armaments, should consult the dictionaries. The Standard Dictionary gives the following definition:

> "The act of disarming; especially, the reduction of a military or naval establishment to a peace footing."

The Century Dictionary gives this:

> "The act of disarming; the reduction of military and naval forces from a war to a peace footing; as 'a general disarmament is much to be desired.'"

The Century Dictionary also gives the following quotation as an instance from Lowe's Life of Bismarck:

> "He (Napoleon) in a fit of irresolution broached in Berlin the question of mutual disarmament."

c. See, for example, the preamble to the Military, Naval and Air Clauses of the Treaty of Versailles: "In order to render possible the initiation of a general limitation of the armaments of all nations, Germany undertakes strictly to observe the military, naval and air clauses which follow."

1

international agreement since the war.[a] Such lessening of armaments as has taken place has been by voluntary national action.

The study of these questions during the last few years has brought about a much clearer understanding of them, both in the minds of statesmen and generally; and the various proposals that have been made have been the subject of detailed and elaborate criticism from all sides.

The latest of these proposals is the paper which is called The Protocol of Geneva.[b] The Protocol of Geneva is, however, much more than a proposal. It has the active support of a considerable number of Governments.[c] It was unanimously recommended for acceptance by the Fifth Assembly of the League of Nations. It deserves the serious attention of all thoughtful minds.

The object of the Protocol of Geneva cannot be better stated than in the words of its authors:[d]

> "to facilitate the reduction and limitation of armaments provided for in Article 8 of the Covenant of the League of Nations by guaranteeing the security of States through the development of methods for the pacific settlement of all international disputes and the effective condemnation of aggressive war."

While this Protocol is, and doubtless always will be, called "The Protocol of Geneva," its official name is "Protocol for the Pacific Settlement of International Disputes."[e]

---

a. The Treaty of Lausanne (A. J. I. L., Vol. XVIII, Supp., pp. 58, 64) with its provisions for demilitarized zones, etc., and the Convention for the Limitation of Armaments in Central America of February 7, 1923 (A. J. I. L., Vol. XVII, Supp. 1923, pp. 114, *et seq.*), are to be noted in this regard.

b. For the text in French and English, see Annex B, p. 132.

c. Sixteen States have signed the Protocol and it has been ratified by Czecho-Slovakia.

d. See Report to the Fifth Assembly, Annex C, p. 156, at p. 164. This Report of MM. Benes and Politis is a notable document, worthy of the ability and learning of the two Rapporteurs.

e. It is herein generally called "the Protocol."

CHAPTER II.

There are various possible points of approach to the consideration of the Protocol of Geneva. In view of the importance of the document, doubtless all such methods are useful. Indeed, in the discussion of such a paper, it is perhaps hardly possible exclusively to adopt only one angle of view, such as the historical, the political, etc. My own consideration of the paper, however, is to be primarily from the legal viewpoint; without attempting wholly to avoid other points of view I shall seek not to stress them.

The Protocol is an elaborate and technical international document; and even in attempting to consider it primarily from the legal viewpoint there are various methods or arrangements of such a discussion. The general starting point which seems to me to be most desirable is that of the legal effect of the Protocol upon the international relations of the States which become parties to it, both as among themselves and as to States not parties.

It will of course in this connection be necessary to consider the obligations fixed by the Protocol in the event of its breach, as well as those which are imposed by its acceptance and performance. These latter may, however, very properly be first considered.

Accordingly, the first discussion will relate to the obligations of the States which become parties to the Protocol as among themselves, particularly in connection with the due performance of these obligations by those parties.

Before coming to this first discussion, however, there are certain general observations which may be made.

In the first place the paper is called a Protocol. The precise reason for the use of this term does not appear; but it is probably due to the fact that the Protocol of Geneva is in a sense supplementary to other international agreements such as the Covenant of the League of Nations and the Statute of the Permanent Court of International Justice; and perhaps because the

3

Protocol is intended to be preliminary to amendments to the Covenant (Article I, paragraph 1, of the Protocol).

Allusion is made to this provisional character of the Protocol of Geneva in the Report[a] made by the First and Third Committees to the Fifth Assembly of the League of Nations, where it is said:

> "When the Covenant has been amended in this way some parts of the Protocol will lose their value as between the said States: some of them will have enriched the Covenant, while others, being temporary in character, will have lost their object.
>
> The whole Protocol will remain applicable to relations between signatory States which are Members of the League of Nations and signatory States outside the League,[b] or between States coming within the latter category.
>
> It should be added that, as the League realizes its aim of universality, the amended Covenant will take the place, as regards all States, of the separate régime of the Protocol."

Of course, as is pointed out in some detail by Satow (Diplomatic Practice, Second Edition, Vol. II, pages 270 *et seq*.), the word "protocol" is used with quite a number of different meanings. In the present case the meaning of the word is nothing more nor less than treaty or convention.

It is naturally impossible to consider or discuss the effect of the Protocol of Geneva without constant reference to the text of the Covenant, to which the Protocol refers throughout. It is also necessary to consider to some extent the Statute of the Permanent Court of International Justice and even certain of the provisions of the Treaties of Peace, other than the Covenant.

Moreover, as any consideration of the legal situation created by the Protocol must assume that the document has come into force, it will be interesting to sum up the provisions of the Protocol in that regard, particularly as they are somewhat unusual.

---

a. The English text of this Report is Annex C, p. 156.
b. From the theory that the Protocol may properly be signed by non-Members of the League, I dissent. See *infra*, p. 10, *et seq*.

CHAPTER III.

THE COMING INTO FORCE OF THE PROTOCOL.

The Protocol is dated at Geneva on October 2nd, 1924. It is drawn up in both French and English and the text of both languages is authentic. It is written in a single original. It was recommended to the Members of the League for acceptance by a resolution[a] unanimously passed in the Assembly by the affirmative vote of 48 Members of the League, and it has been signed by the representatives of various countries.

This recommendation by the Assembly, however, and these signatures, do not, as to any signatories, bring into force the Protocol, which, by its terms, must be ratified, the ratifications to be deposited at the Secretariat of the League at Geneva.

The first preliminary to the coming into force of the Protocol is its formal ratification by at least 13 Members of the League; and these ratifications must include those of at least three of the four Great Powers which are Members—Great Britain, France, Italy and Japan. But even these ratifications do not bring the Protocol into force. The absence of such ratifications by May 1st, 1925, *may* result in the postponement of the Disarmament Conference from the date provisionally fixed, June 15th, 1925. But this is a matter which I shall discuss later.[b]

If and when the ratifications above mentioned are deposited, a procès-verbal to that effect is drawn up; but this procès-verbal does not, as is usual when a procès-verbal of the deposit of ratifications is drafted, bring into force the Protocol. The date of the coming into force of the Protocol is stated as follows (Article 21):

> "as soon as the plan for the reduction of armaments has been adopted by the Conference provided for in Article 17."

In other words, the Protocol will not bind any State that rati-

---

a. Annex D, p. 210 at p. 211, *et seq.*
b. p. 97, *et seq.* It is settled that that Conference will be postponed.

fies it unless and until the Conference for the Reduction of Armaments adopts a Plan for such reduction. *If* such Conference is held and *if* such Plan is adopted, the Protocol will, on the date of the adoption of the Plan, come into force as among the States which have then ratified it. Such is the effect of the provisions of Article 21 of the Protocol.

Other States, which have not at the date mentioned ratified the Protocol, may thereafter accede to it, as is provided by the third paragraph of Article 3, and of course the obligations of these States will commence with the date of such accession.

Furthermore, provision is made[a] by which the Protocol, even after coming into force, may become, as it says, "null and void." It might well be argued that the becoming "null and void" of the Protocol related back to the date when it came into force.

However this may be, it is important to notice here the provisions in this regard. The Conference for the Reduction of Armaments has, under the hypothesis, adopted a Plan for such reduction. That Conference has also to fix the time within which that Plan is to be carried out. The Council of the League is then to consider whether the Plan for the Reduction of Armaments adopted by the Conference has or has not been carried out within that fixed period. Presumably such consideration by the Council of the League would be had immediately after the expiration of the period fixed by the Conference; the Council, if it then considers that the Plan for the Reduction of Armaments has not been carried out, being limited, however, in such consideration to "the grounds" (French text—"conditions") laid down by the Conference in that respect, then declares that the Plan has not been carried out and the Protocol becomes "null and void."

Accordingly, the Protocol can come into force as a legal obligation only on the date of the adoption by the Conference of the Plan for the Reduction of Armaments; and from that date till the date when the Council of the League of Nations declares that the Plan has or has not been carried out, it may be said

---

a. Article 21.

that the Protocol is only *provisionally* in force; it is subject to avoidance.

The question here arises as to what is meant by the language of the Protocol when it speaks of the Plan for the Reduction of Armaments being "carried out," or, in the French text, "exécuté." This is a question rather difficult of answer. Certainly the expression can hardly refer to the actual *physical* carrying out of such a Plan; for that might require a very long period. It seems to me that the expression envisages the formalities requisite for such a Plan. The Conference for the Reduction of Armaments which is to draw up a Plan for such reduction is to draw up, in other words, a Treaty or Treaties between the parties to bring about such reduction. Such Treaty, or such Treaties, will of course be voluntary agreements and will of course require ratification subsequent to the holding of the Conference itself. Accordingly, it is my view that the "carrying out" of the Plan for the Reduction of Armaments adopted by the Conference means in the Protocol the ratification of such Plan, that is to say, the transformation of the Plan into a binding agreement. Of course, the precise terms as to ratification, the number of ratifications required, the time of the deposit of ratifications and all such other formalities are for the Conference to decide; the reference here, however, is to those provisions as they may be drafted.

Accordingly, the "grounds" to be laid down by the Conference for the Reduction of Armaments, on which it may be declared by the Council that the Plan for the Reduction of Armaments has not been carried out, will mean, I take it, the laying down of some requirement that the Plan for the Reduction of Armaments be formally ratified within a time stated by a certain number of States, including certain named States; in default whereof, the Council may and will declare the Plan for the Reduction of Armaments not to have been carried out.

It is to be observed that the Protocol in the last paragraph of Article 21 speaks of the possibility of a Signatory failing to "comply" with the reduction of armaments Plan "after the expiration of the period fixed by the Conference."

This refers, I think, to a failure by a particular Signatory to ratify the Plan for the Reduction of Armaments, the effect being, so far as Article 21 is concerned, that such Signatory would be bound by the terms of the Protocol but could not benefit by them.

The language of this last paragraph of Article 21 is, however, broad enough to include the case of a State which had ratified the Treaty containing the Plan for the Reduction of Armaments and had then failed to carry out its agreement regarding such reduction.

It will thus be seen that the Protocol of Geneva is wholly dependent upon the success of the Conference for the Reduction of Armaments; and the success of that Conference depends wholly upon the voluntary agreement then made. There is nothing in the Protocol which requires the States represented at the Conference to agree to any particular plan for the reduction of armaments; the assent which they may give to such plan must be voluntary.

The question of the proceedings of the Disarmament Conference will be discussed hereafter.[a]

However, there is one point that may be mentioned here. The Plan for the Reduction of Armaments drawn up by the Conference or, in other words, the Treaty or Treaties drawn up by that Conference, will not be perpetual in their operation. No plan for disarmament, no treaty regarding reduction of armaments could possibly be perpetual in its detailed provisions. Not only does this follow from the nature of such an agreement, but it is explicitly laid down in Article 8 of the Covenant that any such Plan is to be subject to reconsideration and revision at least every ten years. Accordingly, the Treaty or Treaties for the Reduction of Armaments to be drawn up by the Conference will be in this sense temporary, that they will have a fixed limit of time for their operation, precisely as the Treaty Limiting Naval Armament drawn up at the Washington Conference may be terminated in 1936.[b]

---

a. *Infra*, p. 97, *et seq.*
b. Article XXIII. See Conference on the Limitation of Armament, Government Printing Office, 1922, p. 1603.

There is no provision made in the Protocol of Geneva for the withdrawal of any State from its obligations, assuming that those obligations come finally into force. On its face the Protocol is therefore perpetual; but it is not really so. The obligations of the Protocol are so intertwined with the obligations of the Covenant that there is no doubt in my mind that the withdrawal from the League by a Member thereof (when bound by the Protocol) would release that State from the obligations of the Protocol as well as from the obligations of the Covenant.

The obligations of the Covenant are terminable by any Member of the League, as to itself, on two years notice. The obligations of the Protocol go much farther than the obligations of the Covenant. The obligations of the Protocol are, by its terms, later to be merged in the Covenant itself, without in any way impairing the withdrawal clause of the latter document.

So clearly it is not to be supposed that the obligations of the Protocol of Geneva, as to a Member of the League, are eternal. If the lesser obligations of the Covenant end as to a particular Member of the League upon withdrawal, surely the greater obligations of the Protocol, as to that League Member, end also.

The foregoing shows the fallacy, as a matter of logic, of the idea that a non-Member of the League may be bound by the Protocol and yet not be a party to the Covenant; for it would mean that a Signatory might be forever bound to a subsidiary instrument (the Protocol) although the primary instrument (the Covenant) was terminable; but I discuss this more at length later.[a]

Furthermore, it should be repeated that the Protocol is intended to be only a temporary document in the sense that, if it comes finally into force, it is contemplated that the Covenant will be amended substantially in accordance with the provisions of the Protocol.

---

a. p. 10, *et seq.*

CHAPTER IV.

PARTIES TO THE PROTOCOL.

The theory of the framers of the Protocol of Geneva is that it may be signed and ratified by non-Members of the League of Nations as well as by Members of the League.

Various words of the Protocol (*e. g.*, Article 12) indicate this, the Report to the Assembly so states,[a] and the Resolution[b] of the Assembly recommending the Protocol for acceptance by the Members of the League of Nations specifically says that the Protocol shall be "open for signature by all other States" as well as by Members of the League.

Now of course all this is conclusive as to the technical question as to whether a non-Member of the League of Nations *may in fact* sign the Protocol. Such a State *may* legally sign, because the other Parties to the Protocol invite such signature. And if any such State should sign, and ratify, it becomes a Party to the Protocol, regardless of logic.

Nevertheless I submit that the whole idea of the possibility of Signatories to the Protocol who are non-Members of the League, is fundamentally contrary to the whole principle, spirit and terms of the Protocol itself.

In the first place, the Protocol is intended as a development of the Covenant; the Protocol is meant to be a temporary paper; its provisions are to be merged in the Covenant itself by amendment of that Document. How then can a State become a party to this temporary and provisional paper if it is not a party to the permanent and definitive document?

If we examine the detailed provisions of the Protocol, the logical conclusion is equally certain. Surely a non-Member of the League cannot really "make every effort" to secure "introduction into the Covenant of amendments" (Article 1). Is this a matter for non-Members of the League?

---

a. Annex C, p. 156 at p. 167.
b. Annex D, p. 210 at p. 212.

Article 3 of the Protocol contemplates that the Signatories thereto shall accede to the special protocol regarding the second paragraph of Article 36 of the Statute of the Permanent Court. But if we turn to the provisions regarding the Permanent Court we find that such States as Russia and Mexico and Egypt are not entitled to accede to that special protocol at all, before entering the League.[a] Accordingly, if any one of these three States, non-Members of the League, should sign and ratify the Protocol of Geneva, it could not legally carry out the engagements of Article 3 thereof.

All the provisions of Articles 4 to 6 inclusive of the Protocol of Geneva relate to disputes between the Signatories and contemplate the possible submission of any such dispute to the Council or Assembly of the League of Nations. But such submission can take place only under the provisions of the Covenant; and under Article 17 of the Covenant a non-Member of the League may not come within the provisions of the Covenant except upon invitation by the Council and upon terms stated.

Without going into further detail, I repeat that the obligations contemplated by the Protocol are, in theory, no more than interpretations, or future elaborations, of the obligations of the Covenant. It seems to me logically impossible to suppose that such interpretations or amplifications may be made applicable to States which are free from the obligations in their primary form.

If this matter is looked at realistically and concretely we find that there is hardly any possibility of the Protocol of Geneva being signed by any State which is a non-Member of the League. The United States and Russia will certainly not sign; the admission of Germany and Turkey to the League is contemplated. The only other States[b] of any international consequence outside the

a. Under the Resolution of the Council of May 17, 1922, *any* State may accept the jurisdiction of the Permanent Court by filing a declaration to that effect; but this is not the same thing as acceding to the Protocol of December 16, 1920.

b. See Membership in the League of Nations, by Manley O. Hudson, A. J. I. L., July, 1924.

League are Mexico and Egypt; and the likelihood of either of these two States becoming a party to the Protocol of Geneva is too remote for serious consideration.

Accordingly, in the subsequent discussion, I shall assume that, whatever may be the legal possibilities, there is no real possibility of any State which is not a Member of the League of Nations becoming a party to the Protocol of Geneva.

CHAPTER V.

It is here assumed that only Members of the League of Nations may become parties to the Protocol of Geneva[a]; the Protocol is a development of the Covenant and it would, in any view, be logically impossible for any State, not a Member of the League, to become a Signatory to the Protocol; on the other hand, Members of the League are, of course, not obligated to sign or to ratify the Protocol of Geneva.

Accordingly, if the Protocol shall come into force, the Powers of the world, from the point of view of the Protocol, will, at least theoretically, be divided into three classes:

    1. Members of the League of Nations who are parties to the Protocol.

    2. Members of the League of Nations who are not parties to the Protocol.

    3. Non-Members of the League of Nations who are not parties to the Protocol.

From this it follows, again looking at the matter from the point of view of the Protocol of Geneva, that the international relations of the various countries of the world would fall into the following six classes:

    1. Relations *inter se* of the Signatories to the Protocol.

    2. Relations *inter se* of the Members of the League not Signatories to the Protocol.

    3. Relations *inter se* of non-Members of the League.

    4. Relations of the Signatories to the Protocol with the Members of the League not Signatories thereto.

    5. Relations of Members of the League not Signatories to the Protocol with States non-Members of the League.

    6. Relations of the Members of the League Signatories to the Protocol with States non-Members of the League.

---

a. Those who framed the Protocol have a different opinion. See the discussion, *supra*, p. 10, *et seq.*

It is proposed in this discussion first to consider the first of the above six classes, namely, the relations of the Signatories to the Protocol, *inter se*; and this discussion will proceed primarily on the assumption that the obligations of the Protocol are carried out.

In numerous places the Protocol speaks of the parties thereto as "the signatory States," *e. g.*, Articles 1, 2, 3, 8, 11, etc. It is curious this is so in view of the meticulous insistence by the British Dominions at the Peace Conference, on the use, throughout the text of the Covenant generally, of the expression "Members of the League" instead of "States Members of the League."[a]

Certainly it is contemplated that ratification of the Protocol may be made on behalf of the British Dominions. Accordingly, I think that the use in the Protocol of the expression "signatory States" is probably an inadvertence, as in no proper international sense of the word are the British Dominions States, despite the fact that they have an international status under the League of Nations and even otherwise.[b]

The first point to be noticed is that under Article 2 of the Protocol there is a very general and a very sweeping obligation on the part of the Signatories not to resort to war. This is a point of the utmost importance. The obligation goes very much farther than anything in the Covenant; the language of this obligation will be examined in detail hereafter.

Before coming to that, however, it is well to look at the provisions of the Protocol regarding the settlement of international disputes. War is one method for the settlement of such disputes, and, in order to make effective the obligation of the Signatories not to resort to war, substitute methods of settlement are provided.

It is very natural and proper that this should be done. A mere obligation not to resort to war, without more, would almost imply that disputes between the parties to the obligation should

---

a. *cf.* the expression in Article 34 of the Court Statute "States or Members of the League of Nations."

b. The exact position of the British Dominions within the League is not yet wholly settled. See the recent British and Irish notes regarding the Irish Treaty, London Times, December 16 and 24, 1924.

find *some* other method of settlement. For if some other method could not be found, feelings due to the continuance of the dispute might well arouse such passions in one country or another as to sweep away the obligation for peace. The two questions of the ending of war and the settlement of disputes between States are not only logically but realistically very closely related.

Disputes between States are often regarded as comprising those that relate to international questions and those that relate to domestic questions, the former being divided into justiciable and non-justiciable disputes.

I prefer, however, *for this discussion,* to classify possible international disputes in three kinds, namely:

1. Disputes as to international questions.

2. Disputes as to domestic questions.

3. Disputes as to *status quo.*

I am aware of the fact that such classification as the foregoing is overlapping. Disputes as to the *status quo* will to some extent fall within the two classes first mentioned; they may relate therefore to questions which are international or which are domestic in their nature. However, I think the classification is justified, at least for reasons of convenience, and also, in my opinion, for reasons which go very much deeper.

Let me illustrate this by reference to questions arising from frontiers. The existence and the location of a frontier are essentially questions of international import. The location of a frontier may, in a given case, not only be an international question in the sense that it should be settled internationally, but also in the sense that it is justiciable, according to the usual idea of justiciable questions. This would be so in a case where the location of the frontier depended wholly upon the interpretation of a treaty between the two neighboring States.

But it is quite possible to imagine an international question regarding a frontier which is not in any way justiciable; such, for example, was the question as to where the frontier between Poland and Russia should be drawn after the World War.[a] That *some* frontier had to be drawn was obvious; but there was no possible legal basis for determining *where* it should be drawn. The question was one of judgment, to be settled by agreement between the parties, if possible; or otherwise, if it was to be peacefully settled, by reference to some sort of tribunal which would decide according to principles[b] of equity, impossible to express in any precise legal formula. In other words, the question was an international political one.

Again, suppose that the frontier between the two States has been settled by agreement and that there is no doubt whatever where it is. One of the two States desires to have that frontier changed; in other words, desires that there shall be a cession of territory. Here is a question of the *status quo.* In a sense it may be called international, because it relates to an international frontier; but it not only falls wholly outside any idea of justiciable questions in the international sense, but also outside any idea of being a political question which any tribunal whatever could decide on *any* basis. In other words, it is within that class of cases of an international nature in regard to which two States *may,* if they choose, negotiate, but in regard to which either one of them may at its pleasure refuse even to consider negotiations.

In any condition of international affairs which it is possible to visualize under the present State system, this must continue to be so. The State system presupposes necessarily the existence of States. One of the inherent conditions of the existence of a State is its right to the possession of its own undisputed territory as against any other State,[c] which does not mean, I mention in passing, as against a revolutionary movement *within* the State; that is another story. The putting in question of this undisputed

a. See Treaty of Versailles, Article 87, third paragraph.
b. Such as, perhaps, the idea of self determination, the economic situation of the inhabitants, etc.
c. See the Declaration of the Rights and Duties of Nations adopted by the American Institute of International Law, specially Paragraph IV, A. J. I. L., Vol. X, pp. 212, 213.

right of one State to hold its own territory as against another State would mean the putting in question of the existing State order as a whole.

Further, while I have included domestic questions as a separate class of questions in the above list, I think that logically many of them fall within the thought of questions which concern the *status quo*. I do not dispute that these domestic questions may at times have an international aspect; but they are questions which each State has an absolute right under law to regulate according to its own pleasure, and it is for this reason that they fall within the class of cases which are, in theory, not to be questioned internationally. Of course a State may, if it chooses, negotiate regarding them, just as it may, if it chooses, negotiate about the cession of part of its territory. But it may also, if it chooses, so to speak end the negotiations by refusing to commence them at all.

However, it is proper, none the less, to consider these domestic questions as a separate group, for the reason that there is a possibility of development toward their international consideration within the present State system. I shall pursue that thought further a little later.

CHAPTER VI.

INTERNATIONAL DISPUTES.

So far as concerns disputes of an international nature, the Protocol, taken in connection with the Covenant, provides for a final and binding settlement of such disputes between Signatories to the Protocol in every case whatsoever.

In order to determine the precise effect of the Protocol in this regard, it is necessary first to examine the provisions of the Covenant.

The provisions of the Covenant which particularly cover this matter are those of Articles 12, 13 and 15. Let us therefore consider the text of these Articles,[a] looking in the first place at the text of Articles 12 and 13 and the first paragraph of Article 15, which follow:

> ARTICLE 12. "The Members of the League agree that, if there should arise between them any dispute likely to lead to a rupture, they will submit the matter either to arbitration or judicial settlement or to enquiry by the Council and they agree in no case to resort to war until three months after the award by the arbitrators or the judicial decision, or the report of the Council.
>
> "In any case under this Article, the award of the arbitrators or the judicial decision shall be made within a reasonable time, and the report of the Council shall be made within six months after the submission of the dispute."
>
> ARTICLE 13. "The Members of the League agree that, whenever any dispute shall arise between them which they recognise to be suitable for submission to arbitration or judicial settlement, and which cannot be satisfactorily settled by diplomacy, they will submit the whole subject matter to arbitration or judicial settlement.
>
> "Disputes as to the interpretation of a treaty, as to any question of international law, as to the existence of any fact which, if established, would constitute a breach of any international obligation, or as to the extent and

---

a. As amended.

nature of the reparation to be made for any such breach, are declared to be among those which are generally suitable for submission to arbitration or judicial settlement.

"For the consideration of any such dispute, the Court to which the case is referred shall be the Permanent Court of International Justice, established in accordance with Article 14, or any tribunal agreed on by the parties to the dispute or stipulated in any convention existing between them.

"The Members of the League agree that they will carry out in full good faith any decision or award that may be rendered, and that they will not resort to war against a Member of the League which complies therewith. In the event of any failure to carry out such an award or decision, the Council shall propose what steps should be taken to give effect thereto."

ARTICLE 15 (first paragraph). "If there should arise between the Members of the League any dispute likely to lead to a rupture, which is not submitted to arbitration or judicial settlement in accordance with Article 13, the Members of the League agree that they will submit the matter to the Council. Any party to the dispute may effect such submission by giving notice of the existence of the dispute to the Secretary-General, who will make all necessary arrangements for a full investigation and consideration thereof."

Looking at these provisions in their entirety, it will be seen that the engagements taken by the Members of the League relate to "any dispute likely to lead to a rupture." This is the language of both Articles 12 and 15. We may say that this means any dispute whatever, any serious dispute from the point of view of international peace. We may lay aside trifling disputes which cannot lead to serious differences between States, whether or not they drag on through years of diplomatic negotiation. Accordingly, we may say that the Covenant in these provisions covers any international dispute whatever as to international questions in the sense above mentioned.

Further examining the provisions above quoted, we see that

the Members of the League agree in every such possible case to do one of three things: they agree to submit all disputes either (a) to arbitration or (b) to judicial settlement or (c) to the Council. They do *not* agree to submit any particular case or any particular class of cases to arbitration; they do *not* agree to submit any particular case or any particular class of cases to judicial settlement; but they do specifically agree that all cases that are not submitted to the one or to the other, go to the Council. The effect of such submission to the Council will be discussed hereafter; at the moment it is only necessary to point out that under these provisions the submission to the Council is *obligatory.* That submission *must,* under Article 15, take place, in the absence of submission to arbitration or to the Court. But the submission to arbitrators or to the Court is voluntary.

The first change made in this scheme of the Covenant is that Parties to the Protocol agree to accept the so-called "compulsory" jurisdiction of the Permanent Court of International Justice in the cases mentioned in paragraph 2 of Article 36 of the Statute of the Court. Thus, in such cases the dispute between the Parties would go, as a matter of right, at the demand of either one of them, to the Court, where it would be finally determined. To that extent the jurisdiction of the Council is lessened.

Under the Protocol, this acceptance of the so-called compulsory jurisdiction of the Permanent Court of International Justice is to take place by the signatory States within a month after the coming into force of the Protocol, which, as we have seen, would mean within a month after the adoption by the Conference on Reduction of Armaments of the plan for such reduction.

The Parties to the Protocol thus agree to accept this so-called compulsory jurisdiction of the Permanent Court; but it is provided that they may do so with appropriate reservations.

Accordingly, it is desirable to consider summarily just what this so-called compulsory jurisdiction of the Permanent Court of International Justice is.

All that the word "compulsory" in this connection means is "agreed to in advance." The general provisions of the Court

Statute[a] describe the jurisdiction of the Court as extending to any case which the Parties, either after it has arisen or by "treaties and conventions in force,"[b] choose to submit. The so-called optional clause relating to the so-called compulsory jurisdiction in effect provides that as to certain defined classes of cases the parties agree, now, in advance of any dispute, that disputes of those particular characters will be submitted to the Court.

The definition of these classes of disputes is found in Article 36 of the Statute of the Court, and in this regard follows generally in its language the provisions of the second paragraph of Article 13 of the Covenant, which declares that these particular classes of disputes are "among those which are generally suitable for submission to arbitration or judicial settlement."

By the so-called optional clause relating to the Court Statute, it is these classes of disputes as to any or all of which the jurisdiction of the Court may be accepted as "compulsory *ipso facto* and without special agreement, in relation to any other Member or State accepting the same obligation."

The classes of "legal disputes" mentioned in Article 36 of the Court Statute are as follows:

"legal disputes concerning:
(a) The interpretation of a treaty;
(b) Any question of international law;
(c) The existence of any fact which, if established, would constitute a breach of an international obligation;
(d) The nature or extent of the reparation to be made for the breach of an international obligation."

rd to these definitions of classes of disputes, it is necake some general observations. No matter what definite be made in advance as to the classes of disputes to be submitted to the Court, a difference of opinion

, first paragraph.
lection of such agreements, see Publications of the Permanent Court o: Justice, Series D, No. 4.

may exist in any given case as to whether the particular dispute which has arisen is or is not within one of the defined classes.

It follows that the mere definition of classes of disputes which, by agreement in advance, are to be submitted to a particular tribunal, is not in itself sufficient; any such definition must be accompanied by a provision for a case when one of the parties to a dispute claims that the particular dispute is within the defined class and the other party to the dispute does not admit that the dispute is within the defined class; some method must be provided for determining that preliminary question of jurisdiction.

Let me put this concretely: let me suppose that two Members of the League have agreed to the optional clause and that a dispute arises between them. One party to the dispute says that the question involved concerns the interpretation of a treaty and accordingly submits the question to the Permanent Court of International Justice in accordance with the procedure under the Statute of that Court. The other party to the dispute says that the dispute does not in any way concern the interpretation of the treaty and submits the matter to the Council of the League under Article 15 of the Covenant.

Clearly there would be here for decision a preliminary point of jurisdiction and, in so far as the optional clause is concerned, the matter is covered by the Statute of the Court in the final paragraph of Article 36, reading as follows:

> "In the event of a dispute as to whether the Court has jurisdiction, the matter shall be settled by the decision of the Court."

In other words, by the Court Statute, it is for the Court to say whether or not it has jurisdiction in any such case; so that in the particular case above supposed, where one party was seeking to go to the Court and the other party was seeking to go to the Council, it would be for the Court in the first instance to decide as to the jurisdiction. If the Court decided that it had jurisdiction, the dispute would come on for decision by the

Court; if the Court decided that it had not jurisdiction, consideration of the dispute would come on before the Council.

The provision in the last paragraph of Article 36 of the Court Statute is a wise and necessary one. It avoids conflicts of jurisdiction and it permits a preliminary and easily realizable method of determining the question of jurisdiction.

It is unnecessary to consider in further detail the described classes of legal disputes mentioned in Article 36 of the Court Statute. Any party to the Protocol may make reservations in acceding to this optional clause and, as the Report of the First and Third Committees to the Assembly points out,[a] these reservations may be of a very extensive character; but the fact that the Signatories to the Protocol agree to accede, even to some extent, to this so-called compulsory jurisdiction of the Permanent Court is of great importance.

However, the most important change which the Protocol makes in regard to the settlement of international disputes concerns the functions of the Council in the case of a dispute submitted to it.

The only respect in which the functions of the Council in such a case under the Protocol are *precisely* the same as the functions of the Council under the Covenant is that the Council must begin along the lines of mediation and conciliation.[b]

This, we may observe, comes directly from the third paragraph of Article 15 of the Covenant, which provides that "the Council shall endeavour to effect a settlement of the dispute." Such language relates to the mediatory and conciliatory functions of friendly governments. The Council is composed of representatives of governments, of governments friendly to the parties to the dispute, because the governments which are Members

a. See the discussion as to this in that Report, *infra*, p. 171.
b. Doubtless the word "conciliation" is not a term of art in this regard. But it seems to me that the functions of the Council under Article 15 of the Covenant go somewhat beyond "mediation" in the strict sense of the writers. See Nys, Droit International, Vol. II, p. 543; also Vattel (1853 edition), p. 276. The Protocol (Article 6) calls a result from these efforts "an amicable settlement." The French text speaks of such efforts as "l'essai de conciliation."

of the Council as well as the governments which are parties to the dispute have joined in a Covenant of Peace.

Accordingly, the first duty of the Council, in the event of any submission of a dispute, is to mediate and conciliate. These are very valuable functions. They permit of delay. The governments which compose the Council may prolong the consideration of the point at issue.[a] The parties to the dispute have come to the Council for a settlement; and the Council may deliberate during a reasonable period so as to permit passions to cool and reason to resume her sway.

Now, as I remarked, these mediatory functions of the Council remain precisely the same under the Protocol as under the Covenant.

Suppose, however, the mediation fails, what is the next duty of the Council? Under the Covenant,[b] the next duty of the Council would be this, to consider the dispute; but under the Protocol (Article 4 [1]), the next duty of the Council is to "endeavour to persuade the parties to submit the dispute to judicial settlement or arbitration." This obviously is a very different thing from consideration of the dispute by the Council itself. Instead of considering the dispute, the Council says to the parties: Is there not some kind of a tribunal to which you are willing to refer it?

Still more striking is the fact that, even if this endeavour fail, it does not even then necessarily become the duty of the Council to consider the dispute on its merits. *Either one* of the parties may demand the setting up of a Committee of Arbitrators. The difference between such a provision as this and the provisions of the Covenant is remarkably great. Under the Covenant, when, as the outcome of the mediation of the Council, the parties do not themselves agree upon a settlement, the Council is inevitably required to consider the merits of the case. Under the Protocol, if the parties do not agree, the dispute goes to the Court or to a tribunal of some kind, if such a reference is agreed on; it next goes to a Committee of Arbitrators if only

a. The period of "six months" is mentioned in Article 12 of the Covenant.
b. Article 15, Paragraph 4, *et seq.*

one of the parties demands it; this means that the Council never gets to consideration of the dispute on the merits, unless the parties to the dispute at the time are unanimous in wishing that this shall happen.

It is obvious that when we have a situation where *any* party to a dispute may demand the appointment of an arbitral committee, the Council of the League can only consider cases of dispute which all parties thereto, *after* the dispute has arisen, *unanimously* agree should be considered by the Council.

The reason why I attach the utmost significance to this change, in connection with some other changes which are to be noticed, is that it is a total departure in theory from the idea of the Covenant that political disputes should be settled by a political body such as the Council of the League of Nations. After all, that was the fundamental idea of Article 15 of the Covenant, that the Council of the League should lay hold of the dispute, at least to the extent of preventing war from arising out of it. *The theory of the Protocol is that every kind of international dispute should be settled either by a Court or by arbitration, that the functions of the Council are those of mediation and conciliation and that the Council is never to consider the merits of the dispute unless the parties thereto at the time of the dispute unanimously wish such consideration.* Even then, as we shall see, a single dissent in the Council regarding the merits is sufficient to render its consideration of no effect, and arbitration again comes into play.

It should be pointed out here that if the dispute goes to a Committee of Arbitrators at the request of one of the parties, any point of law in dispute must be sent by the Committee of Arbitrators to the Permanent Court of International Justice for an opinion.[a]

Now, let us proceed with the duties of the Council. If the dispute has gone to arbitration, the functions of the Council are at an end; but if no party "asks for arbitration,"[b] then and only

---

a. Protocol, Article 4 (2) c.
b. by a Committee of Arbitrators.

then the Council takes up the consideration of the dispute. In this case, the Council in fact becomes an arbitral board, *provided* it can reach a unanimous conclusion; but its deliberations and recommendations have no effect whatever if it cannot reach a unanimous conclusion.

Under the present composition of the Council the arbitral tribunal which it would become in such circumstances would be composed of from eight to ten members. The Council itself would be a body of at least ten members, possibly eleven, possibly twelve (if the dispute were between two outside parties), but the votes of the disputants would not be counted.

It is clear that unanimity would be somewhat difficult to reach in a tribunal of that size. It must be remembered that under the Protocol no dispute can reach the Council for such an arbitral decision unless (a) the mediatory efforts of the Council have failed and (b) the parties have refused to agree upon any form of arbitration and (c) neither party wishes arbitration.[a] Clearly a dispute which had reached that stage would be one upon which unanimous agreement by an arbitral tribunal of representatives of from eight to ten governments would be improbable.

Furthermore, it seems to me almost certain under the new procedure that one of the parties would demand arbitration,[a] because it would always be in the power of one member of the Council to compel such arbitration. This is a point which, so far as I have observed, has not elsewhere been noticed.

The final provision of the Protocol for the settlement of the dispute is that if the matter goes to the Council for consideration; and if the views of the Council are not unanimous (aside from the parties), there is then a "compulsory" arbitration. The Council proceeds itself to determine the composition, the powers and the procedure of the Committee of Arbitrators.

So, taking all the provisions together, the whole result is that a dispute which is past the stage of mediation either goes to arbitration outside the Council or must be unanimously decided

---

a. By a Committee of Arbitrators.

by the members of the Council; and this puts it in the power of any one member of the Council to compel an arbitral award by an outside body.

It should be added that, under the Protocol, as under the Covenant, the Assembly may be substituted for the Council in the consideration of a dispute. It would have in such case the same mediatory powers as the Council and the same arbitral powers as the Council if all the parties refused any other form of arbitration.[a]

A very summary statement of the functions of the Council under the Covenant shows what a radical change is made by the provisions of the Protocol. Under the present provisions of Article 15 of the Covenant, a dispute which passes the stage of mediation is considered by the Council. If the Council is unanimous in making recommendations, their effect is simply to prevent war, not finally to settle the dispute. If the Council is not unanimous, its recommendations may have a moral effect, but have no legal effect whatever.

So far as concerns these provisions of the Protocol, they may be summed up as follows: they provide that every possible dispute between the parties to the Protocol which is subject to international cognizance shall be finally determined by a judicial or arbitral tribunal resulting in a legally binding decision or award; and the parties to the Protocol solemnly agree that they will accept any such decision or any such award as final *and* that they will carry it out in full good faith.[b]

---

a. The powers and duties of the Assembly in such case are stated in the last two paragraphs of Article 15 of the Covenant. They are continued, to the extent stated, by Article 6 of the Protocol.

b. The question as to what may happen under the Protocol if such a decision or award is *not* carried out is discussed *infra*, p. 50, *et seq*.

CHAPTER VII.

THE STATUS QUO.

In many recent discussions of international affairs these two originally innocent Latin words *"status quo"* have attained a really malevolent significance. They seem to be regarded as meaning the same thing as the motto "Whatever is, is wrong," and some who talk about the *status quo* appear to be in the same mind as Omar when he longed

> "To grasp this sorry scheme of things entire
> .... —and then
> Re-mould it nearer to the heart's desire."

It may be well to give some critical examination to this question of the *status quo* and to see what, if anything, is meant by the ideas which lie back of these criticisms.

In the first place, the thought of the critics usually relates to existing international frontiers and, in some instances, to existing international conditions.

Now as to frontiers, if we look at the *status quo* historically, we find that it is practically universally the result of changes in a previous *status quo*. The cause of these changes may have been war, may possibly have been agreements and may have been something other than either of these.[a] I shall refer to them later. But here it should be observed that there is hardly any region of the globe where the *status quo* does not result from some one or more of these changes within times comparatively recent.

Of course there are some exceptions to this observation, the Arctic and Antarctic, for example; but in the populated regions of the globe, the *status quo,* so far as frontiers are concerned, is a thing comparatively new.

If we look at this existing situation, this *status quo* of international frontiers, we find that under modern conditions a com-

---

a. Such as discovery, occupation of *terra nullius,* etc. See the Treaty of Spitzbergen, A. J. I. L., Vol. XVIII, p. 109.

paratively short period of time is all that is necessary to give to the *status quo* the sanctity of universal consent, regardless of its origin. Let me give an instance or two of this.

The Southern frontier of the United States, for part of its extent, is the direct result of a war between the United States and Mexico, a war which by many, and I am among them, is considered to have been a war of aggression. Now no one but a madman would believe that there ought to be a change in the *status quo* of the communities now existing in New Mexico, which in 1850 was uninhabited country, by delivering them over to Mexican rule. It is true that, during the World War, Germany proposed to Mexico in the celebrated Zimmerman note[a] that this should be done; but that incident only emphasizes the truth of my remark.

One of the most recent instances of a change in the *status quo,* so far as the United States is concerned, is the case of the Virgin Islands, which were bought from Denmark in 1916.[b] There was a change made by agreement, made for a purchase price which was satisfactory to the ceding country and made after a plebiscite of the inhabitants, who voted almost unanimously for the change. Here, again, for reasons differing from those of the foregoing instance, no one in his senses would consider that the existing *status quo* was not one of justice and common sense.

Now, if we take the situation generally, we will find, in accordance with the instances that I have mentioned, that the international situation as to frontiers the world over[c] is, as to perhaps 99%, either consecrated by usage which is the equivalent of common consent or at least of common sense, or else is the result of agreement which contains in it both elements.

The fact is, as any realist will admit, that every frontier, no matter how absurd originally or even now, contains, in the very fact of its existence, elements of stability and of reason which to *some extent* justify its existence. The ordinary individual near a

a. A. J. I. L., Vol. XI, at p. 626.
b. A. J. I. L., Vol. XI, Supp. 1917, p. 53.
c. Some regions of Asia may be exceptions.

frontier, as distinguished from the agitator, becomes used to it. Business transactions adjust themselves to it and in a very short time after its creation any proposed change implies inherently a certain amount of undesirability. It is impossible, perhaps, to imagine or to draw a more absurd frontier than that between Switzerland and France in the region of Geneva.[a] It is a monstrosity, geographically and economically, and yet every one is contented with it or at least more contented with it than with the idea of changing it. Naturally there are certain attendant annoyances, as in a motor ride out of Geneva which involves two or more Customs frontier examinations within a few kilometres; and there are certain absurdities involved in catching Swiss fish and French fish in different parts of Lake Leman; and one is amused in reading Customs regulations which permit cows to pasture in one country and be milked in the other without duty; but still every one has gotten used to these matters and gets along with them.

So on the whole these two maligned words represent a rather peaceful condition.

Before the World War the irritation produced in the minds of many by the then existing *status quo* largely related to the frontiers in Eastern Europe and the somewhat similar irritation now existing among alleged liberal thinkers is due to the frontiers created by the Peace Treaties in general which are so usually and inaccurately referred to as the Treaty of Versailles.

Here, I think it is fair to make a certain distinction regarding the causes internationally of a given *status quo* at any particular time and of the existing situation in particular. These causes are two, generally speaking—agreement and war. The instances in modern history of changes in frontiers reached by free agreement are innumerable. I do not see how any one who recognizes the existing state system can object to them or believe that force should be used to change them. Of course there are critics who object to the existing state system and from

a. See the Franco-Swiss Free Zones, by Louis Schulthess, in Foreign Affairs, Vol. 3, No. 2, p. 331, with map.

a theoretical point of view there is something to be said for
these objections. The real answer to them at this time is, that
whether they are good or bad, the present state system is one
that, so far as any human being can see now, is certain to exist
for some more centuries at least; and accordingly, outside of
dreamland, we must take this system as it is. Given that state
system, agreements between states as to their frontiers should be
sacred. If a state can make an agreement about its frontier, and
then, because it made a bad agreement or a stupid agreement or
because circumstances changed after the agreement was made,
may go to war to set aside the agreement, the result would only
be international anarchy—the state system and everything else
would have disappeared together.

The other source of changes in the *status quo* is war or strictly
speaking the treaties of peace that result from war. I pass by
the legal position, which is theoretically correct, that a treaty
of peace made by a vanquished Power with a victor is supposedly a free agreement. This is true enough from the technical point
of view but has no bearing here. The fact is that when one
side wins a war and the other loses it, the treaty of peace is
made under compulsion and constraint.

The argument that is made by those who criticize the *status
quo* of the Peace Treaties of 1919 and 1920 runs about as follows:

> 1.   In certain respects the frontiers and arrangements
> created by the Peace Treaties are unjust.

> 2.   The setting up by the Peace Treaties of an interna-
> tional organization against war is an attempt to sanctify
> the wickednesses of the *status quo*.

> 3.   Both the Treaties and the international organization
> which they set up should at least be denounced and prob-
> ably rejected. This conclusion in various minds is differ-
> ent and uncertain, but I think that I have stated it fairly.

Let us take these points up in their order.

As a preliminary, let me say that the Treaties of Peace in this
connection cannot include the Treaty of Lausanne with Turkey.
Certainly at the time that that Treaty was negotiated there was

no imposed peace on Turkey; as a matter of fact the Turkish negotiators had things pretty much their own way with the Allies. So that we are considering merely the Treaties with Germany, Austria, Hungary and Bulgaria.

In the first place, the question in many cases as to whether or not there is any such thing as a "just" frontier is at least a very doubtful one. I put it this way. If you have a situation where reasonable, impartial and informed minds can differ, you do not have a situation where it can be arbitrarily said by any one that any one frontier is *the* just frontier. Of course I am not talking of the type of mind which insists that the particular line that he would draw is the one and only line, despite the views of anybody else, because to admit such a theory would mean the admission of the existence of perhaps fifty different frontiers between the same two countries at the same time.

Now as to the Peace Treaties, we certainly have that situation to a very large extent. I do not see how any one could contend that the existence of the Polish corridor is a perfect solution, nor do I see how any one could contend that the absence of the Polish corridor would be a perfect solution. One of the Polish Delegation said to me in Paris in December, 1918, in substance, that it would be impossible to draw a frontier between Germany and Poland which would not do an injustice to one country or to the other or to both, and I believe that his observation is perfectly sound.

The same thing is true as between Roumania and Hungary, and perhaps more true.

My sympathies as to Vilna are rather with the Lithunanians than with the Poles, but no one can read the documents without seeing that the Poles have a case.

My own view has always been that the frontier between Poland and Russia is too far to the East, but none the less the Russians, after a fashion, agreed to it.

Most of those whose opinions I respect believe that it was wrong to give the Austrian Tyrol to Italy. Despite those views, I have always believed that the decision was defensible.

Different American experts of the highest qualifications, of the utmost sincerity and of complete impartiality took different views as to Fiume and the Italian-Yugo-Slav frontier generally. In such circumstances, who could say, what tribunal could decide, the "just" frontier?

I am willing to admit that this uncertainty on the question of justice may not exist in every case. I have always believed that some of the cessions of territory forced on Bulgaria were utterly indefensible from any point of view whatsoever. I refer, not to Macedonia, that impossible jumble of contradictions, but more particularly to Western Thrace.

My own view is that, on the whole and taken by and large, the existing frontiers in Europe are more near to justice than ever before in modern history.

But I am going to assume for the rest of this discussion that some of these frontiers are wrong and should be changed. What is our answer to that situation?

Let me point out in the first place that the mere fact that a frontier was imposed by force resulting in a peace treaty is not necessarily anything against it. Take the case of Alsace-Lorraine, for example; or take a still more striking case, the case of Germany and Denmark. Admittedly, in and out of Germany, the result as to Slesvig was just and should continue.

Furthermore, it is necessary to point out that the *imposed* origin of a situation may not continue as the cause of that situation. It *may* become accepted and voluntary, a full agreement. An instance here is the reparations question. The *status quo* as to reparations (a very uncertain one) imposed by the Treaty of Versailles upon Germany, has now, under that very Treaty, become an agreed *status quo* by reason of the voluntary adoption by Germany of the Dawes Report; for in reality as well as in strictness of law that plan could not have been adopted, much less be carried out, without the voluntary assent of Germany to its provisions.

However, taking the frontier *status quo* of the Peace Treaties at its worst, that is to say at its alleged worst, admitting, in other words, that parts of it are unjust and are the result only of force, what are we to say as to the future?

The possibility of change which, under the supposition that I have made, would in itself be admittedly desirable, is along two lines, the line of agreement or the line of war. The so-called fixation or consecration of this *status quo* under the League of Nations in no way precludes a change by agreement, *the utmost that it can do is to preclude a change by war.*

Accordingly, we are confronted at the outset with the question as to whether the continuance of this *status quo* is, or is not, a worse evil than war. Even those who assume or who believe that war is the preferable of the two must, in order to reach that belief, hold that change by agreement is impossible. Such an assumption is contrary to the facts of history, but for the sake of this discussion it may be admitted.

In other words, I am willing to assume that a particular part of the frontier *status quo* is wrong, is unjust, and was brought about by force, and should be changed, and that it cannot be changed by agreement, and come directly to the question if, in these circumstances, it should or should not be changed by war. My answer to this question is: No. And I do not think it is necessary to put this answer merely on the ground of the evil of the war itself, the death, the destruction and so on. It is sufficient to support a negative answer to point out that the effect of the war could not be limited. War never is limited, it goes to lengths that have nothing to do with the supposed injustice for which it is commenced.

Let me give an instance as a concrete supposition. Take the Bulgarian-Greek frontier and suppose, as I do, that it ought to be changed, and suppose further, as the advocates of war assert, that it should be changed by war between Bulgaria and Greece; one of two things would happen in all human probability. Either Greece would be the victor and then not only would the boundary be as unjust to Bulgaria as it is now, but much more so. Or else Bulgaria would be the victor, in which case the injustice would simply be reversed; the frontier would not move to any theoretical point of justice, but would move to the point dictated by the new peace treaty.

In other words, war is not like a litigation which ends in the settlement of a particular dispute. Any war, in its settlement, goes far beyond the dispute which brought it about; every war opens up every possible ambition and desire of the victor.[a] Did the World War end merely in deciding the question about the rights of Austria and Serbia in connection with the murder of the Archduke? Where was the fate of the German colonies decided—in East Africa and in the Pacific, or on the Western Front?

This whole question is of vital importance in connection with the Protocol of Geneva. If that Protocol comes into force and is accepted by Germany, by Austria, by Hungary and by Bulgaria, it will have this effect at least; it will change what I may call the status of the *status quo* in regard to these countries to this extent, that in lieu of that *status quo* being one imposed by force, it will have become one agreed to, at least to the point that it is agreed that the *status quo* may not be changed by war but only by agreement.[b] As a practical example, it will mean, as we now see, that the German effort to regain some of her lost colonies under the mandate system, will again be an effort of negotiation[c] and not an effort of force.

All that the Covenant or the Protocol of Geneva attempts to do about the *status quo* is to say that frontiers shall not be changed *as a result of aggression*. Indeed, the Protocol[d] protects even an aggressor against loss of territory or of independence as a penalty for its aggression; discussion, leading up perhaps to peaceful agreement but to nothing else, is permitted by Articles 11 and 19 of the Covenant, but that is all.

a. "Et il faut bien remarquer, que la Guerre ne décide pas la question; la Victoire contraint seulement le vaincu à donner les mains au Traité qui termine le différend. C'est une erreur non moins absurde que funeste, de dire, que la Guerre doit décider les Controverses entre ceux qui, comme les Nations, ne reconnoissent point de Juge." Vattel, Book III, Section 38.
b. In general, this is the theory of Article Ten of the Covenant.
c. See the Genesis of the War, Asquith, pp. 97, 98.
d. Article 15.

My view is that these provisions are sound and that they should not be extended.

In saying, as I did, that the possibility of change in the *status quo* is along only two lines, the line of agreement and the line of war, I did not lose sight of the proposals made in various forms that there should be some method under the League of Nations or otherwise by which a tribunal of some sort would be empowered to make such changes from time to time. Most of these proposals envisage plebiscites in one form or another.

These proposals by their advocates are thought to have the advantage of adaptability to changing conditions and to be more conformable to the theory of the consent of the governed as a basis of Government.[a]

Of course, changes of frontiers made by any form of tribunal would in a sense be changes of frontiers made by agreement among the parties; for there would be necessarily an agreement in advance setting up such a tribunal and engaging to conform to its conclusions.

It may perhaps be imagined that as between two particular countries some such arrangement is possible along limited lines and relating to a particular area or areas. I doubt even this possibility; but certainly no general agreement in accord with such theories is possible and in my judgment it would be highly undesirable if it were possible.

A tribunal which was charged with the duty of determining changes in frontiers would clearly be a superstate, full-fledged, and in any sense of that much abused term. Obviously, a change of frontier, if it went far enough, might result in the substantial, or even the literal, disappearance of one state by its incorporation within the territories of another. It is inconceivable that any country would agree to such a proposition. Even if it were limited very strictly, it would present enormous difficulties and would certainly arouse fierce passions, as is well illustrated by

---

a. President Wilson's so-called first draft of the Covenant contained a provision along these lines in Article III. See Woodrow Wilson and World Settlement, Baker, Vol. III, p. 89.

the discussion regarding the tribunal which is now sitting to consider the frontier between Northern and Southern Ireland.

Nor would the matter be resolved by the suggested idea of plebiscites. Anyone who will consider this question of plebiscites will realize that the determining factor is not wholly the vote itself but to a large extent the terms in which the plebiscite paper is written. He who drafts the agreement for the plebiscite has much to do with what the plebiscite will determine.[a] The questions are: Is the area to vote as a whole or by districts, and where is the line of the voting area to be drawn? The first of these was one of the great questions in the Upper Silesia case. To apply the idea to an existing episode, let us again refer to the case of Ireland. If the plebiscite were in the whole of Ireland, it would go for Dublin; if it were in Ulster, it would go for Belfast; if it were in Tyrone or Fermanagh, the result would perhaps depend on the exact date when it was taken, as recent elections indicate.

Another difficulty about plebiscites is this: Is their effect perpetual or not, and if not how long does it last? If Tyrone votes for Dublin today, is it an eternal decision or only till another vote in 1930, or till when? There must be some time limit at least; plebiscites cannot be held every year or even every five years, a fact which illustrates the quiet advantages of some kind of a *status quo*.

Another question about a plebiscite is this: Let us concede that an overwhelming vote such as took place in the regions of East Prussia under the Peace Treaties is to be decisive forever. But suppose the vote is very close; how about a vote where a little over half of the population go one way and a trifle under half go the other? Is this conclusive? Does it have the same moral effect as a larger vote? Is a majority of one vote just as good as a majority of ninety per cent.?

---

a. The statistics of language, etc., even when accurate, do not always forecast the popular wish. Upper Silesia is an instance of this fact. The statistics, as stated in the note of Clemenceau of June 16, 1919, showed 1,250,000 Poles and 650,000 Germans. The vote was 717,122 for Germany and 483,514 for Poland.

In reality, the truth about these proposals for changing frontiers by some sort of international procedure is that those who advocate them do not believe in them as a general proposition. An Englishman who believes in this sort of thing, for example, believes in it as regards Macedonia or some such region; he does not for a moment think that such a procedure should enable the people of British Columbia, say, to become part of the United States. I do not mean to intimate that the people of British Columbia have any such idea; but how is it going to be possible to give the privilege (if it be a privilege) to people along a few selected frontiers?

Another point, a fatal objection to such a scheme, is the inevitable uncertainty which it would set up.

It may be a better thing to live in Manitoba than in North Dakota, or to live in North Dakota than in Manitoba; but worse than almost any conceivable place of residence would be a status which might change in the future, so that one could not tell say five years ahead in what country he was going to live. A frontier is not merely a line drawn on a map or demarcated on the ground; a frontier means a *nexus* of customs, of laws, of traditions and of innumerable other things that directly affect the daily life and conduct of every inhabitant. Any lawyer who has had any experience in the matter will realize the enormous difficulties that surround any transfer of territory merely in connection with the drafting of the necessary papers[a]; and any student who wishes to see how far-reaching the practical difficulties may be need only consider the present situation in Alsace-Lorraine in its bearing upon the relations between France and the Vatican.

The impossibility and the undesirability of setting up any system for changing frontiers, such as has been discussed, are equally evident.

There is another phase of this general question of the *status*

---

a. The Convention between Germany and Poland relating to the régime of Upper Silesia is a document of some 300 pages.

quo which is sometimes discussed by those who seem to have a natural antipathy to the two words and that is what I may call the "raw materials" phase. There is, let us say, no coal in Switzerland, and yet Switzerland must have coal for her people to exist. There are no oil wells in Norway, and yet in Norway there must be, if civilization is to continue, automotive engines. It is obvious that there can be no physical change in such a *status quo*. People who live in the territory that is now Switzerland must get their coal somewhere else, and motor transport in Norway must get its gasoline from other lands.

What is the international phase of such situations as this? There are perhaps three possibilities. One is a war of conquest commenced by a country in the situation of Norway in order to obtain dominion over foreign oil lands; the second is some kind of agreement such as has been suggested in a vague way by the Italians and others for some sort of an international supervision in such matters; and the third is that the situation shall continue as it is now—a matter of bargain and sale, of supply and demand.

There is not the slightest doubt in my mind that, among these three, the first would be as impossible as it would be wicked; the second is wholly outside the realm of practical politics for centuries to come; the third is the *status quo,* which has not in any case of world peace resulted in any serious injustice.

Of course, if we go beyond such cases as Norway and Switzerland and take countries much less favored, it is always a mystery as to why people live in them. It is very difficult to understand, for example, why there are settlers in Labrador, or why people are fond of Greenland as a home; none the less these things are so. And under the existing system of exchange of commodities there has perhaps never been a time when even the people who live in these countries without certain particular natural resources have not generally been able to obtain sufficient of them as a result of their own efforts in the occupations which the character of those lands permits.

Of course some countries are naturally richer than others and must remain so. In the Delta of the Nile, the land produces as many as four crops a year and sells for something like $3,000 an acre. Such a condition cannot be duplicated in a climate where only one crop is possible.

But the notion that *any* State or any combination of States, less than world-wide, *could* be substantially self-sufficient in respect of *all* raw materials is untenable. Even the United States lacks (mentioning minerals only) nickel, cobalt, platinum, tin, diamonds. Its supplies of the following are inadequate: antimony, asbestos, kaolin, chromate, corundum, garnet, manganese, emery, nitrates, potash, pumice, tungsten, vanadium, zirconium. Outside of minerals we lack jute, copra, flax fiber, raw silk, tea, coffee, spices, etc. This mere enumeration suggests the absurdity of the "raw materials" argument against the *status quo*.[a]

Without going into it in detail, the mere fact that there are no copper mines in Germany[b] or in England has never prevented either country from obtaining all the copper that it needed by means of the exchange of its own commodities and its own labor for the copper, say, of Spain, or of the United States, or of Chili; and from any possible point of view that is now conceivable it is only by the continuance of such a system that the deficiency of particular articles in particular countries can be supplied.

All that we can say is, in other words, that so long as the people in a particular country are able to produce enough of something that the rest of the world needs, so long will they be able to supply their own necessities. And if in any country, in Labrador, for example, the people are unable, because of the situation of the country, to produce a sufficiency of consumable and exchangeable commodities, the inevitable result will be the evacuation of that country by civilized human beings. If such a result could be changed by conquest, the change would be only temporary. To attempt to change it by agreement would be to attempt a sort of international charity by means of which peo-

---

a. I am greatly indebted to Professor A. A. Young for some of my economic information; but he is in no way responsible for any of my conclusions.

b. Of course this is an over-statement. Germany produces about one-tenth of her consumption of copper.

ple would be able to live in Labrador by the use of part of the
surplus production, say, of Kentucky, given to them for nothing.

There is a very exaggerated notion in the minds of some as
to the effect of what is called "control of raw materials."

Of course, in time of war, control of raw materials *has* importance. But this does not mean "control" in the sense of
ownership of foreign supplies, as, *e. g.,* British ownership of
Persian oil fields or American ownership of Bolivian tin mines.
It means merely either (1) the possession of adequate domestic
supplies, or (2) safe and unimpeded *access* to foreign sources
of supply, as, *e. g.,* German access, during the war, to Swedish
iron ore. The military significance of raw materials, aside from
purely domestic supplies, is related to such things as naval power,
blockade, "freedom of the seas," "free transit," etc., rather than
to national *ownership* of sources of supplies. *Access to the
market* is the important thing, although the question of finance
may be more difficult in respect of foreign supplies than of domestic.

But in time of peace, the "control of raw materials" in the last
analysis means that the owners of those materials can do only
two things with them, use them or to sell them. This is perhaps
most obvious in the case of such raw materials as are perishable,
but it is true of all.

Take such a product as copper, for example. Some countries
have copper mines, others have none. But the ownership of a
copper mine is of no possible advantage unless the copper produced from that mine is manufactured into something else or
is sold. Of course temporarily a mine owner may leave his ore
in the ground or may store a supply of copper above ground;
but these are expedients to be resorted to only in some time of
over-production and impossible of continuance. If the product
of the mine is not either used or sold, its advantage is purely a
theoretical possibility of the future. It has no more value in
present reality than a bank note on a desert island.

The really important factor, as to raw materials, is *access to
the market* on an *equal footing.*

In practice there are only two ways in which a State or its citizens can be discriminated against, in time of peace, so far as the State's access to supplies of raw materials is concerned. They are as follows:

(1) By discriminatory export duties, or similar duties. In practice these are *not* important.

(2) By discrimination in respect of prices, or similar matters, by *monopolistic* producers. To achieve this result it is necessary not merely that one *State* should have a "monopoly" of the supply of some raw materials, but also that *within* that State, the production and sales of the raw materials should be in the hands of monopoly. Further, the domestic monopolistic organization, must, in order that discrimination should be an outcome of the situation, find it *profitable* (not merely "patriotic") to discriminate in favor of the domestic market. There is *no* important instance of such discrimination.

Such conjunction of circumstances is one which is exceedingly unlikely to occur. There is more chance that there will be discrimination *in favor of* the foreign buyer. In short, the matter is not one of great practical importance, for

     (1) a raw material supplied only by one State
and (2) controlled, *within* the State, by a monopoly, which
also (3) finds it profitable to discriminate against foreign buyers

is something to be found only in imagination.

I venture to say that there has never been a time in modern civilization when the people of any country have been prevented by the international situation from obtaining any raw material whatever for which they had the capacity to pay. The only possible exception to this statement has been in time of war[a]; and the only possible change in the situation in time of peace would, as I have suggested, amount to some form of compulsory international charity.

---

a. Or a period due to war, such as 1919-1920.

If we look generally at this question of the *status quo* from the international point of view during the past two centuries, we find two divergent and irreconcilable lines of treatment.

The jurists and the writers have generally considered that the *status quo* is or ought to be sacred from the point of view of outside attack.[a] In most of the books the question is treated under the heading of "Intervention" and, perhaps with some qualifications, the writers do not admit the legality of intervention. They make exceptions on the ground of self preservation of the intervening State, sometimes on the ground of protection of human life and so on. But, at least with these exceptions, they generally maintain that the State against which the intervention is directed may legally object to it—that is, may legally insist upon the maintenance of the *status quo* (or of its right, in a proper case, to change the *status quo*[b]) and furthermore that such a State might justly, if able (as it usually is not), resort to war against the intervention.

On the other hand, the history of international affairs during this period is quite to the contrary.[c] Over and over again States, sometimes individually, sometimes some of them collectively, have interfered with the affairs of another State with which they had strictly no legal concern, on many different occasions and on all sorts of pretexts. They have defended such intervention at times on the vague grounds of the rights of humanity, the interests of commerce, the restoration of order and so on.

Any one who is familiar, even in a cursory way, with the history of Europe will be able to recall numerous such instances; and it must in fairness be admitted that in some of them the result has seemed beneficent.[d]

And it must not be forgotten that it is not only the wicked powers of Europe that have acted along these lines. In reference

a. See Hall, International Law (Seventh Edition), Chapter VIII, for an illuminating discussion.

b. Such as the right of State A to cede territory to State B, notwithstanding the objection of State C to such a cession.

c. See Moore's Digest, Vol. VI, pp. 2-367.

d. Such as the intervention in Greece in 1827 by Great Britain, France and Russia. See Hertslet's Map of Europe by Treaty, Vol. I, p. 769.

to the affairs of other countries, though not its own, the United States has maintained this privilege of paternal intervention by force. We maintained it, for example, in Cuba in 1898, chiefly on the ground of the sake of humanity.[a] In connection with the Panama Canal, Mr. Root set up the famous proposition[b] that the sovereignty of Columbia over the Isthmus was limited and qualified by the general right of mankind to have a canal between the Atlantic and the Pacific, and to have that canal kept open for the commerce of all.

Many other instances might be cited. It is, however, worth while to recall in connection with this alleged limited right of sovereignty of Columbia over part of its territory that the United States subsequently paid $25,000,000 to the owner of the qualified fee.

It is perhaps unnecessary to add that this alleged right of intervention, as between great powers, was recognized by another name as a method of changing the *status quo,* namely, the method of war.

The effect of the Protocol is unquestionably to consecrate the international *status quo* with a definite position of legality, not to be disturbed by force.[c] The views of the writers, as opposed to the practice of Great Powers, have been adopted.

Article 2 of the Protocol forbids a resort to war[d] as against any

---

a. See the Message of President McKinley, April 11, 1898, Foreign Relations, 1898, p. 750 at p. 757.

b. The Ethics of the Panama Question, Sen. Doc. 471, 63rd Congress, 2nd Session, p. 39.

c. There is a reference to the *status quo* in the General Report (Annex C, p. 181), which uses this language:

"There is a third class of disputes to which the new system of pacific settlement can also not be applied. These are disputes which aim at revising treaties and international acts in force, or which seek to jeopardise the existing territorial integrity of signatory States. The proposal was made to include these exceptions in the Protocol, but the two Committees were unanimous in considering that, both from the legal and from the political point of view, the impossibility of applying compulsory arbitration to such cases was so obvious that it was quite superfluous to make them the subject of a special provision. It was thought sufficient to mention them in this report."

d. For the view that this includes acts of force, even in the absence of a state of war, see *infra,* p. 55.

other State, a party to the Protocol, "except in case of resistance to acts of aggression."[a]

Under Article 8, every Signatory agrees to abstain from any act which might constitute a threat of aggression.

Under these provisions and the provisions of the Protocol for the settlement of international disputes, intervention to upset the *status quo* (or to prevent a state from changing it where it legally may) becomes aggression and is an international crime.

---

a. The other exception "when acting in agreement with the Council," etc., is not here material. It is discussed *infra,* p. 50.

CHAPTER VIII.

DOMESTIC QUESTIONS.

The treatment in the Protocol of so-called domestic questions aroused a great deal of discussion not only at the Assembly last September, but since the adoption there of the text.

It may be remembered that there was a similar public discussion at the time of the drafting of the Covenant; in that document[a] a domestic question is defined as "a matter which by international law is solely within the domestic jurisdiction" of a State.

Among instances of domestic questions which have been mentioned from time to time, perhaps the two most commonly referred to in this country are the tariff and immigration. Of course it has been pointed out very often that even such questions as these, however inherently domestic, may become international as soon as they are made the subject of a treaty, as they so frequently are. It should be added that almost any question, no matter how "domestic" in its nature originally, *may* become the subject of international cognizance by virtue of a treaty. There are many treaties of the United States which have related to such questions as the inheritance of land, the right to administer the estates of decedents, etc.; a very recent instance is a treaty between this country and Canada regarding the protection of migratory birds, a treaty which has been upheld as valid by the Supreme Court.[b]

None the less, the absolute right of a country to regulate these matters in its own discretion must be recognized as a matter of strict law. Any country, in the absence of treaty, may, at its pleasure, exclude foreigners from entering into its territory, for example. I think no one questions this.[c]

However, as a matter of fact and as a result of the development of the world's commerce, there is hardly any such question which remains exclusively domestic. For example, even in our

a. Article 15, paragraph 8.
b. Missouri *v.* Holland, 252 U. S., 416.
c. See Moore's Digest, Vol. IV, p. 67, *et seq.,* also p. 151, *et seq.*

drastic Immigration Law of 1924,[a] there are various treaty rights of entry into the country for the purposes of commerce and so on which are expressly and in terms saved by the statute. Furthermore, there is, I suppose, hardly a country in the world which does not have various most-favored-nation treaties which directly affect tariffs.

Again, modern developments necessitate the extension of international discussions and agreements to matters previously undreamed of; the erection of wireless stations near frontiers is a very practical instance; there must be some kind of agreement to prevent jamming in the air. The negotiations about the opium traffic have gone to the length of discussions as to what areas in certain regions should be planted with the poppy; a more essentially domestic question than the crops to be grown within a country could hardly be imagined.

In my opinion, the Protocol follows the Covenant in its treatment of these domestic questions and goes no farther. The Covenant provides that if, upon reference to the Council, it is found that a dispute arises "out of a matter which by international law is solely within the domestic jurisdiction," the Council shall report to that effect and shall not even make a recommendation as to its settlement (Article 15, paragraph 8). In practice the Council will doubtless refer this question of law to the Permanent Court for an advisory opinion.[b]

The Protocol (Article 5, paragraphs 1 and 2) continues this provision and applies it also to any arbitration which takes place by its terms. It is provided that if one of the parties to the dispute claims that the dispute "or part thereof" arises out of a domestic question, the arbitrators must take the advice of the Permanent Court on the point. The opinion of the Permanent Court is binding on the arbitrators and if the Court holds that the matter is "domestic," the power of the arbitrators to decide

---

a. Act of May 26, 1924.
b. As in the case of the Tunis and Morocco nationality decrees, Advisory Opinion No. 4, February 7, 1923.

the question is at an end and they are confined merely to recording the Court's opinion.

The further provision of Article 5 on this question is the last paragraph of that Article, which reads as follows:[a]

> "If the question is held by the Court or by the Council to be a matter solely within the domestic jurisdiction of the State, this decision shall not prevent consideration of the situation by the Council or by the Assembly under Article 11 of the Covenant."

So far as this provision goes, I do not think that it adds anything to the effect of Article 11 of the Covenant. The matter would stand precisely where it does now, even if this last paragraph of Article 5 of the Protocol had been omitted.

Under Article 11 of the Covenant, both the Council and the Assembly have the right to consider any circumstance which threatens to disturb international peace. This does not mean any right of decision or even recommendation in any binding sense. What it does is to give to the Council or to the Assembly the privilege of attempting, by friendly offices, to avert war.

To my mind there is nothing very new in this; indeed, it is rather inherent in the idea of any international association for the prevention of war. After all, there is no doubt that these so-called domestic questions have their international repercussions. The case that was put by way of argument at Geneva was the control of the quinine of the world by the Dutch, which is said to be practically absolute. What would happen if the Dutch put an embargo upon the exportation of this drug? It would be idle to say that such an act, legal as it would be in the strict sense, would not have a profound effect upon civilization generally. Under Article 11,[b] such an act could be discussed before the Council with a representative of the Dutch Government present, in an effort to obtain some adjustment, some change in what had been done; but that would be all.

In 1898, the United States went to war with Spain over what

---

a. This is one part of the so-called Japanese Amendment, as to which see *infra*, p. 64, *et seq.*
b. of the Covenant.

was, technically at least, from the point of view of Spain, a domestic question, namely, the internal situation in Cuba. Shortly before hostilities broke out, the six then Great Powers of Europe addressed to the United States a friendly note in the matter, to which this Government replied.[a] In principle, I cannot see any difference between such diplomatic correspondence and the discussion of the matter by the Council of the League, a discussion to which presumably Spain and not the United States would have been the party to object, for the question was a Spanish domestic question of which we were complaining.

There are other aspects of the treatment by the Protocol of domestic questions, in connection with the Covenants against War, and with Aggression, under which headings it will be discussed.[b]

---

a. Foreign Relations (U. S.), 1898, pp. 740-741.
b. See *infra*, p. 50 and p. 54. Also "The Japanese Amendment," p. 64.

CHAPTER IX.

COVENANTS AGAINST WAR.

Under the Protocol, the agreement of the parties thereto (Article 2) not to resort to war with one another is, if the terms of the Protocol are carried out, absolute. The only stated exceptions in Article 2 of the Protocol are (1) in case of resistance to acts of aggression and (2) when acting in agreement with the Council or the Assembly under the Covenant or the Protocol.

The first exception relates to defence and, if there be no aggression, as there would not be if the Protocol is lived up to, there would never be any need of defence against aggression.

The second exception, so far as it relates to a Party to the Protocol against whom force might be used, relates primarily to an aggressor, as defined in the Protocol. Of course this second exception in this regard goes beyond the question of defence, strictly speaking, because it would permit a State, not attacked, to go to the defence of another State attacked if and when the application of the Sanctions of the Protocol is called for by the Council[a]; but if the Parties to the Protocol carry out their agreements as therein expressed, there could never be any war between two or more of them.

There appears to be another possibility of the use of force within the language of this second exception; this is the case where a State, against which has gone a decision of the Court or an arbitral award, fails to carry out the decision or award.

The provision of the Covenant regarding such a situation is contained in Article 13, where it is said that the Council shall "propose what steps should be taken to give effect" to such decision or award. Obviously such proposals by the Council would not have any binding effect upon the Members of the League.

However, under the Covenant, the State in whose favor the decision or award had gone *might* lawfully have resorted to war against the State refusing to carry out the decision or award,

---

a. See the discussion on this point, *infra,* p. 72, *et seq.*

provided merely that it delayed resort to war for three months thereafter, under the language of Article 12 of the Covenant. In other words, if an award or decision was made and a State refused to carry it out, the successful party, under the Covenant, agreed merely to refrain from war against the defeated party for a period of three months.

The Protocol (Article 4 [6]), as interpreted by the Report to the Assembly, still permits the successful party to use force in such a case but only when the Council authorizes the use of force, such authorization being brought within the terms of Article 13 of the Covenant.

It is true that the Council is first to exert its influence to secure compliance with the decision or award and that, if the use of this influence fails, the Council may then propose measures short of force before authorizing the use of force itself.

Indeed, the Report[a] says that the Council may "institute[b] against the recalcitrant party collective sanctions of an economic or financial order." If this means that the Signatories to the Protocol are obligated to employ such sanctions in such a case when called on by the Council, I can only say that, in my opinion, the statement is not warranted by any language of the Protocol or of the Covenant.

However, the final effect of these provisions is that with the authorization of the Council the successful party *may* use force to execute a judicial decree or arbitral award.

Furthermore, the Report to the Assembly says that in such a case the defeated party could not resist, and that, if it did resist, it would become an aggressor against whom all the Sanctions of the Protocol might be brought into play.

To see how this would work out, let us suppose that in an arbitration between State A and State B, State A obtained an award to the effect that State B should pay to it the sum of twenty million dollars. Thereupon State B refuses to pay the award and, notwithstanding the efforts of the Council, maintains that

---

a.   Annex C, p. 180; see also pp. 168, 169.
b.   The word in the French text of the Report is "déclencher."

refusal, thereby violating its agreement in the Protocol (and in the Covenant also) to carry out any such award.

Thereupon the Council authorizes State A to use force to collect the money. It is no answer to this to say that the Council would not authorize the use of force, for we are considering what may be done, not what would be done. State A then begins to use force and, if State B resists at all, the entire machinery of the Sanctions of the Protocol can be brought into play and these include military and naval Sanctions.

Of course, such a result would be highly improbable, but I submit that it ought to be legally impossible. The provisions of the Protocol in this regard go very much farther than they ought to go, and very much farther, in my opinion, than the States of the world are now willing to go.

The case which I have supposed is one of a money judgment. A more difficult case would be one where the award was for the recovery by State A of certain territory in the possession of State B which State B thereupon refused to give up. In such a case there is more to be said for the use of force than in the other.

In any case, the refusal of a State to carry out the judicial decision or the arbitral award after solemnly agreeing to do so is a very serious breach of a treaty; but the idea of the authorization of force to execute such a decision seems to me to present a question of the very gravest character. My own view is against it. I am inclined to think that the penalty of expulsion from the League under the fourth paragraph of Article 16 of the Covenant should be the utmost permissible.

Whether this view of mine be correct or not, certainly the countries of the world are not going to accept any provision by which they will be obligated in advance to join in measures to enforce the result of an arbitration or of a litigation before the Permanent Court. Whether they will agree to a provision permitting the successful party, so to speak, to execute the decision or award on its own account is perhaps doubtful; but certainly they will go no farther, if as far; and this is one of the provisions of the Protocol which will have to be changed before the document becomes a reality.

Subject to the foregoing exceptions, the general covenant under Article 2 of the Protocol not to go to war is, in my opinion, all inclusive. It obviously includes all cases where there is a dispute of international cognizance, for in such cases all parties agree upon a final and binding method of decision and agree to carry out the decision. It also includes, as pointed out previously,[a] all cases in which one State would seek to change by force the *status quo,* or to prevent by force a lawful change in the *status quo.*[b] Neither the lawful maintenance of the *status quo* nor its lawful change would come within the general exceptions of Article 2.

Furthermore, the covenant against war in Article 2 would also exclude the going to war about domestic questions. All that any Signatory agrees to do regarding such a question, if, when raised internationally, it is not settled by negotiation, is to discuss it before the Council or the Assembly.[c] A State which did that would have fulfilled all its obligations regardless of any action or inaction as to the domestic question itself; and an attack made on it by any other State would then be aggression under the terms of the Protocol. There is no exception. As the Report to the Fifth Assembly says,[d] "Our purpose was to make war impossible, to kill it, to annihilate it." This, if lived up to by the Parties, the paper does, as among them.

The detailed provisions of Articles 7 to 10 inclusive of the Protocol confirm the views above expressed. The provisions of these Articles will be more specially considered in connection with the question of Aggression.[e]

---

a. p. 45.
b. An instance of this would be if States A and B agreed on a cession of territory from one to the other, to which State C objected.
c. Under Article 11 of the Covenant.
d. p. 208, *infra.*
e. p. 54, *et seq.*

CHAPTER X.

AGGRESSION.

The preamble to the Protocol asserts that a war of aggression is an international crime. I have discussed above[a] the agreement of the parties to the Protocol not to resort to war except in defence against aggression or in aid of defence against aggression or perhaps in execution of a judicial decision or arbitral award. This is the general covenant of Article 2 of the Protocol. It is this resort to war, contrary to the terms of the Protocol, which is the chief breach of the Protocol against which its chief Sanctions are ordered.

By Article 10 of the Protocol[b] every State which resorts to war in violation of the undertakings either in the Covenant or in the Protocol, is an aggressor.

It will be necessary to consider only the provisions of the Protocol forbidding a resort to war, for it would be impossible to have a resort to war contrary to the Covenant which would not also be a resort to war contrary to the Protocol. The provisions of the Protocol go farther than those of the Covenant in this regard.

It is true that there are in the Covenant certain engagements by Members of the League not to resort to war. These are found in Articles 12, 13 and 15; but it is unnecessary to consider them in detail, for any resort to war contrary to the provisions of those Articles of the Covenant would clearly also be contrary to the general engagements of Article 2 of the Protocol.

The Report to the Assembly[c] seems to infer that a violation of the obligation of Article 10 of the Covenant on the part of all Members of the League to respect the territorial integrity and political independence of other Members might be a resort to war not included in the language of the Protocol; but I think that

---

a. p. 50, *et seq.*
b. First paragraph.
c. Annex C, p. 156 at p. 186.

any such forcible violation would be within the terms of the
Protocol also.

It is against the aggressor that the Sanctions of the Protocol
are set up and accordingly the provisions of the Protocol defining
an aggressor and the procedure for determining what State is
an aggressor are of the utmost consequence.

The definitions of an aggressor under the Protocol are complex in their language though not in their fundamental idea,
which is that aggression is a resort to war instead of to arbitration.[a] The language of the definitions is obscured by certain presumptions (Article 10) and by the procedure laid down for the
determination of an aggressor.

The general definition of an aggressor in the first paragraph
of Article 10 of the Protocol I have mentioned above. It is well,
however, to quote it in full:

> "Every State which resorts to war in violation of the
> undertakings contained in the Covenant or in the present
> Protocol is an aggressor. Violation of the rules laid down
> for a demilitarized zone shall be held equivalent to resort
> to war."

This is the general definition of principle. It relates back in
its meaning to Article 2 of the Protocol, the general engagement
not to resort to war. Beyond that, it makes the violation of the
rules for an agreed demilitarized zone the equivalent of a resort
to war, the two are assimilated.

The first question that arises regarding this general definition
is whether the words "resort to war" mean necessarily an actual
and technical state of war only, or whether they include all acts
of violence and force, even if such acts did not in a particular
case result in an actual state of war, because, for example, not
resisted.

The view of the Report to the Assembly[b] in this matter is that
such acts of violence are included in the expression. I am in-

---

a. I use the word here in its largest sense.
b. Annex C, p. 156 at p. 187.

clined to agree with this view, though as a mere matter of language an argument to the contrary is possible.

Suppose, however, that there is an actual state of war; how is it to be determined which one of the two[a] belligerents is the aggressor?

The Protocol attempts to meet this difficulty by laying down two different methods of determining the aggressor. One is by creating certain presumptions, which I shall discuss later; the other is for the case in which none of the presumptions is applicable.

In this case, that is to say, in the absence of the presumptions, it is for the Council to determine the aggressor and, in order to come to such a determination, the Council must act unanimously under the general rule of Article 5 of the Covenant.

I have no doubt of this conclusion, which is the conclusion of the Report to the Assembly. It is true that the language of Article 10 of the Protocol is not as clear as it might be, since the duty and power of the Council to determine the aggressor are not directly stated, but rather to be inferred from the language.

What Article 10 of the Protocol says as to this in its last paragraph but two[b] is that, apart from the cases when there is a presumption,

> "if the Council does not at once succeed in determining the aggressor, it shall be bound to enjoin upon the belligerents an armistice, and shall fix the terms, acting, if need be, by a two-thirds majority and shall supervise its execution."

---

a. Of course there may be more than two.

b. The reason why I have used in regard to Article 10 of the Protocol this uncouth language, "its last paragraph but two," is that in the English text of Article 10 there is a textual error which is extremely confusing. Article 10 really consists of five paragraphs, and the second of these five paragraphs has two sub-heads or sub-paragraphs numbered 1 and 2. The third paragraph of Article 10, in referring to these two sub-heads of the second paragraph calls them "paragraphs 1 and 2." In other words, the first words of what is here referred to as the third paragraph of Article 10 (the paragraph which I call "the last paragraph but two") read as follows: "Apart from the cases dealt with in paragraphs 1 and 2 of the present Article." They should read something like this: "Apart from the cases dealt with in sub-heads 1 and 2 of the second paragraph of the present article." Compare the French text which is perfectly clear: "Hors les hypothèses visées aux numéros 1 et 2 du présent article." See the English and French Texts of Article 10 in full, *infra*, pp. 144, 145.

So that in those cases where the presumptions hereafter considered do *not* arise, it is the duty of the Council to determine the aggressor; it must act unanimously in coming to such a determination; as the Report to the Assembly says,

> "Where there is no presumption, the Council has to declare the fact of aggression; a decision is necessary and must be taken unanimously";

and, if the Council is not unanimous, it *must* enjoin an armistice upon the belligerents.

Before coming to the procedure before the Council, I now enumerate those cases in which, because of the existence of certain facts, a State is "presumed" to be an aggressor; any such presumption can be upset only by the *unanimous* decision of the Council to the contrary. These cases are as follows:

> 1. If hostilities have broken out and a State has refused to submit the dispute to the procedure for pacific settlement contemplated by the Protocol.
>
> 2. If hostilities have broken out and a State has refused to comply with a decision, award, etc.
>
> 3. If hostilities have broken out and a State has disregarded a determination that the matter in dispute is a domestic matter *and* has not submitted the question for discussion by the Council or Assembly under Article 11 of the Covenant.
>
> 4. If hostilities have broken out and a State has violated the provisional measures against mobilization, etc., contemplated by Article 7 of the Protocol (and which will be mentioned later).

Certainly the theory of the first three of the four instances above mentioned is the theory stated by Herriot in his speech before the Assembly that the State that refuses arbitration is an aggressor.[a] In other words, law is substituted for force.

Now it is to be observed that in each of the four foregoing

a. September 5, 1924.

cases *hostilities must have broken out* and in each one of them at least one additional fact must have occurred.

In other words, given certain facts, there is a presumption as to the aggressor; but who is to say, how it is to be determined, whether or not at any particular moment these facts exist? It is not sufficient to say that the facts will be open and notorious, for they might not be. Indeed, if we look critically at each one of what I may call the required facts, we find that doubt might arise.

Take the primary fact, which is always required for any presumption to arise; this fact is that hostilities shall have broken out. One's first impression might be that this could never be a matter of doubt; but this is not so. Take the case of Corfu, for example. Italian officers had been murdered in Greece by somebody; various individuals had been killed at Corfu by a bombardment of the Italian fleet. Had or had not hostilities broken out within the meaning of Article 10 of the Protocol? Surely the point is at least debatable.

Take the next required fact, that a State has refused to submit a dispute to the procedure for pacific settlement. It is very easy to suppose cases where there would be a difference of view as to this. A State might claim, for example, that the matter was a domestic question which it did not have to submit to the procedure for pacific settlement. There might be a difference of opinion as to whether or not the matter had been actually decided by the tribunal. It is not at all uncommon in municipal law for parties to disagree as to whether a particular question is or is not *res judicata;* there have been many litigations over this very point; and there have been international arbitrations in which it was raised.[a]

Similarly, difference of opinion might exist as to whether or not a State had disregarded a determination that the matter in dispute was domestic or as to whether or not a State had sub-

a. *e. g.,* the Pious Fund case reported in the Hague Arbitration Cases, p. 1, and the Interest Case between Russia and Turkey, op. cit., p. 260. These two cases are also in Stowell and Munro's International Cases, Vol. I, p. 58, *et seq.*

mitted a question for discussion under Article 11 of the Covenant. Such differences of opinion could easily arise because of the non-formulation in precise terms of just what the dispute was. Parties do not always agree as to what it is they are differing about and they may in fact be at the same time differing as to more than one question. As to whether or not a State had violated the provisional measures against mobilization contemplated by Article 7 of the Protocol, that document itself recognizes that such a question would require investigation, and in such case and in such case only the Protocol gives the Council the power to determine the question of fact, acting by a two-thirds majority.

So we come back to the situation that a presumption as to the aggressor can exist only if certain facts exist; and that the existence of one or more of these facts may very likely be in doubt or dispute and that, with one exception, there is no procedure for determining such questions of fact so as to be able to say with certainty that the presumption *does* exist.

What is the answer to this difficulty? If we look at the matter technically, we must conclude that none of the presumptions created by Article 10 of the Protocol can ever arise unless the facts[a] were admitted by the two[b] disputants. Such an admission would mean, in other words, that one of the parties openly admitted that it was an aggressor.

If the facts were in dispute or, in other words, if the existence of the presumption was in dispute, the Council could not determine the aggressor on the basis of a presumption requiring the unanimous vote of the Council to upset it; but would be required to determine the aggressor under the general provision which was first mentioned, under which no presumption exists and when the Council is required by affirmative unanimous vote to determine the aggressor.

Here again, however, there would unquestionably be disputed facts; that is to say, unless one of the parties said that it was the aggressor, it would require an elaborate investigation to deter-

a. I mean the facts from which the presumption as to the aggressor would arise.
b. I assume only two, for convenience.

mine under the language of Article 10 of the Protocol whether a
State *had* resorted to war in violation of its undertaking, or *had*
violated the rules laid down for a demilitarized zone. It is
utterly impossible to suppose that the Council could ever immediately determine the aggressor under such circumstances by
unanimous vote; and such determination *must* be immediate.
The language of the text is: "at once"; and in the French: "dans
le plus bref délai."

Let us look at the matter concretely and take up the question
of procedure, supposing an actual case before the Council.
There is a crisis; hostilities have or are supposed to have broken
out; there are two States which either are or are thought to be
at war; the Council meets. Not only under the realities of the
situation, but under the express language of the Protocol, the
Council must act instantly; the peace of the world is at stake.

Now, under those circumstances, there could be only two situations. One would be when some Great Power, either by open
and announced defiance or by its refusal even to meet with the
Council, proclaimed itself an aggressor. In that case of course
neither the language of Article 10 nor any other language would
make any difference. The other situation would be that the two
States were there before the Council, each claiming that the
other was in the wrong, each disputing the allegations of fact
made by the other's representative. In such case clearly no presumption could arise and in such case the Council could not ever
immediately determine the aggressor by unanimous vote. The
mere fact that it would require time to examine into the truth
of the respective allegations would prevent this. So the Council,
by the compelling facts of the situation and indeed in accordance
with the strictest construction of the Protocol, would be con-
strained to declare and would declare an armistice.

Any dispute as to what State was guilty of aggression prior
to that time would be put over for subsequent adjustment; the
armistice would be laid down and would be obeyed. Of course,
in theory, it could be violated and the violator of the armistice

would become the aggressor; but a State that was going to refuse or violate the armistice, knowing the procedure, would doubtless not go to the Council at all.

So, to my mind, the vital part of the procedure laid down by Article 10 for determining an aggressor is found in the provision giving the Council the power immediately to declare an armistice; and, under the procedure, this, in my judgment, is the only power that the Council would ever exercise, except in the case suggested, in which a State itself denounced itself as an aggressor.

I am aware that the framers of the Protocol are not in accord with these views. In their opinion, the presumptions of Article 10 establish "an automatic procedure which would not necessarily be based on a decision of the Council." They say that where a presumption has arisen and is not unanimously rejected by the Council, "the facts themselves decide who is an aggressor" and otherwise that "the Council has to declare the fact of aggression."

I can only say that their conclusions, while perhaps admissible as a mere matter of language and nothing but language, take no account of the inevitable certainty that there will always be at least two views of what the facts are; to put it from a legalistic viewpoint, tribunals do not deal with facts; they deal with what lawyers call facts, but which are merely conclusions based on such evidence as is available. This sort of a "fact" is arrived at only after a hearing or a trial of some kind; and to suppose that the Council could ever conduct such a hearing and at the same time come to a unanimous and immediate conclusion is to suppose a contradiction in terms.[a]

So while from the language of Article 10 of the Protocol difficulty may arise in determining an aggressor under its provisions (for there might in any case be a disputed or doubtful question of fact; and the Council under the provisions of the Covenant would in general have to act unanimously) the Protocol provides a solution of any such difficulty by saying that if the Council does not immediately determine the aggressor, it *must*

---

a. In the Dogger Bank case, the Commission of Inquiry sat for more than two months. Hague Court Reports, Scott, p. 403.

(the language is mandatory) proceed to enjoin an armistice, to fix its terms and to supervise its execution, acting for these purposes by two-thirds majority. Then the Protocol provides that any belligerent which refuses the armistice or violates it shall be the aggressor.

These provisions regarding an armistice seem to me to meet any possible objection that might be raised to the absence of a more complete and detailed system of determining in fact and in law what State is an aggressor.

No matter what the presumptions were or even what procedure was laid down, it is clear that, after hostilities in any given case had actually commenced, there would be enormous difficulty for any tribunal whatever in laying down conclusively which State was the aggressor. After all, the vital thing is to prevent war; and the opening of hostilities, to be immediately followed by an armistice, would not be very much of a war. So I regard these provisions as to an armistice as the most ingenious and, except its statements of principle, the most important of all the provisions of Article 10 of the Protocol.

The power given to the Council to formulate an armistice would be the power exercised if hostilities broke out rather than the power of adjudging the aggressor; unless the aggression was openly admitted, which would mean that one of the parties to the Protocol really defied the others; and, in that case, of course, it would defy the terms of an armistice as well as any other terms. But in any other case a new consideration would immediately arise. The Council would formulate an armistice and in the absence of an open defiance by one State, or possibly by a group of States, of all the others, the armistice would introduce a new situation, a situation in which hostilities were *not* going on; and human experience shows that, given an armistice, the recommencement of hostilities on the old grounds is a real impossibility.

In the view that I take, the Sanctions of the Protocol become less important in the light of its provisions as to the determination of an aggressor, for it is only against an aggressor that the

main Sanctions of the Protocol can be brought into play; and
these provisions for determining the aggressor really mean that
an aggressor is a State or a combination of States which has
finally and deliberately determined to begin war and to carry it
on regardless of its most solemn engagements to the contrary.
In other words, there could be no war as between the parties
to the Protocol without a wilful, wanton and wicked disregard of
its provisions.

CHAPTER XI.

During the framing of the Protocol of Geneva by the Committees of the Fifth Assembly of the League of Nations, the language of the document was changed by what has been called the Japanese Amendment; and while the provisions which constitute that amendment as part of the Protocol have been generally considered in the previous discussion in connection with the application of various Articles, still that amendment attained such prominence in the discussions in the Fifth Assembly and since, that it may well be separately reviewed.

The Japanese Amendment related to domestic questions, questions within the domestic jurisdiction of a State; and before coming to its terms, it will be well to see what the situation as to these domestic questions is under the Covenant, taken by itself.

The Covenant, as we have seen,[a] provided for the submission to the Council of all disputes between Members of the League which were not otherwise adjusted by some kind of agreement or by some kind of Tribunal. In regard to those disputes submitted to the Council, the eighth paragraph of Article 15 of the Covenant said that if one of the parties claimed, and if the Council found, that the dispute related to a question which by international law was entirely within the jurisdiction of a State, the Council should so report and make not even a recommendation regarding a settlement. In other words, if the dispute related to a domestic question and one of the parties to the dispute raised the point, the Council could not proceed at all to make any recommendation which would bind the parties to the dispute or either of them to anything whatever.

At the same time, under the Covenant, by Article 11, either the Council or the Assembly might consider *any* circumstance tending to threaten or disturb international peace. The language in this regard is general. It means no more than discussion and

---

a. *Supra,* p. 18, *et seq.*

suggestion, except perhaps publicity; but under this language of Article 11, the parties were left with their liberty of action in the matter; and indeed, under the Covenant, the Members of the League entered into no commitment against going to war in the case of a dispute about a domestic question.

So we may sum up the provisions of the Covenant as to a dispute regarding a domestic question by saying that while such a dispute might go to the Council,[a] still the Council,[a] if the point were raised, could make no recommendation about it; but the Council (or the Assembly) might take the matter into consideration as a subject of discussion when it threatened peace, with the hope and duty to preserve the peace if possible; but in regard to this the parties remained free to act as they might themselves finally determine.

The Protocol of course, as we have also seen,[b] makes a great change in this situation because it contains a general agreement by the parties not to resort to war, an agreement which is applicable to disputes about domestic questions to the same extent that it is applicable to disputes about international questions; this general agreement not to go to war includes all questions of both kinds.

Furthermore, the Protocol makes it very much more likely that disputes between Members of the League will go for a hearing to a Committee of Arbitrators than to the Council; we have seen[c] that the likelihood of any dispute going to the Council under the new régime, for consideration on the merits, is remote. The functions of the Council regarding disputes are to some extent delegated to the Permanent Court of International Justice, but even more largely to Committees of Arbitrators agreed on or appointed *ad hoc*.

Now the Japanese amendment is not strictly a single amendment; it is in two parts. The first part is the last (third) paragraph of Article 5 of the Protocol, reading as follows:

---

a.   or the Assembly.
b.   *Supra,* p. 50, *et seq.*
c.   *Supra,* p. 23, *et seq.*

"If the question is held by the Court or by the Council to be a matter solely within the domestic jurisdiction of the State, this decision shall not prevent consideration of the situation by the Council or by the Assembly under Article 11 of the Covenant."

We must bear in mind that by the second paragraph of Article 5, any Committee of Arbitrators, in its consideration of a dispute is subject to the same limitations concerning a dispute about a domestic question as are provided for the Council. The method of so limiting the Committee of Arbitrators is that the question of law is decided by the Permanent Court of International Justice, and if that Court decides that the question is domestic, the Committee of Arbitrators simply so declares and proceeds no farther.

What the paragraph of Article 5 above quoted says is that although neither the Council nor a Committee of Arbitrators may consider a dispute regarding a domestic question if the point is raised, still none the less the Council or the Assembly, under Article 11 of the Covenant, may consider the situation in its bearing upon the peace of the world. Now such consideration under Article 11 of the Covenant would have been possible without this statement, so that, to my mind, this portion of the Japanese amendment makes no change in that regard. The paragraph does not change the legal situation at all, but simply makes explicit what was otherwise implied.

The other portion of the Japanese Amendment is the clause which is added to sub-head 1 of the second paragraph of Article 10, beginning with the word "nevertheless."

In order to see just what this other portion of the Japanese Amendment is, I cite here the second paragraph of Article 10 (omitting certain phrases not here material) with the words of the Japanese Amendment italicised:

"In the event of hostilities having broken out, any State shall be presumed to be an aggressor, unless a decision of the Council, which must be taken unanimously, shall otherwise declare:

1.   If it * * * has disregarded a unanimous report of
the Council, a judicial sentence or an arbitral award
recognizing that the dispute between it and the other
belligerent State arises out of a matter which by
international law is solely within the domestic jurisdiction of the latter State; *nevertheless, in the last
case the State shall only be presumed to be an
aggressor if it has not previously submitted the
question to the Council or the Assembly, in accordance with Article 11 of the Covenant.*"

The language of Article 10 of the Protocol is quite involved.
I have already discussed it at some length,[a] endeavoring to
show that its real effect differs greatly from the theory of its
framers, a theory borne out, perhaps, by the language of Article
10 considered as language only. I sum up *that theory* as follows:

Laying down the general principle that a State which resorts
to war contrary to the Covenant or to the Protocol is an aggressor,
and prescribing a general procedure by which it is for the Council to decide, unanimously of course, whether such a violation
has taken place (and in the absence of such unanimous decision
to declare an armistice) none the less Article 10 limits or qualifies
this general procedure by enumerating certain classes of cases
in which the facts would *supposedly* be so open, so notorious, so
impossible to question, that they would create a presumption as
to the State which was the aggressor; and such presumption
could be upset only by unanimous vote of the Council against it.

I repeat that this is the theory of MM. Benes and Politis; it is
not mine.

My own view, heretofore expressed, is that in no case could
the supposedly notorious facts create a presumption because
there would always be a difference of opinion as to those very
facts themselves.

But proceeding on the other theory, and looking only at the
language, the presumptions are important; here it is necessary
to refer to only one of them.

a. pp. 54-63.

This presumption arises when a State has "disregarded" a decision by the Council, by the Court or by the Arbitrators following the Court, that a dispute arises out of a domestic question *and has also not submitted*[a] the question to the Council or the Assembly for discussion, under Article 11 of the Covenant.

Before the Japanese amendment, the text was that the presumption arose when a State "disregarded" such a decision to the effect that the dispute arose out of a domestic question.

Now let us see what the difference between the two is, that is to say, the difference between the text *prior* to the Japanese amendment and the text *with* the Japanese amendment.

In either case the decision on the question of law has gone against the complaining State. The proper tribunal has decided that the question is a domestic question and that decision in either case is and remains conclusive.

In either case, the State "disregarding" that decision and going to war is an aggressor. We may see that this is so by supposing that the entire original text as well as the text of this portion of the Japanese amendment was stricken out.[b] Then, clearly, the State would be an aggressor under Article 2 of the Protocol and under the first paragraph of Article 10; and there is nothing either in the original text that we are considering or in the Japanese addition thereto which changes that conclusion.[c]

The difference then between the original text and the text with the amendment is this: in the original text, a complaining State disregarding such a binding decision as to the domestic character of the question was *presumed* an aggressor if it went

a. The text says "previously." Presumably this means before hostilities broke out. It *might* mean before the "disregard" of the decision that the dispute was domestic. Precisely how a State could "disregard" such a decision, except by resort to war, is not very clear. The French is "qui aura passé outre à un rapport," etc.

b. That is, all the text above quoted as part of sub-head 1 of the second paragraph of Article 10, beginning "has disregarded a unanimous report of the Council."

c. The Japanese proposal regarding this Article as it first stood, was to strike out all the words referring to the "domestic jurisdiction," etc.; the addition of the clause commencing "nevertheless" was a compromise; it would have been a much simpler result and a better one, I think, to have omitted the whole clause, as the Japanese proposed.

to war *either before or after* the consideration of the matter by the Council or the Assembly under Article 11 of the Covenant. Under the text as amended, such a State is *presumed* to be an aggressor only if it resorts to war *before* such consideration under that Article 11.

In other words, the difference between the original and amended texts would arise only in the following circumstances: State A brings a dispute against State B before a tribunal (Council, Committee of Arbitrators, etc.). The tribunal renders a binding decision that the dispute arises out of a domestic question. The complaining State, bound by that decision, then brings the matter before the Council or the Assembly under Article 11 of the Covenant and no adjustment results; thereupon the complaining State resorts to war.

Under those circumstances, in the original text, the State resorting to war would be *presumed* an aggressor, a presumption to be upset only by the unanimous vote of the Council against it. Under the amended text, the complaining State would be an aggressor, but there would be no presumption; and the determination that it was an aggressor would come on to be made by the Council, which would either have to vote unanimously that the complaining State was an aggressor, or else proclaim an armistice.

I confess that it is difficult to see why such a refined and subtle and technical distinction about the presumption of aggression should be made. If there is a binding decision by a tribunal that a dispute arises out of a domestic question, surely a complaining State, under the principles of the Protocol, is bound not to go to war, because it is legally wrong in its claim and has been so adjudged. Just why a State going to war under such circumstances should be *presumed* to be and be an aggressor if it goes to war *before* a discussion of the matter subsequent to the decision and not be *presumed* to be an aggressor but merely be an aggressor, if it goes to war *after* such discussion, is not logically to be explained.

However, the foregoing discussion resulting in such an

obscure and technical distinction is, as I intimated, based solely
on the language of the Article and on the legalistic theory of its
framers as to its meaning and result. Earlier in my discussion,[a]
I pointed out that I do not agree with the conclusions of MM.
Benes and Politis, for I do not think that the presumptions laid
down in Article 10 of the Protocol would ever have any material
bearing on the decision reached by the Council. In other words,
repeating in substance what I said before, I believe that the
power to declare an armistice is the only power under Article 10
of the Protocol which the Council would ever exercise, except in
a case where a State itself denounced itself as an aggressor.

Furthermore, it seems to me that the very intricacies of the
language of Article 10 of the Protocol are themselves a very real
indication that my conclusion is correct.

As a matter of reality, I cannot see that the Japanese amendment in any conceivable case would cause any difference in
what would happen. We must suppose that war has commenced, for unless there is a resort to war, Article 10 of the
Protocol is out of the picture entirely. Assuming then a resort
to war, there are, under Article 10, with all its provisions and
exceptions and presumptions, only two real possibilities:

a. There is an open and admitted and defiant aggression.

b. There is a difference as to the facts and it follows
that it is not possible for the Council *at once* to reach a
unanimous conclusion in the case; accordingly the Council declares an armistice which each belligerent must accept or become an aggressor.

What these two cases come to is obviously one of two alternatives, namely, either some State is going on with its fighting,
with its war, regardless of the Council and regardless of the
Protocol, or else there is an armistice and the fighting stops.
Under the first circumstance, the provisions as to presumptions
and as to the decisions of the Council are alike of no conse-

a. pp. 61, 67.

quence; and, in the second case, the war ends with an armistice as soon as it commences.

The drafting of Article 10 of the Protocol is unfortunately obscure; but when the language of the whole Japanese amendment is carefully looked at, it seems to me that it certainly adds nothing to the powers of either the Council or the Assembly in considering disputes arising from domestic questions, and that the legal right of any State to determine and control its own domestic matters remains unquestioned; indeed, it may be said to remain more unquestioned than it is now; for, under the Protocol, that right cannot be questioned by the League, either in Council or in Assembly; it cannot be questioned by the Permanent Court or by Arbitrators; and it cannot be questioned by war. All that is possible is friendly discussion and consideration under Article 11 of the Covenant and that, so far as Members of the League are concerned, is possible now.

Of course it might be argued that the various possible decisions and presumptions under Article 10 of the Protocol might make some difference as to the charging of the costs of the aggression under Article 15 of the Protocol; but the possibilities involved are too remote to be worthy of discussion.

CHAPTER XII.

SANCTIONS.

The Protocol of Geneva provides for sanctions or penalties for its breach by a Signatory.

Before considering the main sanctions which are set up by the Protocol, it may be mentioned that there are certain provisional measures which may be taken which fall short of the chief sanctions.

Under Article 7, in the event of a dispute between Signatories they agree, pending its settlement, not to increase their armaments, take mobilization measures, etc., and the Council is given the right, upon complaint being made, to make enquiries and investigations as to the maintenance of these agreements, and to decide upon measures in regard thereto, so as to end a threatening situation. Similar powers are given to the Council under Article 8 concerning threats of aggression or preparations for war, and in all these cases, the Council may act by a two-thirds majority.

The preventive measures which the Council may take as to such preliminary matters are not precisely defined. It is to be pointed out, however, that a State violating the engagements of Article 7 or Article 8 would not be an aggressor against which the main sanctions of the Protocol could be directed, assuming that hostilities had not broken out. Accordingly, the measures which could be "decided upon" by the Council would perhaps be limited to those of warning, of advice and of publicity; certainly they could not be measures of force; and in my opinion, they could not go as far as sanctions of any kind, economic or otherwise; the General Report[a] speaks of "the evacuation of territories" as a possibly appropriate measure; this indicates that the "measures" are to be "taken" by the State guilty of violation of the agreements mentioned; *certainly* there would be no obligation on the part of any Signatory to take any steps against a violation of these agreements of Articles 7 and 8; but the lan-

---

a. Annex C, p. 156 at p. 196.

guage is very vague and all doubt should be set at rest by changing it, particularly as the Council may decide by a two-thirds vote.

In considering the main sanctions provided by the Protocol, the first point to be emphasized is that they cannot come into play until a state of war, in the real sense, exists; hostilities must have broken out, so that the world is confronted with fighting actually taking place. It is true that there is a theoretical exception to this in the fact that a violation of the rules of a demilitarized zone is equivalent to a resort to war; but this exception is more apparent than real for the violation of a demilitarized zone would be only a brief prelude to hostilities.

The second condition precedent to the application of the sanctions is the determination of the aggressor.[a] And in any case the determination by the Council as to which State is the aggressor must have taken place before the sanctions are to be applied.

This is laid down in the last paragraph of Article 10, which provides that the Council shall "call upon" the Signatories to apply the sanctions.[b] As the sanctions contemplated by the Protocol are *in theory* merely a development of the sanctions contemplated by Article 16 of the Covenant, it is interesting to note that this preliminary calling by the Council upon the States to apply the sanctions introduces a new system, at least a system which develops from the view taken by the Assembly under Article 16 of the Covenant in 1921; for in the elaborate resolutions then adopted,[c] it was stated, among other things, that the Council was to give merely an "opinion" as to whether there had been a breach of the Covenant by resort to war, but that it was for each State to decide "for itself" whether or not its duty to apply the sanctions provided by Article 16 of the Covenant had arisen.

---

a. If there were two parties to the conflict, either one or both might be aggressor. See Article 11 of the Protocol.

b. I think this means upon *all* the Signatories. The system of the Protocol is flexible as to the *extent* to which the Sanctions are to be applied by a particular Signatory; but all Signatories come under the same legal obligation.

c. On October 4, 1921. Official Journal, October, 1921, Special Supplement No. 6, p. 24.

The reason for this development is easy to see. Even though the sanctions of the Protocol may in theory be the same as those of Article 16 of the Covenant, *they are applicable to a very different state of facts.* The sanctions of Article 16 of the Covenant were to be applied to any Member of the League which resorted to war in disregard of certain provisions of the Covenant in Articles 12, 13 and 15, and the difficulty of determining whether or not, in a given case, a resort to war *was* a violation of those other Articles of the Covenant was not solved, particularly as the Covenant does not preclude a resort to war in *every* case. Under the Protocol, however, every resort to war by the parties to it is forbidden (except by way of defense or in aid of defense or perhaps in execution of a judgment of some tribunal), and a procedure which, in theory at least and probably in practice, would always determine the aggressor, is provided. For if my view is correct, an "aggressor" is a State which openly and wilfully defies the other Signatories when summoned by the Council under Article 10 of the Protocol. Consequently, it is now for the Council, upon the determination of the aggressor, to call for the application of the sanctions.

Of course, in all cases of a serious decision such as this would be, the Council is not an outside body "calling" upon Governments to do something. The words used lead one almost unconsciously to visualize the Council as a sort of entity like a Court, laying down a rule of conduct for some one; but this is a false vision; for in any such case the Council is a group of representatives of Governments agreeing, in the first instance, as such representatives of their own Governments, upon a course of action to be taken by those very Governments pursuant to a treaty obligation. We must think of any such action by the Council as meaning primarily that the British representative and the French representative, and so on, agree that the respective countries which they represent will follow a certain course of action in accord. If the Council were composed of all the Members of the League, it would be proper to describe its action under such a provision as this as being a conference of the parties to the treaty to decide as to what, if anything, those parties should do, and to come to such decision unanimously, if any decision is to be reached. It is only as to the Governments which are *not* represented on the Council that the Council "calls" for action; so far as the Governments represented on the Council are concerned, what they do is to *agree* upon a course of action.

In theory, as I have said, the sanctions of the Protocol are no more than a development of those of Article 16 of the Covenant. The language of the Protocol indeed, in Article 11, incorporates the provisions of Article 16 of the Covenant by reference.

No provisions of the Covenant have been more debated since it was written than those of Article 16. In 1921, various amendments to this Article of the Covenant were proposed, none of which has gone into force; and, as mentioned above, the Assembly then adopted various interpretative resolutions regarding Article 16 which, with the proposed amendments (one of which was textually modified in 1924), are *provisionally* in force.[a]

It is unnecessary to attempt any detailed consideration of the exact legal effect of Article 16 of the Covenant at the present time in view of these interpretative resolutions and proposed amendments; in general they are intended to make the system of the economic blockade more flexible in its application so far as may be consistent with the purpose of the first paragraph of Article 16 of the Covenant, namely, to institute a complete economic and financial boycott of an aggressor.

This first paragraph of Article 16 of the Covenant says also that the aggressor shall *ipso facto* be deemed to have committed an act of war against the other Members of the League; this provision does not create a state of war; it simply gives the other Members of the League the right to consider themselves at war with the aggressor if they see fit; this provision is supplemented by the language of Article 10 of the Protocol which gives to any signatory State called upon to apply sanctions the privilege of exercising the rights of a belligerent, if it chooses.

---

a. See League of Nations Official Journal, October, 1921, Special Supplement No. 6, pp. 14-15, 24-26, also October, 1924, Special Supplement No. 21, p. 9.

Paragraph 2 of Article 16 of the Covenant made it the duty of the Council to "recommend" to the various governments what armed forces they should severally contribute for use in protecting the covenants of the League.

Now what Article 11 of the Protocol does in its first paragraph is to say that the obligations of all States in regard to the sanctions mentioned in paragraphs 1 and 2 of Article 16 of the Covenant will, when the call for the application of the sanctions is made by the Council, immediately become operative, in order that such sanctions may forthwith be employed against the aggressor.

So far as the first paragraph of Article 16 of the Covenant is concerned—the economic and financial blockade—I do not see that this first paragraph of Article 11 of the Protocol adds anything to that first paragraph of Article 16 of the Covenant, even when the former is read in connection with the second paragraph of Article 11 of the Protocol.

It is true that in the resolutions about the economic weapon in the Assembly of 1921, it was recognized that from practical points of view the application of the economic pressure cannot be made equally by all countries. But undoubtedly, subject to the practical difficulties mentioned, a definite obligation exists in Article 16 of the Covenant to impose economic sanctions against the aggressor, and, as I said, in my judgment this obligation is not changed by the Protocol; but it can now become an operative obligation only if and when the Council says so.

The vital question regarding sanctions under the Protocol arises under the second paragraph of Article 16 of the Covenant in connection with the first and second paragraphs of Article 11 of the Protocol. Indeed, it is because of this second paragraph of Article 11 of the Protocol that the question regarding the use of the British Fleet has been raised in England.

Article 16, paragraph 2 of the Covenant reads as follows:

"It shall be the duty of the Council in such case to recommend to the several Governments concerned what effective naval, military or air force the Members of the

League shall severally contribute to the armed forces to be used to protect the covenants of the League."

Article 11, paragraphs 1 and 2 of the Protocol read as follows:

"As soon as the Council has called upon the signatory States to apply sanctions, as provided in the last paragraph of Article 10 of the present Protocol, the obligations of the said States, in regard to the sanctions of all kinds mentioned in paragraphs 1 and 2 of Article 16 of the Covenant, will immediately become operative in order that such sanctions may forthwith be employed against the aggressor.

"Those obligations shall be interpreted as obliging each of the signatory States to co-operate loyally and effectively in support of the Covenant of the League of Nations, and in resistance to any act of aggression, in the degree which its geographical position and its particular situation as regards armaments allow."

On its face, paragraph 2 of Article 11 of the Protocol merely interprets paragraph 2 of Article 16 of the Covenant; but unquestionably *it greatly changes it*. Under the provisions mentioned of the Covenant, the Council had merely the duty of recommendation as to forces to be contributed by Members of the League. Undoubtedly under Article 16 of the Covenant, paragraph 1, any Member of the League had the right, if it chose, to consider itself at war with an aggressor, but equally under that paragraph any Member of the League had the right, if it chose, *not* to consider itself at war with an aggressor. Consequently there was no duty whatever under that Article 16, not even a moral duty, in my judgment, on the part of any Member of the League to contribute any armed forces whatever. The Council had the duty (under Article 16, Paragraph 2, of the Covenant) of making a recommendation; but it was merely a recommendation, and there was no obligation of the Member of the League to which the recommendation applied; there was merely a possible privilege to the Member of the League to which the recommendation applied— and that is a very different thing.

Now, let us look at paragraph 2 of Article 11 of the Protocol, quoted above. Each signatory State is "to cooperate loyally and effectively" not only "in support of the Covenant," but "in resistance to any act of aggression." Well, certainly resistance to an act of aggression means force and this fact is not qualified but emphasized by the words: "in the degree which its geographical position and its situation as regards armaments allow." I grant that these words have a qualifying effect in some cases. They would mean, for example, that if Denmark had no army, she could not be under any obligation to use infantry. But they also refer to the other side of that picture, that the British do have a navy, that is their particular situation as regards armaments, a very particular situation; and under this Article, as I read it, the British would be bound "loyally and effectively" to cooperate in resistance to an act of aggression in the degree which their particular naval situation allowed.

Furthermore, paragraph 1 of Article 11 of the Protocol says that the "obligations   *   *   *   in regard to the sanctions of all kinds mentioned" not only in paragraph 1 but also in paragraph 2 of Article 16 of the Covenant "will immediately become operative." This indicates that there are military, naval and air sanctions to be employed and that the parties to the Protocol are under obligations to employ them.

Now, it is no answer to this to say that as to the *extent* of the armed forces to be used, the signatory State has its own discretion; and it is true that there would be no international command, there would be no turning over of the forces of one country to the General Staff of another or to an international Staff of all; however, even that did not take place during the first three years of the World War, except with specific detachments. So, for example, the British could say that they would send five destroyers or ten cruisers under their own Admiral, or the Grand Fleet if they chose; but clearly it would be bad faith for them to say with this commitment that they would not send even a gunboat.

I am entirely satisfied that these provisions greatly extend the provisions of the Covenant; for the first time[a] there is intro-

---

a. Except as to the possibilities of Article 10 of the Covenant, as to which see *infra,* p. 84, *et seq.*

duced in the League system a definite military commitment—definite in the sense that it is obligatory, and not in the sense that it is defined as to extent of force.[a]

It may be argued that the first paragraph of Article 13 of the Protocol looks somewhat the other way, but I do not think that it does. That paragraph merely provides that the parties to the Protocol, if they see fit, may give to the Council "undertakings"[b] as to the military forces which they would use in applying the sanctions of the document. There is no obligation to give any such undertaking; it is purely optional with each State. Doubtless if such an undertaking was given and accepted by the Council, the State giving it would at least not have to do anything more in the way of military action than provided in the undertaking; but as the giving of the undertaking is optional, the fact of its not having been given would not, in my opinion, limit or qualify the obligation "interpreted" in the second paragraph of Article 11 of the Protocol.

I point out here that the word "contingent" in the first paragraph of Article 13 of the Protocol does not relate to the obligatory character of the sanctions but to the necessary uncertainty as to the future existence of the breach required for their applicability (see the French text); and the debate in the Third Committee and more particularly the Report unanimously adopted by the Assembly, in its discussion of Article 11,[c] make it clear that the above interpretation as to the military sanctions is correct; uniform in obligation, they are flexible in application.

Consideration of the third paragraph of Article 11 of the Protocol in connection with the third paragraph of Article 16 of the Covenant tends to support the views already expressed. Without further elaboration, I call particular attention to the last clause of the paragraph of the Protocol mentioned and cite

---

a. The debates in the Third Committee of the Fifth Assembly are of interest in this regard.
b. The French is "engagements."
c. Annex C, p. 156 at p. 197, *et seq.*

the respective paragraphs of the two documents in parallel columns:

Paragraph 3 of Article 16 of the Covenant.	*Paragraph 3 of Article 11 of the Protocol.*
"The Members of the League agree, further, that they will mutually support one another in the financial and economic measures which are taken under this Article, in order to minimize the loss and inconvenience resulting from the above measures, and that they will mutually support one another in resisting any special measures aimed at one of their number by the Covenant-breaking State, and that they will take the necessary steps to afford passage through their territory to the forces of any of the Members of the League which are co-operating to protect the covenants of the League."	"In accordance with paragraph 3 of Article 16 of the Covenant the signatory States give a joint and several undertaking to come to the assistance of the State attacked or threatened, and to give each other mutual support by means of facilities and reciprocal exchanges as regards the provision of raw materials and supplies of every kind, openings of credits, transport and transit, and for this purpose to take all measures in their power to preserve the safety of communications by land and by sea of the attacked or threatened State."

There are certain other provisions of the Protocol regarding sanctions which should be mentioned at least for the sake of completeness.

It is the Council[a] which declares that sanctions are at an end and that "normal conditions be re-established" (Article 14).

To the "extreme limit of its capacity," all costs of an aggression are to be borne by the aggressor (Article 15). The language concerning the extent of the liability involved is very sweeping, going much farther than the categories of damage mentioned in Annex I of the Reparation clauses of the Treaty of Versailles.

---

a. by unanimous vote.

The plans to be drawn up by the Council for the detailed application of the economic and financial sanctions are to be "communicated" to the Signatories—in other words, they are advisory, not binding (Article 12).

Here it should be said that the final words of this Article 12 mention "the Members of the League and the other signatory States." These words imply the possibility of States signatory to the Protocol which are non-Members of the League. As pointed out above,[a] no such possibility exists, in my opinion. Even if such a theoretic possibility existed, it would be absurd to suppose that any State would sign the Protocol, with obligations going beyond those of the Covenant, while still being outside the privileges of the Covenant; however, the question is of no special importance here.

The main sanctions of the Protocol, *as among the Parties to the Protocol,* may be thus summed up: a war of aggression is an international crime; a Signatory which either avows itself an aggressor or refuses an armistice after hostilities have broken out, commits this crime; and accordingly the other Signatories, upon the call of the Council, unite in the defence of the Signatory which is not the aggressor, according to their respective capacities; which means that if and to the extent that they are able to do so, they contribute by force to the defence against the aggression, as well as by economic and financial measures.

But in view of the other agreements of the Protocol regarding pacific settlement of disputes and its covenants against war, the chief sanctions of the Protocol would never come into play against a Signatory, unless that State finally decided to defy the public opinion of the world and to make into a scrap of paper its own solemn written pledge.

---

a. p. 10, *et seq.*

CHAPTER XIII.

SEPARATE DEFENSIVE AGREEMENTS.

The general character of the Protocol of Geneva is such that separate defensive agreements between the parties to it lose substantially all of their former importance. The Protocol itself is, among other things, a general defensive agreement; and under such an agreement, faithfully lived up to, substantially the only part that could be played by separate agreements would be to make more detailed and more regional, perhaps, in their obligation and execution, the general obligations binding all signatories.

The possibility of these separate defensive agreements is mentioned in Article 13 of the Protocol. It is laid down that they must be public; furthermore, action under them cannot take place until the Council "has called upon the signatory States to apply sanctions." Finally, there is a most significant provision which illustrates the relatively unimportant character of such separate agreements under the Protocol—any such agreement must remain open to all Members of the League which desire to accede thereto.

This last mentioned provision takes away every possible idea that such defensive agreements under the Protocol could be anything like the former "defensive" alliances. Obviously, a defensive agreement which is open to any Member of the League is merely a part of the general agreement; particularly is this so when the performance of the agreement depends and is conditioned upon the request of the Council.

Indeed, in view of the other provisions of the Protocol, it is very difficult to see any substantial difference between these so-called defensive agreements and the undertakings[a] which, by Article 13, States which are signatory to the Protocol may voluntarily give to the Council regarding the armed forces which might be used in the application of the sanctions. I say that the

---

a. Whether these "undertakings" would have the same legal quality as a treaty is at least doubtful.

82

two things are similar for this reason: if in a given case the Council decides that the military sanctions are to be applied, any Signatory is then entitled, at least if it chooses, to use the whole of its armed forces against the aggressor. This being so, the use of a specified portion of these forces in any given case comes to just the same thing whether it arises from the general agreement to apply sanctions or from a particular undertaking with the Council or from a particular agreement with another Signatory.

We may go to this length in thinking of these defensive agreements hereafter; in view of the fact that they must be public, that any Member of the League may adhere to them and that they cannot be performed until the Council of the League says so, there could be in such a paper no effective provision which would go beyond the engagements under the Protocol itself.

Article 13 of the Protocol says that these separate agreements may be acceded to by any Member of the League of Nations. This language would include a Member of the League which was not a signatory of the Protocol. Under Article 13, it is only the States signatory to the Protocol which may make separate agreements. The point is doubtless of no real importance; but it cannot be intended that these separate agreements, if any be made, shall be acceded to by States other than those bound by the Protocol, for any such separate agreement would be in reality a paper subsidiary to the Protocol.

CHAPTER XIV

THE PROTOCOL AND ARTICLE TEN OF THE COVENANT.

It is to be remembered that in this portion of the discussion consideration is given only to the relations *inter se* of the Signatories to the Protocol.

As among these States the famous Article 10 of the Covenant will have lost all its significance.

Article 10 of the Covenant has two distinct aspects. The more important of these is the undertaking by the Members of the League to "preserve as against external aggression the territorial integrity and existing political independence" of other Members. Because of these guarantees Article 10 was objected to in this country and in Canada chiefly for the reason that it might involve the use of armed force by the guarantor States. The further idea that this use of armed force would necessarily come into play upon a decision of the Council of the League of Nations was largely fallacious and was practically removed by the resolution of the Assembly regarding Article 10.[a]

The other side of these guarantees of Article 10, which has perhaps not always been very well appreciated, is that the obligation of a guarantor State under Article 10 *may* be very limited indeed and may even be nothing at all, even in the case of a wilful attack. Article 10 goes only to two things, territorial integrity and political independence. If an aggressor State respects these two things it can do otherwise what it chooses, so far as the guarantor States are concerned. For example, under Article 10 alone *and taking nothing else into consideration,* one State could attack another, destroy every building in the country, blow up every mine, and lay waste every field, and then retire, saying: The territorial integrity of the country attacked is now preserved, and its remaining inhabitants retain their full political independence. Under such circumstances, no guarantor State under Article 10 of the Covenant of the League of Nations would be obliged to do anything.

---

a. September 25, 1923. Technically, the resolution was not adopted, the vote not being unanimous, 29 in favor, one, Persia, opposed, and 22 absent or abstaining. League of Nations Official Journal, October, 1923, Special Supplement No. 11, p. 34.

Now I say that under the Protocol any significance of Article 10, as among the parties to the Protocol, has disappeared; clearly this is so. Article 10, so to speak, waited, or at least might wait, till the end of the war.[a] If the aggressor State did not in the Treaty of Peace or otherwise annex any territory and left the attacked State independent, Article 10 did nothing at all.[b] But the Protocol commences to work even before any war commences and certainly at its commencement; there must be no attack.[c] It is not a question of the final result of the attack; it is merely a question of the existence of the aggression; and it is *then* that all the other parties to the Protocol come to the defence of the attacked State. The lesser Article 10 of the Covenant is swallowed up in the greater Protocol.

The other aspect of Article 10 of the Covenant was the undertaking by each Member of the League to *respect* the territorial integrity and political independence of the other Members. This, of course, is an undertaking in regard only to the acts of the State giving it. Such a self-denying clause would be implied in the Covenant if it were not expressed and equally, of course, it is inherent in the Protocol.

Indeed, in the Protocol it was thought necessary to insert a provision regarding the political independence and territorial integrity, not of the attacked State but of the aggressor. All that is left now of Article 10, so far as the signatories to the Protocol *inter se* are concerned, is to be found in the second paragraph of Article 15 of the Protocol, which says that the territorial integrity and the political independence of the aggressor State shall not be affected by the application of the sanctions of the Protocol.

A development of the Covenant by which Article 10 becomes unimportant, except as a measure of protection *for* an aggressor, is perhaps the most remarkable and unforeseen of all possible developments.

---

a. *i. e.,* so far as the Guarantor States are concerned.

b. In the debates of the First Committee of the Fourth Assembly it was asserted that "no forcible invasion" is possible without a violation of Article 10 of the Covenant; but in certain circumstances war is permissible under the Covenant (Article 15, paragraph 7); and with a permissible war, there could be a permissible invasion. See Oppenheim, 3rd edition, Vol. 1, page 739.

c. *i. e.,* no aggression, in the sense intended by the Protocol.

CHAPTER XV.

At the beginning of this discussion[a] it was pointed out that upon the coming into force of the Protocol, there would, in theory at least, and from the point of view of its provisions, be three classes of Powers in the world, to wit, the parties to the Protocol, the Members of the League not parties to the Protocol and the non-Members of the League, the last named of course being also not parties to the Protocol.

It should also be mentioned again that the possibility of this second class of States, namely, the Members of the League not parties to the Protocol, is a temporary possibility only. For certainly if the Protocol comes finally into force, its provisions will in due course be embodied in the Covenant, as indeed is contemplated by Article 1 of the Protocol; and thereupon those Members of the League who have not ratified the Protocol will either become parties to the amended Covenant or will, under the provisions of Article 26 of the Covenant, cease to be Members of the League.

However, temporarily, there will doubtless be certain Members of the League of Nations who do not ratify the Protocol and the relation of these States to others during this provisional period is to be considered.

So far as concerns the relations *inter se* of this temporary or provisional class of States (those which remain Members of the League without ratifying the Protocol) it may be said at once that these relations, from this point of view, will continue to be governed by the Covenant and by the Covenant alone. The Protocol does not make or purport to make any change in this regard; so that, as among those States, we might envisage during this temporary period the theoretic possibility of a war not forbidden by the Covenant, just as we might envisage the possibility, during that period, of a dispute among those Powers remaining unset-

---

a. *Supra*, p. 13.

tled. It is, I suppose, fair to add that both of these speculations are here of juristic interest only.

Similarly, the relations of non-Members of the League *inter se* will continue, as they are now, to be governed neither by the Covenant nor by the Protocol. These States would not have bound themselves by either document and so far as concerns their relations with each other, neither the Covenant nor the Protocol attempts to regulate them.

The only provision of either document which has any bearing in this regard is to be found in Article 17 of the Covenant, which says in substance that in case of a dispute between States not Members of the League, such non-Members shall be invited to become *ad hoc* members upon conditions laid down by the Council. If they refuse, the Council, under the last paragraph of Article 17 of the Covenant, may take measures toward the prevention of hostilities; but these measures would be in the nature of good offices or mediation only and could be accepted or rejected by the two non-Members of the League as they saw fit; they could decline them wholly and go to war at their pleasure.

There is indeed one question which suggests itself to the mind under Article 17 of the Covenant concerning a dispute between two non-Members of the League. Suppose they should be both invited for the purpose of settling the dispute to become members *ad hoc,* and one of them accepted the invitation and the other refused, would the dispute then be considered as being a dispute between a Member and a non-Member? The real answer to this question probably is that on issuing the invitation the Council would make it a condition that both parties to the dispute should accept it. The legal answer as to the possibility of the case supposed is a matter of some doubt. I incline to the view that the invitation contemplated by Article 17 of the Covenant in a case when the dispute is between two non-Members, is a joint invitation and a joint invitation only. I do not think that it is intended that a non-Member of the League may temporarily seek the protection and guarantees of the Covenant against another non-Member.

However, the question is of interest only from the point of view of the meaning of language; if the possibility should arise, it would doubtless be taken care of by the Council.

Another and also comparatively unimportant point may be here noticed and that is in regard to the relations between the signatories to the Protocol and the Members of the League not signatory thereto, another phase of the temporary situation heretofore considered. As to this, it may be said very briefly that such relations would continue to be governed wholly by the Covenant. The Members of the League which do not ratify the Protocol could not during this temporary period be regarded as being in any way affected by what, as to them, would be in the nature of proposed amendments to the text of the Covenant itself. These non-Signatories of the Protocol would therefore continue to look only to the Covenant for the regulation of their relations with any Member of the League. The Protocol does not contemplate a League within a League; it simply contemplates, during this temporary phase, a situation where certain Members of the League had assumed certain obligations without any constraint or effect whatever upon such Members as might not choose to assume them.

The really vital question is as to the effect of the Protocol and of the Covenant upon non-Members of the League in their relations with Signatories to the Protocol.

Even assuming that the plans now proposed for the admission of Germany to the League are carried out, there will remain for a considerable period two Great Powers, the United States and Russia, outside the League; and there are two other States of occasional international importance, the admission of which to the League is not, so far as I know, presently contemplated, these being Mexico and Egypt.

Accordingly, the possible effect of the Covenant and the Protocol on non-Members of the League is one of very great consequence. It is a question which is being actively discussed in so far as it may have a bearing on the relations between Great Britain and the United States.

It is unquestionably true that the Protocol may have a real effect on non-Members of the League. Of course there is a legal formula which correctly says that a treaty cannot bind States not parties thereto, *res inter alios acta;* but even in the strictest legal sense this formula is only part of the truth in international matters. Any one who questions this will be convinced by reading Roxburgh's International Conventions and Third States.[a] A treaty between State A and State B may harm State C or it may benefit State C, as the Treaty of Versailles benefited Denmark by the cession of Slesvig, though Denmark was a neutral and not a party to the Treaty of Peace.[b]

Let us consider the matter first from the point of view of the Covenant. There are sanctions which may be applied under the Covenant and the application of these sanctions might affect a non-Member of the League either because they were applied against that particular non-Member or because they were applied against some other State.

It is rather curious that this question has not been very much considered under the Covenant; interest in it has been greatly revived by the Protocol; but the possible realities under the Covenant are, it seems to me, *in some respects* more important than those under the Protocol alone.

In considering this question it is well to look at it from the concrete point of view with a specific instance or example before us.

The sanctions of the Covenant[c] are an economic and financial blockade. These sanctions may be applied either as against a Member of the League which resorts to war contrary to the provisions of the Covenant or they may be applied against a non-Member of the League which resorts to war against a Member after refusing to settle its dispute with that Member (Covenant, Article 17, paragraph 3).

Suppose at the time of the Corfu dispute, Italy had gone on

---

a. Longmans, Green & Co., 1917.
b. A subsequent treaty between Denmark and the Principal Allied Powers confirmed the cession. A. J. I. L. Supplement 1923, Vol. XVII, p. 42.
c. Article 16.

to war against Greece, and the British had deemed it their duty
to apply an economic blockade against Italy.

Suppose another case; suppose that Russia attacked Poland
and that the British deemed it their duty to apply the economic
blockade against Russia. We are speaking here in both of these
cases merely of the provisions of the Covenant; and the question
raised is what attitude might the United States take in such a case
as one of these.

I have suggested two instances for the reason that there is a
slight difference between them. That difference lies in the fact
that in the first instance supposed, Italy, as a Member of the
League, would have agreed to the application of the sanctions;
they would have been applied by the British as a result of Italy
breaking her treaty. But in the second instance, Russia never
having agreed to the Covenant, the sanctions would be applied
by the British solely as a result of the British agreement to apply
them and not because of any legal breach by Russia, however
morally wrong her attack on Poland might be.

I do not think that the difference between the two supposed
cases would make any difference legally in the attitude that the
United States might take in the one case or the other. The blockade would arise from the provisions of the Covenant in either
case. To that document the United States is not a party. In
each case our correct legal position would be that our international rights were not limited by the agreement of others.

Accordingly, let us consider the case of the blockade of Russia
by the British, recalling that, under the hypothesis, Russia has
attacked Poland and that the economic and financial blockade
of the first paragraph of Article 16 of the Covenant has come
into full force. Now, so far as that blockade cut off relations
between Great Britain and Russia, it would be none of our business. But the language of Article 16 includes

"the prevention of all financial, commercial or personal
intercourse between the nationals (residents)ᵃ of the
Covenant-breaking State (Russia, under the hypothesis;

a. The discussions in the Assembly of Article 16 of the Covenant show that the
word "nationals" is to be read as "residents."

see Covenant, Article 17) and the nationals (residents) of any other State, whether a Member of the League or not."

What this would mean would be that all intercourse between Russia and the United States would be cut off by the British Fleet so far as they could do it. The questions suggested are: Could the United States protest; and would we protest?

The first question is a question of law. Would the United States have the right under international law to object to such a blockade? As a preliminary to the answer to this question, it must be pointed out that a blockade of Russia by the British might result in two different situations. Russia could undoubtedly regard such a blockade as being war, and if she did, no other country, neither the United States nor any other country, could then object to the blockade. The reason for that is that, without going into the much debated question as to the "legality" of war, under present international law it can at least be said that a neutral may not object to the belligerent status of two countries at war with each other. Of course a neutral may object to the manner of carrying on the war, or to particular incidents during the fighting; a neutral may protest that a particular blockade is not binding because not effective, and so on; but these things are not immediately important here. The important thing here is that if the blockade resulted in war, we could not object to the fact of war and its incidents.

On the other hand, a blockade *might* continue merely as a blockade, without the technical status of war arising. This is, I suppose, not very likely in the case of the blockade of a Great Power, but still it is legally possible under the terms of the Covenant.

The situation created would be new under international law. It would have to be considered as arising wholly from treaty and consequently not a situation binding on Third States, but as to them simply a situation in which their rights were governed by the principles of international law. Under these rules, the nearest approach to such a situation is the so-called pacific blockade of the past.

In my view, which is the view of the vast majority of writers on the question, Third States do not have to respect a pacific blockade. (See Oppenheim, 3rd edition, Vol. II, page 56.) Accordingly, it seems to me that the United States would be entitled to regard such a blockade as not affecting her commerce with Russia.[a]

If the United States took such a position, as probably she would, the practical value of such a blockade would be very largely diminished, for I do not think there is any doubt that the Members of the League would admit that the blockade only applied to such Third States outside the League of Nations as might acquiesce in it.

Under the Protocol, precisely the same legal situation as to the blockade of Russia exists as under the Covenant and the same conclusions would follow. However, the probability of such a blockade under the Protocol, without an actual state of war resulting, is much less than under the Covenant. The Protocol provides definitely for military sanctions and it can hardly be doubted, as a matter of reality, that if the sanctions of the Protocol commenced to be applied to a State in or out of the League and that State resisted, the result would be war as between that resisting State and at least those of the Members of the League, like Great Britain, that were taking a real part in the application of the sanctions.

And, as pointed out above, the legal situation is much clearer in the case of war than in the case of this economic and financial boycott of the Covenant. It would be much "easier"[b] to go to war than it would be to apply the economic and financial sanctions alone. The world has gotten more or less used, in a legal sense, to the legalities and illegalities of war; but there are no precedents as to the corresponding situations[c] in such a block-

a. See Moore's Digest, Vol. VII, pp. 135-142.
b. That is, in the sense that there would to some extent be known and applicable rules of conduct for all States.
c. Innumerable questions of difficulty as to private contracts might be suggested; but I am thinking here of relations between States.

ade as has been suggested; and it is, above all, custom and general agreement that make international law.

I may sum up my views on this point as follows:

If under either the Covenant or the Protocol, the economic sanctions were applied either against a Member of the League or a non-Member of the League and the application of these sanctions did not result in war, the United States legally could, and very likely would, contend that any resulting blockade was not applicable to the United States and the commerce and intercourse of her residents; and this view would be accepted by the Members of the League as being legally sound; and the result of course would be that the practical effect of any such blockade would be very much weakened.

However, if the application of the sanctions either of the Covenant or of the Protocol resulted in war between the State against which the sanctions were applied and the States applying them, the United States could not object to that state of war, although of course it would have its rights as a neutral in such a war as in any other war and these neutral rights would not be affected by any provision of either the Covenant or the Protocol.

The next consideration is the possible application of sanctions against the United States. From the foregoing review of the provisions of the Covenant and of the Protocol it is evident that such action against the United States is possible from a theoretic point of view. It is, however, important here to repeat that there is no possible sanction in either paper against a non-Member of the League except after war breaks out, a war which the non-Member of the League has commenced against a Member or against a Signatory to the Protocol as the case may be. In other words, the sanctions of either paper could only become operative against the United States after the United States had gone to war against a Member of the League.

Continuing the theoretic view of the matter, it would be idle to discuss any difference between one kind of sanction and another in such a case. If the United States went to war with State A, a Member of the League, and any other State undertook to apply economic or any other sanctions on behalf of State A and against the United States, it would here be regarded simply as an act of war, creating two or more enemies instead of one.

Perhaps from the common sense outlook, such contingencies are not worthy of discussion, for what they would mean if they happened would be either that there was another world war, in which case the provisions of no document would be very important, or else there would be some kind of a minor war such as that between the United States and Spain, in which the other Powers of the world would find some way of keeping their hands off, regardless of legalistic arguments based on the Covenant or on the Protocol or on both.

It may be suggested that in the foregoing discussion I have omitted any thought of the possibility of war between the United States and Japan; but I have kept that possibility in mind. Its theoretical possibilities, so far as they might exist by reason of the United States attacking Japan have been considered above.

Let us consider the opposite possibility, an attack by Japan on the United States.

Suppose, then, that Japan attempted to raise before the League the question of the treatment of her nationals by the United States; there is no way in which such a question could be considered by the League except under the vague general clauses of Article 11 of the Covenant; all that the League could do, even in theory, would be to ask if the United States cared to discuss the matter; and the United States would presumably decline to take part in any such discussion. Further, it may be supposed that the United States would not have the slightest desire to commence a war in the matter as the United States is satisfied with the situation as it is—it is Japan which is dissatisfied. The United States would merely refuse to discuss a question which it deemed domestic.

Suppose then that Japan went to the length of declaring war on the United States for this cause. While immaterial from the point of view of the United States, I cannot see that such a war would violate the Covenant in its letter; of course it would vio-

late its spirit of peace; but I do not think there is any specific provision of the Covenant which, in terms, forbids it.

The Protocol in this regard goes farther in its language.
The general covenant not to resort to war in Article 2 includes
such a resort to war, not only against a signatory, but also against
a State which "accepts all the obligations hereinafter set out";
in other words, against a sort of *ad hoc* adherent to the Protocol
(Article 16), but we may assume that these last words would not
include the United States.

The preamble asserts that a war of aggression constitutes a
violation of the solidarity of the members of the international
community, and also an international crime.   Article 10 of the
Protocol says that every State which resorts to war in violation
of the undertakings contained in the present Protocol is an aggressor; and in Article 8 the document goes to its greatest length,
so far as non-Signatories are concerned, by saying that the signatory States undertake to abstain from any act which might constitute a threat of aggression against another State.   These last
words "against another State" are the important words, because
they include every State in the world, not only a Signatory.   Furthermore, in that same Article 8 any Signatory can bring to the
notice of the Council its view that "another State" is making
preparations for war, which of course would include another
Signatory.

So it is perhaps arguable that under the Protocol an attack by
a Signatory against a State which is not a Signatory might be an
aggression and that the sanctions of the Protocol might be
brought into play in favor of the non-Signatory.   If that view be
correct, then, in the case supposed, namely, an attack by Japan
upon the United States, it would seem that, if the matter were
brought before the Council by *any* Signatory (as it undoubtedly
would be) the Council *might* declare Japan to be an aggressor
under the Protocol; and it would then become the duty of the
other Signatories to apply against Japan all the sanctions of the
Protocol, at least unless the United States objected to such a
course and preferred to go it alone.

However, there is at least grave doubt as to all this. The provisions of Article 16 of the Protocol and of Article 17 of the Covenant rather indicate that a State which pays no attention to an invitation to become an *ad hoc* Member or Signatory takes its chances as they exist *dehors* the Covenant or the Protocol. I think myself that this is the better view. To suppose otherwise would be to suppose that States outside the League (or the Protocol) had all the advantages of States within, and none of the burdens or obligations, a difficult thing to envisage.

So, on the whole, I conclude that an attack by Japan upon the United States because of a "domestic" or other question would permit the Members of the League, both under the Covenant and under the Protocol, to be interested onlookers and nothing more.

CHAPTER XVI.

THE DISARMAMENT CONFERENCE.

Under Article 17 of the Protocol, a Disarmament Conference to which all States of the world are to be invited is to meet at Geneva on June 15th, 1925. It is made the duty of the Council to draw up a general programme for reduction and limitation of armaments to be laid before the Conference and to be communicated to the various Governments not later than March 15th, 1925. The provision to this effect says that the Council shall give due regard to the undertakings of the Protocol regarding sanctions, but the preparation of this general programme is in substantial accord with Article 8 of the Covenant.

The Assembly adopted a quite elaborate resolution[a] regarding this Conference. This resolution makes seven or eight suggestions in general terms for the agenda of the Disarmament Conference. While the resolution was adopted, it was pointed out in the discussion that the Council has a perfectly free hand in the matter and that the requests of the Assembly regarding the agenda were nothing more than requests. There is perhaps no occasion to go over them in detail, but one or two points may be mentioned.

The matter of demilitarized zones figures in this Assembly list. As such zones are specifically mentioned in Articles 9 and 10 of the Protocol there is no doubt that this is one of the questions that would be on the agenda. Another suggestion of the Assembly for the agenda of the Conference is "the control and investigation of armaments in the contracting States." Such control and investigation were a part of the so-called American Plan,[b] and in view of the fact that the control and investigation of the armaments of the former enemy States are now before the League, there can be no doubt that this matter also would be on the agenda of the Disarmament Conference prepared by the Council.

a. See Annex D, p. 210 at p. 213, *et seq.*
b. Annex F, p. 263.

It was pointed out previously[a] that the date of the Disarmament Conference may be postponed. It now seems very likely that it will be.[b] Indeed, I feel that there was a little too much optimism at Geneva in fixing the date as early as June 15th, 1925, involving the completion of a programme by March 15th.

Of course, in getting up a programme of general disarmament, and an agenda for the Conference on Disarmament, it is true that the Council would have available the advice of the Permanent Military Commission and of the different bureaus of the Secretariat. Even so, the task of finishing these preparations in three or four months, getting them approved by the Council and also by at least the chief of the interested Governments, is one that seems to me to be very doubtful of accomplishment.

It is perhaps not generally understood what an amount of work and how great a number of questions are involved in such discussions as are proposed. There are something like twenty European Governments that are vitally interested. Some of these Governments have quite different points of view and all of them have their military, naval, air and chemical programmes in force and subject to the control of their own Parliaments.[c] The idea of a general reduction of armaments involves, at least provisionally, the recasting of the entire military system of Europe. It is complicated by numerous possibilities of regional agreements which in themselves would create new problems of complexity.

Furthermore, it is not generally recognized that a great deal of the work of such a Conference as this has to be done in advance. Doubtless no Conference in plenary session ever drew up a paper; no Legislature ever wrote a law. The utmost that any such body can do is to consider concrete proposals drawn up often by one individual, but certainly always by very small groups. I venture to say that ten lawyers could hardly draw a

---

a. p. 5.
b. This was written before the meeting of the Council in Rome in December, 1924. The Disarmament Conference certainly cannot meet before 1926. The present situation of the preliminaries is stated in a note to the Resolution of the Council of October 3, 1924, *infra,* p. 215.
c. For a statement of existing European armaments, see note to page 100.

deed without appointing a sub-committee. The success or failure of the Disarmament Conference will very largely depend on the care and judgment used in the preparations for its meeting.

We can look back on the Washington Conference and see the truth of some of these observations there. That Conference dealt with only a portion of the field of naval armaments, among only five Powers, only three of which had any substantial naval force. The naval staffs of the countries particularly interested had to prepare in advance elaborate studies, and yet with all this the Conference lasted nearly three months. Certainly the task of a general conference on disarmament is very much greater than that of the Washington Conference was.

It took nearly four months to draw up the Treaty of Versailles, which is by far the most elaborate and complex international agreement ever written. In the circumstances this was a remarkably short time. The most serious detailed criticism that I have seen of the time involved suggests that it might have been two or three weeks less. It is to be remembered, however, that the Peace Conference worked at that time under a perfectly enormous pressure from all sides to complete its task, which, as a matter of fact, would never have been completed within anything like the time taken if the decisions had not finally been left to three or four men to take.

I need not dwell further on the difficulties of the details. Any one who reads the Disarmament Treaty drawn up at the Washington Conference will appreciate something of their nature; but, looking at the matter from the larger point of view, there is a question of real statesmanship involved. The possible field to be covered by a general conference on disarmament cannot perhaps be limited; but the extent to which the first discussion shall go will determine its success or failure. If it attempts to go too far, that will be fatal; if, on the other hand, the attempt is only to go a short distance now and to continue on the road further later on, the Conference may be a success, despite the fact that it will meet with the criticisms of those who want to do everything at once.

The question of a permanent, or rather of a recurrent, Conference on Disarmament, as proposed by the so-called American Plan,[a] is one that is inevitably bound to come up at any such Conference, for whatever the Conference does or whatever it tries to do, it will have to leave much undone. Many questions will remain open, many changes of the future will not be foreseen, and those who meet in the Conference will see when they end their work that they have only begun it.

It is also to be noted again that the Conference is to fix the period within which the plan of reduction which it adopts is to be carried out. If within that time the plan is not carried out, the Council is to make a declaration rendering the Protocol null and void. The Conference is also to lay down the grounds on which the Council may make such a declaration.

In other words, the Protocol itself is to depend wholly upon the work of the Conference; it is to the Conference that the whole responsibility is transferred. If the Conference does not adopt the plan, and then if that plan is not carried out[b] within the time and on the conditions that the Conference declares, the Protocol falls.

Never, I venture to say, has any important treaty ever been drawn up depending upon a more impressive condition subsequent.

---

a. Annex F, p. 263.

b. See the discussion as to this, *supra*, p. 7, showing that the "plan" will be another Treaty or Treaties and that the "carrying out" probably means ratification thereof.

NOTE.—A statement of existing European Forces was made to Parliament on June 18, 1924 (Hansard, Parliamentary Debates [Commons], N. S., Vol. 174, page 2151). It gave the following figures:

Great Britain	155,935	Latvia	20,000
Germany	100,000	Lithuania	15,000
Austria	21,500	Poland	250,000
Hungary	35,000	Norway	16,000
Jugo Slavia	130,000	Sweden	32,000
Rumania	125,000	Denmark	27,000
Czecho Slovakia	149,877	Greece	110,000
Netherlands	163,262	Bulgaria	20,000
Italy	250,000	Turkey	88,000
Switzerland	500,000	France	732,248
Soviet Union	1,003,000	Belgium	86,531
Finland	30,000	Spain	240,113
Esthonia	16,000	Portugal	40,000

Total armed forces in Europe, 1924 4,356,466

CHAPTER XVII.

DEMILITARIZED ZONES.

Emphasis is laid by the Protocol on the creation and maintenance of demilitarized zones along frontiers. Article 9 of the Protocol treats of such zones, and their violation is, by Article 10, made the equivalent of a resort to war.

Any question of the real value, in the strict military sense, of agreements for demilitarized zones, may be left at one side. Undoubtedly, expert opinions differ in this matter. At least it may be said that such agreements have a value in the realm of feeling, which is as much a reality in international affairs as is a fleet of battleships.

If countries feel more secure because of the creation of such zones, certainly agreements regarding them are worth while on each side of a frontier.

As mentioned above, the question of demilitarized zones will certainly be one of the items of the agenda of the Conference on Disarmament. There are quite a number of precedents for the creation of such zones in recent international agreements. For example, the Treaty of Versailles[a] creates a demilitarized zone for fifty kilometres east of the Rhine. The Aaland Islands were demilitarized by the Treaty[b] which attributed them to Finland; and the Treaty of Lausanne[c] creates certain demilitarized zones, not only on each side of the Straits, but also in Western Thrace.

It is such agreements as these that are referred to in Article 9 of the Protocol as those "already existing under the terms of certain treaties." It is these zones, and others which may be established by consent of the neighboring States, which, according to Article 9, may be placed under a system of supervision by the League, either temporary or permanent. Obviously, any such supervision would come about by means of the voluntary agreement of the States concerned; and, in view of the fact that the Protocol makes a violation of a demilitarized zone the equiv-

a. Articles 42 to 44.
b. A. J. I. L. Supplement 1923, Vol. XVII, p. 1.
c. A. J. I. L., Vol. XVIII, January, 1924, pp. 58, 63.

alent of a resort to war (Article 10), supervision by the League of the carrying out of these essential agreements would seem to be highly desirable.

Indeed, it may be said here that it will almost certainly be found that a system of international inspection will inevitably be a part of agreements for the reduction and limitation of armaments. A system of general international inspection was suggested as one of the parts of the so-called American Plan,[a] and the proposal for a system of supervision of demilitarized zones under the League of Nations is a part of that general idea.

I do not think it should be lost sight of that the thought of certain places where violence is forbidden has roots which go far back in human history. The idea of "sanctuary" is as old as any records that we have; and, if it be thought that I am going very far afield in speaking of sanctuary, I mention that the legal development of this general notion is a very early development. At least as long ago as Anglo-Saxon law in England, it was a peculiarly heinous offence to commit a crime on the King's Highway. It was a much more serious matter to break the peace there than elsewhere, because it was a breach of the King's peace; and this notion of the King's peace is said by high authority to be as old as the Salic Law.

We have heard much in the past of strategic frontiers. A great deal of ability and learning have been devoted toward the problem of making frontiers available for attack or for defence. It is perhaps true, as some critics appear to think, that the development of war in the air and of chemical warfare has made questions of strategic frontiers in general less important than heretofore. Perhaps that is so. I suggest, however, that even if it is so, that same ability and learning may be able to find in a combination of the ideas of demilitarized zones and international supervision a real solution of the problems arising from these new methods and discoveries; and, as I have pointed out, there is a very ancient human feeling behind this whole idea of peaceful places, on which popular support for such a programme may be based.

---

a. Annex F, p. 263.

CHAPTER XVIII.

SECURITY AND THE PROTOCOL.

For me to discuss the bearing of the Protocol of Geneva upon the security of States means that I go outside my brief.

No technical juristic reasoning is applicable to a feeling which lies at the heart of national sentiments, sentiments of patriotism and of devotion to country, which are as deep rooted in the souls of millions as are the love of family and the belief in religion.

This matter of security is in verity a matter of national feeling, a state of mind in the truest sense. For no human agency, no belief, no will, outside of the country concerned, can alter or affect it. Ourselves alone must say, we and our rulers, whether or not we are in fact secure—if we say yes, that is enough; but if we say no, it is not for any one else to question, much less for any one else to seek to argue the matter.

So I shall merely seek to state the theory of the Protocol in regard to this matter of security. That theory is this: if the nations of the world will agree to outlaw war, if they will agree to substitute law for force, to settle by pacific means all disputes among them, if they will agree to unite against any people which so agrees but then betrays humanity by tearing up its own agreement, then we may develop intra-nationally a belief in security, a confidence in a settled order, a hope for the future, which will slowly but inevitably disarm the forces for war and lift the curtain on a new day.

Such is the theory of the Protocol of Geneva.

CHAPTER XIX.

Article 20 of the Protocol provides that any dispute as to its interpretation shall be submitted to the Permanent Court of International Justice. No provision similar to this is to be found in the Covenant.

The importance of this provision does not consist chiefly in its application to the Protocol. Even if and when the Protocol comes into effect the provision in itself will not be very important, because the Protocol is only a temporary document to be transformed into amendments to the Covenant. If these amendments include the incorporation into the Covenant of a similar provision to the effect that any dispute as to its interpretation shall be submitted to the Permanent Court of International Justice, such an amendment will be of supreme importance. With the Protocol embodied in the Covenant, the latter document will be by far the most important international treaty in existence. If all questions of its interpretation are to be submitted to the Permanent Court, that tribunal will have judicial powers of the most far-reaching character.

It is true that the extension of the powers of the Court so that they would include the interpretation of the Covenant is logical in so far as it relates to the settlement of disputes between Members of the League or other States; but the Covenant contains many other provisions bearing only indirectly upon such disputes. The Covenant provides for the Council and the Assembly and for their meetings, their powers and procedure, powers which under Articles 11 and 19 of the Covenant, for example, are expressed in the most general terms. The Covenant provides for the mandate system for certain territories and for the supervision by the League of numerous international agreements and bureaus of all sorts. Now, in most of these matters the method of interpreting the Covenant has been by consent. Members of the Council or, as the case may be, of the Assembly agree on what they may do and proceed accordingly. If differences of view as to the interpretation of the Covenant in this regard are to be submitted to the Permanent Court, that tribunal would have in some respects a power superior to that of either the Council or the Assembly.

Let me give an instance. The fifth paragraph of Article 4 of the Covenant provides as follows:

> "Any Member of the League not represented on the Council shall be invited to send a Representative to sit as a Member at any meeting of the Council during the consideration of matters specially affecting the interest of that Member of the League."

This paragraph gave rise to a difference of opinion as to what States are entitled to sit on the Council when it considered questions arising under Article 213 of the Treaty of Versailles and similar Articles in the other Peace Treaties relating to the investigations by the Council of the armaments of Germany and other countries. When the question came up, the Council took the opinion of Jurists on it and reached a common sense result.[a] Under a general clause giving jurisdiction to the Court in all matters of interpretation,[b] it would seem that any Member of the League could require a question as to the composition of the Council on a particular occasion to be decided by the Court before the Council could meet. It is obvious that any such method of regulating procedure would give rise to impossibilities which should be avoided.

---

a. See League of Nations Official Journal, July, 1924, p. 922 and Cmd. 2287 (Miscellaneous No. 20, 1924), p. 16.

b. Many people suppose that the Supreme Court of the United States has such general powers regarding our Constitution, but this is not so. Read, for example, Article I, Section 5 of the Constitution; and see Massachusetts v. Mellon, 262 U. S., 447.

CHAPTER XX.

I trust that no one appreciates better than myself that examination of a document bit by bit and piece by piece tends to blind the vision. One sees the trees and not the forest. Worse than that, one gets a false vision, a picture, if I may change the metaphor, of the buttons on the coat but not of the man wearing the coat and still less of the soul within the man.

A critical examination of an international legal document leads to a discussion of trivialities and to hypotheses of almost impossible possibilities. Of course it is true that the carrying out of a great international agreement in the light of the facts and conditions of international life as they arise does not proceed along the technical lines that I have followed, but rather along those lines of policy which really control international action. I do not mean necessarily selfish policy, but policy in the larger sense of decisions based upon the best judgment of those in power for the time being.

What really ought to be done in studying any proposal such as the Protocol of Geneva, is to realize, if possible, the ultimate purpose of the document and to visualize, so far as we can, what would happen if it came into force, not so much what *might* happen under a particular phrase, but how the international relations of the world would proceed if the whole agreement were a reality.

I have mentioned more than once that the Protocol of Geneva contemplates that its provisions shall form part of the Covenant; in other words, that the two documents shall be amalgamated, forming an amended Covenant. With the hope of facilitating a general view, I have endeavored to put the two documents together in the form of an "amended" Covenant, and the result of this effort is set out below.[a]

Looking at the text of this "amended" Covenant, one may observe that while twenty of the present twenty-six Articles re-

---

a. See Annex G, p. 271.

106

main unchanged in form, Articles 12 to 17, inclusive, are expanded and somewhat rewritten; and eight Articles are added; and I do not think that the text of the "amended" Covenant could be phrased in much less language than it appears below.

Of course the length of a document in itself is not of much consequence; but it is not unimportant to observe that the "amended" Covenant is very much longer than the Covenant as it now reads. This fact, I say, is important, because it is the visible evidence of a reality. The Protocol of Geneva is not a mere completion of the provisions of the Covenant. Advocates of the Protocol make a very serious mistake when they erroneously say that the Protocol of Geneva is merely a rounding out of incomplete and partial agreements of the Covenant.

And it must be borne in mind that new or varied phrases in one Article may change the whole; the amended Covenant is altered not only in those Articles which may be textually amended, but throughout; I attempted to show this in detail as to Article 10 of the Covenant[a]; like any other document, the entire new paper must be read together.

What the Protocol of Geneva does is to create a new and a different League of Nations. It is true that what I may call the procedural and structural functions of the League are not changed; but the system of international relations which is now set up under the League is so much changed that one may properly say that it is an entirely new and different system.

To my mind, there are three outstanding features of the "amended" Covenant. It creates a complete system of compulsory arbitration; it consecrates the legality of the *status quo;* and it is a general defensive alliance.

Now let us compare these three features of the "amended" Covenant with the ideas of the existing Covenant.

The first mentioned, the system of compulsory arbitration, is by far the most important and the one that should be the starting point for any view of the "amended" Covenant as a whole. In this arbitration system is contained the idea of outlawry of

---

a. *Supra,* p. 84.

war which the document embodies. The arbitration of disputes under the new system is to take the place of war, which is outlawed.

All that the Covenant did was to forbid some wars, to provide for delay in every case, and otherwise to rely wholly upon voluntary arbitration and, in cases where they could be obtained, upon unanimous recommendations of the Council. The framers of the Covenant were most careful to avoid the idea of compulsory arbitration, for all that even the unanimous recommendation of the Council could do was to prevent hostilities.

Under the "amended" Covenant, the defensive alliance of the Members of the League becomes complete. It is intended to see to it that arbitral decrees are carried out; to see to it that the *status quo* remains untouched, except by voluntary agreement; and to see to it that the violator is met by the combined forces of other States.

Contrast the provisions of the Covenant, which contemplate no concerted action, unless agreed to at the time, other than economic and financial pressure; and the preservation of the *status quo* only so far as Article 10 of the Covenant extends.

It would be unfair and untrue to call this new system a super-State, for it is nothing of the sort; but it would be in a sense untrue also to say that this new system is merely a development of the Covenant itself; it is the sort of change that one might call a development if it had taken two or three generations or a century to bring it about; but not properly to be called a development when it all comes at once.

The natural conclusion to be reached is that such a complete change cannot be realized at this time, and that is the sound conclusion. That a system of law should be built up governing the international relations of the States of the world, by which their differences should be adjusted by the orderly processes of legality, excluding as a method of adjustment the chaos of war, may be admitted. Thus far, the changes proposed by the Protocol of Geneva are desirable; the question is merely as to the length to which the countries of the world are willing to go in this direction at this time; and I include as a part of this development, the outlawry of war, the agreement that war is not to be resorted to by any State, that it should disappear from international relations, except in so far as force must necessarily remain as defence.

It is to be hoped that this part of the Protocol may stand; and it must be admitted that there is inherently and *ipso facto* to some extent a consecration of the legality of the *status quo* by the outlawry of war and by peaceful settlement of disputes by legal means.

On the other hand, various features of what I may call the defensive alliance portion of the Protocol seem to me to be impossible and at this time inadvisable. They are supposed to flow logically from the system of compulsory arbitration; and certainly the problem which they attempt to solve does follow logically from any system of compulsory arbitration and outlawry of war. If we assume war to be outlawed and a system by which there is to be a legal settlement of disputes in place of war, the question of course arises: Well, what is to happen in a given case if some State which has accepted this system and has agreed to it should refuse to abide by it, should not carry out an award or decision or should even take up arms against it, what then?

The Continental mind very logically answers this question by saying there must be a system of execution of decrees and that if you outlaw war, you must have a combination for defence. This is true from the point of view of logic; but it is not true from the point of view of life. Compulsory arbitration and outlawry of war are untried ideas, and we cannot say now, under all circumstances, what should be done in the course of their working, if they are put to work; much less can Nations now bind themselves as to a definite and complete course of action under all possible and varying future circumstances. That such a system of concerted action against aggression as is proposed by the Protocol of Geneva may perhaps in time be worked out along with the growth and development of the ideas of outlawry of war and of arbitration, may be admitted. That it can be done now is, to my mind, contrary to the realities of life and to the lessons of history.

There is another phase of this last discussion which should be particularly noticed. It is impossible for any such agreement for concerted action not to have a direct bearing upon countries which are not parties to the agreement; in other words, Russia and the United States. We must admit at least the theoretic possibility of a conflict between one of the Members of the League and one of these two Great Powers, insisting, if we will, that such a possibility is highly remote so far as the United States is concerned, and utterly unknowable so far as Russia is concerned; but none the less a possibility.

And certainly, in view of that possibility, any provisions of a document which looks toward force as a last resort of defence should, in my judgment, be drawn with the utmost care to avoid the idea of a possible conflict between the parties to the document on the one hand and an outside State on the other. Outlawry of war and arbitration are things to be agreed upon and not to be compelled against those who are unwilling to agree; for the breach of such an agreement is a much more serious and a very different thing than a refusal to arbitrate, or even than going to war when there is no agreement.

That the hospitality, if I may call it so, of the League of Nations should be extended to States which are unwilling to join it; that its facilities should be offered to these States for the settlement of disputes in every case where they are willing to accept them; that the covenants of the Members of the League for justice toward an outside State should be as explicit and complete as its covenants toward a Member, I quite agree; the covenants of the Members of the League should be covenants of peace among themselves, and of justice toward all. This is the road to a universal League of all Nations.

If it be said that to Finland or the Baltic States or Poland or Roumania or Turkey there is danger from their great neighbour,

I cannot deny such a possibility; and if any Members of the League are willing to join with such States in protection against such danger, either in advance of its occurrence or when it happens, I would see no objection to it, if such agreements were coupled with all the offers of peaceful settlement that could be written, as well as with offers of membership in the League, either permanent or *ad hoc*.

To a state which is contemplating the possibility of signing the Protocol of Geneva, it may well be that the provisions of that document regarding sanctions stand out as the most important, the ones having the greatest possibilities as to obligations of future action. This is a very natural point of view, and even a very proper one. And, while I myself am very deeply convinced that, from the point of view of world politics, the most far-reaching and vital provisions of this document are those which refer to arbitration and to the outlawry of war, yet perhaps for that very reason, I am equally convinced that the most serious changes which are necessary in the paper are changes in its provisions for sanctions and for enforcement.

With the principles of compulsory arbitration I am wholly in accord; with the principle that outlawry of war should follow as the necessary and natural consequence of the substitution of a reign of law for a reign of force I quite agree; and that some tribunal should determine, if need arise, that the agreement has been broken and that there is an "outlaw," is a natural consequence of those principles; and that there may be defence against aggression, if it comes, almost no one will deny. But there, I think, we must stop so far as present agreement is concerned. That any State may, *if it chooses,* go to the defence of another against an adjudged aggressor I would concede; but that all States can be or should be now required to sign an agreement so to go to such defence, I deny. In the present state of world opinion and when its own direct interests are not involved, any free people can well say that it will not or ought not to sign such an undertaking.

So I say that, while arbitration may be agreed to in advance and outlawry of war may be agreed to in advance, sanctions and assistance in defence must be voluntary.

Where does all this leave the problems of disarmament and security?

I answer by saying that the solution of these problems is very difficult, because with it are involved feelings of national fear and haunting doubts of possible national disaster. The feeling of security must be a plant of slow growth, and progress toward disarmament cannot be realized except to the extent that that growth comes. All that can be done now is to make a beginning, and, if too much is attempted, less will be accomplished. The world must rely on the development of the new idea of the reign of law and reach its feeling of security as that reign succeeds and triumphs.

The Protocol of Geneva is one of the most important of modern international documents. This is true whether it comes into force as a binding treaty or whether it does not; and it is true because the Protocol represents a development of international thought since the World War along lines of what may be called international morality, of what may almost be called international religion, which, while not novel in the realm of thought, were wholly novel in the diplomatic field of action.

The belief that international law must be strengthened, the thought that it must lay hold of international questions before the time of war and the idea that the security of a country is to be a security for peace and not simply a security in war, were the principles upon which the Covenant of the League of Nations was based; but in that document they were to some extent formulated only as hopes for the future.

These ideas which the Protocol of Geneva seeks to make complete realities have fundamentally become a part of international life. To my mind, they are certain to be carried out in some document in the near future and one of their incidents will be the realization of schemes for the reduction of armament as an incident of the development of the feeling which exists as to security.

The Protocol of Geneva will undoubtedly be much changed as a result of the consideration which is now being given to it by the various important governments of the world.[a] In various respects the Protocol goes farther than cautious public sentiment of countries like Great Britain and her Dominions is, or ought to be, willing now to proceed; but it is these very matters which can easily be changed and which will be changed.

The Conference on Disarmament and its result are the cornerstones on which the Protocol of Geneva rests. That Conference must be held and it must have a result; the public sentiment of the world demands it; and the satisfaction of that demand involves the adoption by the Members of the League of the Protocol of Geneva, not the document as it now is, but as it will be.

---

a. Since this monograph was written, I have received the text of the Report of the British Delegates regarding the Protocol of Geneva (Miscellaneous No. 21, 1924, Cmd. 2289). It is reprinted as Annex E, page 217. It is a most valuable and interesting document. I have carefully considered its conclusions, some of which are not the same as my own, and despite my very high regard for its authors, I see no reason to change anything that I have written.

ANNEXES

ANNEXES

ANNEX A.

THE COVENANT

OF THE

LEAGUE OF NATIONS.[a]

The High Contracting Parties,

In order to promote international co-operation and to achieve international peace and security

by the acceptance of obligations not to resort to war,

by the prescription of open, just and honourable relations between nations,

by the firm establishment of the understandings of international law as the actual rule of conduct among Governments, and

by the maintenance of justice and a scrupulous respect for all treaty obligations in the dealings of organised peoples with one another,

Agree to this Covenant of the League of Nations.

ARTICLE 1.

The original Members of the League of Nations shall be those of the Signatories which are named in the Annex to this Covenant and also such of those other States named in the Annex as shall accede without reservation to this Covenant. Such accession shall be effected by a Declaration deposited with the Secretariat within two months of the coming into force of the Covenant. Notice thereof shall be sent to all other Members of the League.

Any fully self-governing State, Dominion or Colony not named in the Annex may become a Member of the League if its admission is agreed to by two-thirds of the Assembly, provided that it shall give effective guarantees of its sincere intention to observe its international obligations, and shall accept such regulations as may be prescribed by the League in regard to its military, naval and air forces and armaments.

---

a. Including Amendments adopted to December, 1924.

Any Member of the League may, after two years' notice of its intention so to do, withdraw from the League, provided that all its international obligations and all its obligations under this Covenant shall have been fulfilled at the time of its withdrawal.

ARTICLE 2.

The action of the League under this Covenant shall be effected through the instrumentality of an Assembly and of a Council, with a permanent Secretariat.

ARTICLE 3.

The Assembly shall consist of Representatives of the Members of the League.

The Assembly shall meet at stated intervals and from time to time as occasion may require at the Seat of the League or at such other place as may be decided upon.

The Assembly may deal at its meetings with any matter within the sphere of action of the League or affecting the peace of the world.

At meetings of the Assembly each Member of the League shall have one vote, and may have not more than three Representatives.

ARTICLE 4.

The Council shall consist of Representatives of the Principal Allied and Associated Powers, together with Representatives of four other Members of the League. These four Members of the League shall be selected by the Assembly from time to time in its discretion. Until the appointment of the Representatives of the four Members of the League first selected by the Assembly, Representatives of Belgium, Brazil, Spain and Greece shall be members of the Council.

With the approval of the majority of the Assembly, the Council may name additional Members of the League whose Representatives shall always be members of the Council; the Council with like approval may increase the number of Members of the League to be selected by the Assembly for representation on the Council.

The Council shall meet from time to time as occasion may require, and at least once a year, at the Seat of the League, or at such other place as may be decided upon.

The Council may deal at its meetings with any matter within the sphere of action of the League or affecting the peace of the world.

Any Member of the League not represented on the Council shall be invited to send a Representative to sit as a member at any meeting of the Council during the consideration of matters specially affecting the interests of that Member of the League.

At meetings of the Council, each Member of the League represented on the Council shall have one vote, and may have not more than one Representative.

ARTICLE 5.

Except where otherwise expressly provided in this Covenant or by the terms of the present Treaty, decisions at any meeting of the Assembly or of the Council shall require the agreement of all the Members of the League represented at the meeting.

All matters of procedure at meetings of the Assembly or of the Council, including the appointment of Committees to investigate particular matters, shall be regulated by the Assembly or by the Council and may be decided by a majority of the Members of the League represented at the meeting.

The first meeting of the Assembly and the first meeting of the Council shall be summoned by the President of the United States of America.

ARTICLE 6.

The permanent Secretariat shall be established at the Seat of the League. The Secretariat shall comprise a Secretary General and such secretaries and staff as may be required.

The first Secretary General shall be the person named in the Annex; thereafter the Secretary General shall be appointed by the Council with the approval of the majority of the Assembly.

The secretaries and staff of the Secretariat shall be appointed by the Secretary General with the approval of the Council.

The Secretary General shall act in that capacity at all meetings of the Assembly and of the Council.

The expenses of the League shall be borne by the Members of the League in the proportion decided by the Assembly.

ARTICLE 7.

The Seat of the League is established at Geneva.

The Council may at any time decide that the Seat of the League shall be established elsewhere.

All positions under or in connection with the League, including the Secretariat, shall be open equally to men and women.

Representatives of the Members of the League and officials of the League when engaged on the business of the League shall enjoy diplomatic privileges and immunities.

The buildings and other property occupied by the League or its officials or by Representatives attending its meetings shall be inviolable.

ARTICLE 8.

The Members of the League recognise that the maintenance of peace requires the reduction of national armaments to the lowest point consistent with national safety and the enforcement by common action of international obligations.

The Council, taking account of the geographical situation and circumstances of each State, shall formulate plans for such reduction for the consideration and action of the several Governments.

Such plans shall be subject to reconsideration and revision at least every ten years.

After these plans shall have been adopted by the several

Governments, the limits of armaments therein fixed shall not be exceeded without the concurrence of the Council.

The Members of the League agree that the manufacture by private enterprise of munitions and implements of war is open to grave objections. The Council shall advise how the evil effects attendant upon such manufacture can be prevented, due regard being had to the necessities of those Members of the League which are not able to manufacture the munitions and implements of war necessary for their safety.

The Members of the League undertake to interchange full and frank information as to the scale of their armaments, their military, naval and air programmes and the condition of such of their industries as are adaptable to war-like purposes.

ARTICLE 9.

A permanent Commission shall be constituted to advise the Council on the execution of the provisions of Articles 1 and 8 and on military, naval and air questions generally.

ARTICLE 10.

The Members of the League undertake to respect and preserve as against external aggression the territorial integrity and existing political independence of all Members of the League. In case of any such aggression or in case of any threat or danger of such aggression the Council shall advise upon the means by which this obligation shall be fulfilled.

ARTICLE 11.

Any war or threat of war, whether immediately affecting any of the Members of the League or not, is hereby declared a matter of concern to the whole League, and the League shall take any action that may be deemed wise and effectual to safeguard the peace of nations. In case any such emergency should arise the Secretary General shall on the request of any Member of the League forthwith summon a meeting of the Council.

It is also declared to be the friendly right of each Member of the League to bring to the attention of the Assembly or of the Council any circumstance whatever affecting international relations which threatens to disturb international peace or the good understanding between nations upon which peace depends.

ARTICLE 12.

The Members of the League agree that, if there should arise between them any dispute likely to lead to a rupture they will submit the matter either to arbitration or judicial settlement or to enquiry by the Council, and they agree in no case to resort to war until three months after the award by the arbitrators or the judicial decision, or the report by the Council.

In any case under this Article the award of the arbitrators or the judicial decision shall be made within a reasonable time, and the report of the Council shall be made within six months after the submission of the dispute.

ARTICLE 13.

The Members of the League agree that whenever any dispute shall arise between them which they recognise to be suitable for submission to arbitration or judicial settlement and which cannot be satisfactorily settled by diplomacy, they will submit the whole subject-matter to arbitration or judicial settlement.

Disputes as to the interpretation of a treaty, as to any question of international law, as to the existence of any fact which if established would constitute a breach of any international obligation, or as to the extent and nature of the reparation to be made for any such breach, are declared to be among those which are generally suitable for submission to arbitration or judicial settlement.

For the consideration of any such dispute, the court to which the case is referred shall be the Permanent Court of International Justice, established in accordance with Article 14, or any tribunal agreed on by the parties to the dispute or stipulated in any convention existing between them.

The Members of the League agree that they will carry out in full good faith any award or decision that may be rendered, and that they will not resort to war against a Member of the League which complies therewith. In the event of any failure to carry out such an award or decision, the Council shall propose what steps should be taken to give effect thereto.

ARTICLE 14.

The Council shall formulate and submit to the Members of the League for adoption plans for the establishment of a Permanent Court of International Justice. The Court shall be competent to hear and determine any dispute of an international character which the parties thereto submit to it. The Court may also give an advisory opinion upon any dispute or question referred to it by the Council or by the Assembly.

ARTICLE 15.

If there should arise between Members of the League any dispute likely to lead to a rupture, which is not submitted to arbitration or judicial settlement in accordance with Article 13, the Members of the League agree that they will submit the matter to the Council. Any party to the dispute may effect such submission by giving notice of the existence of the dispute to the Secretary General, who will make all necessary arrangements for a full investigation and consideration thereof.

For this purpose the parties to the dispute will communicate to the Secretary General, as promptly as possible, statements of their case with all the relevant facts and papers, and the Council may forthwith direct the publication thereof.

The Council shall endeavour to effect a settlement of the dispute, and if such efforts are successful, a statement shall be made public giving such facts and explanations regarding the dispute and the terms of settlement thereof as the Council may deem appropriate.

If the dispute is not thus settled, the Council either unanimously or by a majority vote shall make and publish a report containing a statement of the facts of the dispute and the recommendations which are deemed just and proper in regard thereto.

Any Member of the League represented on the Council may make public a statement of the facts of the dispute and of its conclusions regarding the same.

If a report by the Council is unanimously agreed to by the members thereof other than the Representatives of one or more of the parties to the dispute, the Members of the League agree that they will not go to war with any party to the dispute which complies with the recommendations of the report.

If the Council fails to reach a report which is unanimously agreed to by the members thereof, other than the Representatives of one or more of the parties to the dispute, the Members of the League reserve to themselves the right to take such action as they shall consider necessary for the maintenance of right and justice.

If the dispute between the parties is claimed by one of them, and is found by the Council, to arise out of a matter which by international law is solely within the domestic jurisdiction of that party, the Council shall so report, and shall make no recommendation as to its settlement.

The Council may in any case under this Article refer the dispute to the Assembly. The dispute shall be so referred at the request of either party to the dispute, provided that such request be made within fourteen days after the submission of the dispute to the Council.

In any case referred to the Assembly, all the provisions of this Article and of Article 12 relating to the action and powers of the Council shall apply to the action and powers of the Assembly, provided that a report made by the Assembly, if concurred in by the Representatives of those Members of the League represented on the Council and of a majority of the other Members of the League, exclusive in each case of the Representatives of the parties to the dispute, shall have the same force as a report by the Council concurred in by all the members thereof

other than the Representatives of one or more of the parties to
the dispute.

ARTICLE 16.

Should any Member of the League resort to war in disregard
of its covenants under Articles 12, 13 or 15, it shall *ipso facto*
be deemed to have committed an act of war against all other
Members of the League, which hereby undertake immediately
to subject it to the severance of all trade or financial relations,
the prohibition of all intercourse between their nationals and
the nationals of the covenant-breaking State, and the prevention
of all financial, commercial or personal intercourse between
the nationals of the covenant-breaking State and the nationals
of any other State, whether a Member of the League or not.

It shall be the duty of the Council in such case to recommend to the several Governments concerned what effective military, naval or air force the Members of the League shall severally contribute to the armed forces to be used to protect the covenants of the League.

The Members of the League agree, further, that they will
mutually support one another in the financial and economic
measures which are taken under this Article, in order to minimise the loss and inconvenience resulting from the above measures, and that they will mutually support one another in resisting any special measures aimed at one of their number by the
covenant-breaking State, and that they will take the necessary
steps to afford passage through their territory to the forces of
any of the Members of the League which are co-operating to
protect the covenants of the League.

Any Member of the League which has violated any covenant
of the League may be declared to be no longer a Member of
the League by a vote of the Council concurred in by the Representatives of all the other Members of the League represented
thereon.

ARTICLE 17.

In the event of a dispute between a Member of the League and a State which is not a Member of the League, or between States not Members of the League, the State or States not Members of the League shall be invited to accept the obligations of membership in the League for the purposes of such dispute, upon such conditions as the Council may deem just. If such invitation is accepted, the provisions of Articles 12 to 16 inclusive shall be applied with such modifications as may be deemed necessary by the Council.

Upon such invitation being given the Council shall immediately institute an inquiry into the circumstances of the dispute and recommend such action as may seem best and most effectual in the circumstances.

If a State so invited shall refuse to accept the obligations of membership in the League for the purposes of such dispute, and shall resort to war against a Member of the League, the provisions of Article 16 shall be applicable as against the State taking such action.

If both parties to the dispute when so invited refuse to accept the obligations of membership in the League for the purposes of such dispute, the Council may take such measures and make such recommendations as will prevent hostilities and will result in the settlement of the dispute.

ARTICLE 18.

Every treaty or international engagement entered into hereafter by any Member of the League shall be forthwith registered with the Secretariat and shall as soon as possible be published by it. No such treaty or international engagement shall be binding until so registered.

ARTICLE 19.

The Assembly may from time to time advise the reconsideration by Members of the League of treaties which have become inapplicable and the consideration of international conditions whose continuance might endanger the peace of the world.

ARTICLE 20.

The Members of the League severally agree that this Covenant is accepted as abrogating all obligations or understandings *inter se* which are inconsistent with the terms thereof, and solemnly undertake that they will not hereafter enter into any engagements inconsistent with the terms thereof.

In case any Member of the League shall, before becoming a Member of the League, have undertaken any obligations inconsistent with the terms of this Covenant, it shall be the duty of such Member to take immediate steps to procure its release from such obligations.

ARTICLE 21.

Nothing in this Covenant shall be deemed to affect the validity of international engagements, such as treaties of arbitration or regional understandings like the Monroe doctrine, for securing the maintenance of peace.

ARTICLE 22.

To those colonies and territories which as a consequence of the late war have ceased to be under the sovereignty of the States which formerly governed them and which are inhabited by peoples not yet able to stand by themselves under the strenuous conditions of the modern world, there should be applied the principle that the well-being and development of such peoples form a sacred trust of civilisation and that securities for the performance of this trust should be embodied in this Covenant.

The best method of giving practical effect to this principle is that the tutelage of such peoples should be entrusted to advanced nations who by reason of their resources, their experience or their geographical position can best undertake this responsibility, and who are willing to accept it, and that this tutelage should be exercised by them as Mandatories on behalf of the League.

The character of the mandate must differ according to the stage of the development of the people, the geographical situation of the territory, its economic conditions and other similar circumstances.

Certain communities formerly belonging to the Turkish Empire have reached a stage of development where their existence as independent nations can be provisionally recognized subject to the rendering of administrative advice and assistance by a Mandatory until such time as they are able to stand alone. The wishes of these communities must be a principal consideration in the selection of the Mandatory.

Other peoples, especially those of Central Africa, are at such a stage that the Mandatory must be responsible for the administration of the territory under conditions which will guarantee freedom of conscience and religion, subject only to the maintenance of public order and morals, the prohibition of abuses such as the slave trade, the arms traffic and the liquor traffic, and the prevention of the establishment of fortifications or military and naval bases and of military training of the natives for other than police purposes and the defence of territory, and will also secure equal opportunities for the trade and commerce of other Members of the League.

There are territories, such as South-West Africa and certain of the South Pacific Islands, which, owing to the sparseness of their population, or their small size, or their remoteness from the centres of civilisation, or their geographical contiguity to the territory of the Mandatory, and other circumstances, can be best administered under the laws of the Mandatory as integral portions of its territory, subject to the safeguards above mentioned in the interests of the indigenous population.

In every case of mandate, the Mandatory shall render to the Council an annual report in reference to the territory committed to its charge.

The degree of authority, control, or administration to be exercised by the Mandatory shall, if not previously agreed upon by the Members of the League, be explicitly defined in each case by the Council.

A permanent Commission shall be constituted to receive and examine the annual reports of the Mandatories and to advise the Council on all matters relating to the observance of the mandates.

ARTICLE 23.

Subject to and in accordance with the provisions of international conventions existing or hereafter to be agreed upon, the Members of the League:

(a) will endeavour to secure and maintain fair and humane conditions of labour for men, women, and children, both in their own countries and in all countries to which their commercial and industrial relations extend, and for that purpose will establish and maintain the necessary international organisations;

(b) undertake to secure just treatment of the native inhabitants of territories under their control;

(c) will entrust the League with the general supervision over the execution of agreements with regard to the traffic in women and children, and the traffic in opium and other dangerous drugs;

(d) will entrust the League with the general supervision of the trade in arms and ammunition with the countries in which the control of this traffic is necessary in the common interest;

(e) will make provision to secure and maintain freedom of communications and of transit and equitable treatment for the commerce of all Members of the League. In this connection, the special necessities of the regions devastated during the war of 1914-1918 shall be borne in mind;

(f) will endeavour to take steps in matters of international concern for the prevention and control of disease.

ARTICLE 24.

There shall be placed under the direction of the League all international bureaux already established by general treaties if the parties to such treaties consent. All such international bureaux and all commissions for the regulation of matters of international interest hereafter constituted shall be placed under the direction of the League.

In all matters of international interest which are regulated by general convention but which are not placed under the control of international bureaux or commissions, the Secretariat of the League shall, subject to the consent of the Council and if desired by the parties, collect and distribute all relevant information and shall render any other assistance which may be necessary or desirable.

The Council may include as part of the expenses of the Secretariat the expenses of any bureau or commission which is placed under the direction of the League.

ARTICLE 25.

The Members of the League agree to encourage and promote the establishment and co-operation of duly authorised voluntary national Red Cross organisations having as purposes the improvement of health, the prevention of disease and the mitigation of suffering throughout the world.

ARTICLE 26.

Amendments to this Covenant will take effect when ratified by the Members of the League whose Representatives compose the Council and by a majority of the Members of the League whose Representatives compose the Assembly.

No such amendments shall bind any Member of the League which signifies its dissent therefrom, but in that case it shall cease to be a Member of the League.

The text of the Protocol of Geneva, which follows as Annex B, is printed in French and English on opposite pages.

PROTOCOLE POUR LE REGLEMENT PACIFIQUE DES DIFFERENDS INTERNATIONAUX.

Animés de la ferme volonté d'assurer le maintien de la paix générale et la sécurité des peuples dont l'existence, l'indépendance ou les territoires pourraient être menacés;

Reconnaissant la solidarité qui unit les membres de la communauté internationale;

Affirmant que la guerre d'agression constitue une infraction à cette solidarité et un crime international;

Désireux de faciliter la complète application du système prévu au Pacte de la Société des Nations pour le règlement pacifique des différends entre les Etats et d'assurer la répression des crimes internationaux; et

Afin de réaliser, comme l'envisage l'article 8 du Pacte, la réduction des armements nationaux au minimum compatible avec la sécurité nationale et avec l'exécution des obligations internationales imposées par une action commune,

Les Soussignés, dûment autorisés à cet effet, sont convenus des dispositions suivantes:

ARTICLE PREMIER.

Les Etats signataires s'engagent à faire tous efforts en leur pouvoir pour l'introduction dans le Pacte d'amendements conformes au sens des dispositions contenues dans les articles suivants.

Ils conviennent que ces dispositions deviendront obligatoires dans leurs rapports respectifs à la date de la mise en vigueur du présent Protocole et que, vis-à-vis d'eux, l'Assemblée et le Conseil de la Société des Nations seront, dès lors, autorisés à exercer tous les droits et devoirs qui leur sont conférés par ce Protocole.

ARTICLE 2.

Les Etats signataires conviennent qu'en aucun cas ils ne

ANNEX B.

PROTOCOL FOR THE PACIFIC SETTLEMENT
OF INTERNATIONAL DISPUTES.

Animated by the firm desire to ensure the maintenance of general peace and the security of nations whose existence, independence or territories may be threatened;

Recognising the solidarity of the members of the international community;

Asserting that a war of aggression constitutes a violation of this solidarity and an international crime;

Desirous of facilitating the complete application of the system provided in the Covenant of the League of Nations for the pacific settlement of disputes between States and of ensuring the repression of international crimes; and

For the purpose of realising, as contemplated by Article 8 of the Covenant, the reduction of national armaments to the lowest point consistent with national safety and the enforcement by common action of international obligations;

The Undersigned, duly authorised to that effect, agree as follows:

ARTICLE 1.

The signatory States undertake to make every effort in their power to secure the introduction into the Covenant of amendments on the lines of the provisions contained in the following articles.

They agree that, as between themselves, these provisions shall be binding as from the coming into force of the present Protocol and that, so far as they are concerned, the Assembly and the Council of the League of Nations shall thenceforth have power to exercise all the rights and perform all the duties conferred upon them by the Protocol.

ARTICLE 2.

The signatory States agree in no case to resort to war either

133

doivent recourir à la guerre, ni entre eux ni contre tout Etat qui, le cas échéant, accepterait toutes les obligations ci-après définies, excepté dans le cas de résistance à des actes d'agression ou quand ils agissent en accord avec le Conseil ou l'Assemblée de la Société des Nations, selon les dispositions du Pacte et du présent Protocole.

ARTICLE 3.

Les Etats signataires s'engagent à reconnaître comme obligatoire, de plein droit et sans convention spéciale, la juridiction de la Cour permanente de Justice internationale dans les cas visés au paragraphe 2 de l'article 36 du Statut de la Cour, mais sans préjudice de la faculté pour un Etat quelconque, lorsqu'il adhérera au protocole spécial ouvert le 16 décembre 1920, prévu par ledit article, de formuler les réserves compatibles avec ladite clause.

L'adhésion à ce protocole spécial ouvert le 16 décembre 1920 devra être faite dans le délai d'un mois qui suivra la mise en vigueur du présent Protocole.

Les Etats qui adhéreront au présent Protocole après sa mise en vigueur devront s'acquitter de l'obligation ci-dessus dans le mois qui suivra leur adhésion.

ARTICLE 4.

En vue de compléter les dispositions des alinéas 4, 5, 6 et 7 de l'article 15 du Pacte, les Etats signataires conviennent de se conformer à la procédure suivante:

1° Si le différend soumis au Conseil n'a pu être réglé par lui ainsi qu'il est prévu au paragraphe 3 dudit article 15, le Conseil engagera les Parties à soumettre le différend à un règlement judiciaire ou arbitral.

2° a) Si les Parties s'y refusent, il est procédé, à la demande d'au moins l'une des Parties, à la constitution d'un Comité d'arbitres. Le Comité sera constitué, autant que possible, par l'accord des Parties.

with one another or against a State which, if the occasion arises, accepts all the obligations hereinafter set out, except in case of resistance to acts of aggression or when acting in agreement with the Council or the Assembly of the League of Nations in accordance with the provisions of the Covenant and of the present Protocol.

ARTICLE 3.

The signatory States undertake to recognise as compulsory, *ipso facto* and without special agreement, the jurisdiction of the Permanent Court of International Justice in the cases covered by paragraph 2 of Article 36 of the Statute of the Court, but without prejudice to the right of any State, when acceding to the special protocol provided for in the said Article and opened for signature on December 16th, 1920, to make reservations compatible with the said clause.

Accession to this special protocol, opened for signature on December 16th, 1920, must be given within the month following the coming into force of the present Protocol.

States which accede to the present Protocol, after its coming into force, must carry out the above obligation within the month following their accession.

ARTICLE 4.

With a view to render more complete the provisions of paragraphs 4, 5, 6, and 7 of Article 15 of the Covenant, the signatory States agree to comply with the following procedure:

1. If the dispute submitted to the Council is not settled by it as provided in paragraph 3 of the said Article 15, the Council shall endeavour to persuade the parties to submit the dispute to judicial settlement or arbitration.

2. (*a*) If the parties cannot agree to do so, there shall, at the request of at least one of the parties, be constituted a Committee of Arbitrators. The Committee shall so far as possible be constituted by agreement between the parties.

b) Si, dans le délai que le Conseil aura fixé, elles ne se sont pas entendues en tout ou en partie sur le nombre, le nom et les pouvoirs des arbitres, ainsi que sur la procédure, le Conseil réglera les points en suspens. Il choisira d'urgence—en consultant les Parties—les arbitres et leur président, parmi les personnes qui, par leur nationalité, leur caractère et leur expérience, lui paraîtront donner les plus hautes garanties de compétence et d'impartialité.

c) Après que les conclusions des Parties auront été formulées, le Comité d'arbitres, à la demande de toute Partie, sollicitera, par l'entremise du Conseil, sur les points de droit contestés, l'avis consultatif de la Cour permanente de Justice internationale qui, dans ce cas, se réunira d'urgence.

3° Si aucune des Parties ne demande l'arbitrage, le Conseil reprendra l'examen du différend. Au cas où le Conseil établit un rapport voté à l'unanimité de ses membres autres que les représentants de toute Partie au différend, les Etats signataires conviennent de se conformer aux solutions recommandées par lui.

4° Au cas où le Conseil ne peut établir un rapport accepté par tous ses membres autres que les représentants de toute Partie au différend, il soumettra le différend à l'arbitrage. Il réglera lui-même la composition, les pouvoirs et la procédure du Comité d'arbitres et aura égard, dans le choix des arbitres, aux garanties de compétence et d'impartialité visées au N° 2*b* ci-dessus.

5° En aucun cas ne pourront être remises en question les solutions ayant déjà fait l'objet d'une recommandation unanime du Conseil acceptée par l'une des Parties intéressées.

6° Les Etats signataires s'engagent à exécuter de bonne foi les sentences judiciaires ou arbitrales et à se conformer, comme il a été dit à l'alinéa 3 ci-dessus, aux solutions recommandées par le Conseil. Dans le cas où un Etat manquerait à ces engagements, le Conseil exercera toute son influence pour en assurer le respect. S'il ne peut y réussir, il proposera les mesures qui doivent en assurer

(b) If within the period fixed by the Council the parties have failed to agree, in whole or in part, upon the number, the names and the powers of the arbitrators and upon the procedure, the Council shall settle the points remaining in suspense. It shall with the utmost possible despatch select in consultation with the parties the arbitrators and their President from among persons who by their nationality, their personal character and their experience, appear to it to furnish the highest guarantees of competence and impartiality.

(c) After the claims of the parties have been formulated, the Committee of Arbitrators, on the request of any party, shall through the medium of the Council request an advisory opinion upon any points of law in dispute from the Permanent Court of International Justice, which in such case shall meet with the utmost possible despatch.

3. If none of the parties asks for arbitration, the Council shall again take the dispute under consideration. If the Council reaches a report which is unanimously agreed to by the members thereof other than the representatives of any of the parties to the dispute, the signatory States agree to comply with the recommendations therein.

4. If the Council fails to reach a report which is concurred in by all its members, other than the representatives of any of the parties to the dispute, it shall submit the dispute to arbitration. It shall itself determine the composition, the powers and the procedure of the Committee of Arbitrators and, in the choice of the arbitrators, shall bear in mind the guarantees of competence and impartiality referred to in paragraph 2 (b) above.

5. In no case may a solution, upon which there has already been a unanimous recommendation of the Council accepted by one of the parties concerned, be again called in question.

6. The signatory States undertake that they will carry out in full good faith any judicial sentence or arbitral award that may be rendered and that they will comply, as provided in paragraph 3 above, with the solutions recommended by the Council. In the event of a State failing to carry out the above undertakings, the Council shall exert all its influence to secure compliance therewith. If it fails

l'effet, ainsi qu'il est dit à la fin de l'article 13 du Pacte. Dans le cas où un Etat, manquant à ces engagements, recourrait à la guerre, les sanctions prévues à l'article 16 du Pacte, interprétées de la manière indiquée au présent Protocole, lui deviendraient immédiatement applicables.

7° Les dispositions du présent article ne s'appliquent pas au règlement des différends qui pourraient s'élever à la suite des mesures de guerre prises par un ou plusieurs Etats signataires en accord avec le Conseil ou l'Assemblée.

ARTICLE 5.

La disposition de l'alinéa 8 de l'article 15 du Pacte demeure applicable devant le Conseil.

Si, pendant le cours d'une des procédures d'arbitrage prévues à l'article 4 ci-dessus, l'une des Parties prétend que le différend, ou une partie du différend, porte sur une question que le droit international laisse à la compétence exclusive de cette Partie, les arbitres consulteront sur ce point la Cour permanente de Justice internationale par l'entremise du Conseil. L'avis de la Cour liera les arbitres qui se borneront, si cet avis est affirmatif, à le constater dans leur sentence.

Si la question est reconnue par la Cour permanente ou par le Conseil comme étant de la compétence exclusive d'un Etat, la décision intervenue n'empêchera pas que la situation soit examinée par le Conseil ou par l'Assemblée, conformément à l'article 11 du Pacte.

ARTICLE 6.

Si, conformément à l'alinéa 9 de l'article 15 du Pacte, le différend est porté devant l'Assemblée, celle-ci aura, pour le règlement du différend, tous les pouvoirs dévolus au Conseil en ce qui concerne l'essai de conciliation des Parties, tel qu'il est prévu aux alinéas 1, 2 et 3 de l'article 15 du Pacte et au N° 1 de l'article 4 ci-dessus.

A défaut de règlement amiable obtenu par l'Assemblée:

therein, it shall propose what steps should be taken to give effect thereto, in accordance with the provision contained at the end of Article 13 of the Covenant. Should a State in disregard of the above undertakings resort to war, the sanctions provided for by Article 16 of the Covenant, interpreted in the manner indicated in the present Protocol, shall immediately become applicable to it.

7. The provisions of the present article do not apply to the settlement of disputes which arise as the result of measures of war taken by one or more signatory States in agreement with the Council or the Assembly.

ARTICLE 5.

The provisions of paragraph 8 of Article 15 of the Covenant shall continue to apply in proceedings before the Council.

If in the course of an arbitration, such as is contemplated in Article 4 above, one of the parties claims that the dispute, or part thereof, arises out of a matter which by international law is solely within the domestic jurisdiction of that party, the arbitrators shall on this point take the advice of the Permanent Court of International Justice through the medium of the Council. The opinion of the Court shall be binding upon the arbitrators, who, if the opinion is affirmative, shall confine themselves to so declaring in their award.

If the question is held by the Court or by the Council to be a matter solely within the domestic jurisdiction of the State, this decision shall not prevent consideration of the situation by the Council or by the Assembly under Article 11 of the Covenant.

ARTICLE 6.

If in accordance with paragraph 9 of Article 15 of the Covenant a dispute is referred to the Assembly, that body shall have for the settlement of the dispute all the powers conferred upon the Council as to endeavouring to reconcile the parties in the manner laid down in paragraphs 1, 2 and 3 of Article 15 of the Covenant and in paragraph 1 of Article 4 above.

Should the Assembly fail to achieve an amicable settlement:

Si l'une des Parties demande l'arbitrage, il est procédé par le Conseil à la constitution du Comité d'arbitres, dans les conditions prévues au N° 2 de l'article 4 ci-dessus, lettres *a, b* et *c;*

Si aucune des Parties ne demande l'arbitrage, l'Assemblée reprend, avec les mêmes pouvoirs que le Conseil, l'examen du différend. Les solutions recommandées par le Rapport de l'Assemblée, dans les conditions d'approbation prévues à la fin de l'alinéa 10 de l'article 15 du Pacte, ont la même valeur et produiront les mêmes effets, en tout ce qui concerne le présent Protocole, que celles recommandées par le Rapport du Conseil dans les conditions prévues au N° 3 de l'article 4 ci-dessus.

Si la majorité nécessaire ne peut être obtenue, le différend sera soumis à l'arbitrage et le Conseil réglera lui-même la composition, les pouvoirs et la procédure du Comité d'arbitres, comme il est dit au N° 4 dudit article 4.

ARTICLE 7.

Dans le cas d'un différend s'élevant entre deux ou plusieurs Etats signataires, ceux-ci conviennent que, soit avant que le différend ait été soumis à une procédure de règlement pacifique, soit au cours d'une telle procédure, ils ne procéderont à aucune augmentation d'armements ou d'effectifs qui pourrait modifier la situation fixée par la Conférence pour la réduction des armements prévue à l'article 17 du présent Protocole; ils ne procéderont non plus à aucune mesure de mobilisation militaire, navale, aérienne, industrielle ou économique, ni en général à aucun acte de nature à aggraver ou à étendre le différend.

Conformément aux dispositions de l'article 11 du Pacte, il est du devoir du Conseil d'examiner toute plainte en violation des engagements ci-dessus, qui pourrait lui être adressée par un ou plusieurs des Etats parties au différend. Si le Conseil considère que la plainte est recevable, il doit, s'il l'estime convenable, organiser des enquêtes et des investigations dans un ou plusieurs des pays intéressés. Ces enquêtes et ces investigations doivent être faites dans les délais les plus brefs, et les Etats signataires s'engagent à donner toutes facilités pour leur exécution.

If one of the parties asks for arbitration, the Council shall proceed to constitute the Committee of Arbitrators in the manner provided in sub-paragraphs (*a*), (*b*) and (*c*) of paragraph 2 of Article 4 above.

If no party asks for arbitration, the Assembly shall again take the dispute under consideration and shall have in this connection the same powers as the Council. Recommendations embodied in a report of the Assembly, provided that it secures the measure of support stipulated at the end of paragraph 10 of Article 15 of the Covenant, shall have the same value and effect, as regards all matters dealt with in the present Protocol, as recommendations embodied in a report of the Council adopted as provided in paragraph 3 of Article 4 above.

If the necessary majority cannot be obtained, the dispute shall be submitted to arbitration and the Council shall determine the composition, the powers and the procedure of the Committee of Arbitrators as laid down in paragraph 4 of Article 4.

Article 7.

In the event of a dispute arising between two or more signatory States, these States agree that they will not, either before the dispute is submitted to proceedings for pacific settlement or during such proceedings, make any increase of their armaments or effectives which might modify the position established by the Conference for the Reduction of Armaments provided for by Article 17 of the present Protocol, nor will they take any measure of military, naval, air, industrial or economic mobilisation, nor, in general, any action of a nature likely to extend the dispute or render it more acute.

It shall be the duty of the Council, in accordance with the provisions of Article 11 of the Covenant, to take under consideration any complaint as to infraction of the above undertakings which is made to it by one or more of the States parties to the dispute. Should the Council be of opinion that the complaint requires investigation, it shall, if it deems it expedient, arrange for enquiries and investigations in one or more of the countries concerned. Such enquiries and investigations shall be carried

Les mesures ainsi prises par le Conseil sont destinées uniquement à faciliter le règlement pacifique des différends et ne doivent préjuger en rien du règlement lui-même.

Si, à la suite de ces enquêtes et investigations, une infraction quelconque aux dispositions du premier alinéa du présent article est établie, il est du devoir du Conseil de sommer l'Etat ou les Etats coupables de l'infraction de la faire disparaître. Si l'Etat ou les Etats en question ne se conforment pas à cette sommation, le Conseil déclare lesdits Etats coupables d'une violation du Pacte ou du présent Protocole et doit décider les mesures à prendre en vue de faire cesser au plus tôt une situation de nature à menacer la paix du monde.

Pour l'application du présent article, le Conseil prendra sa décision à la majorité des deux tiers.

ARTICLE 8.

Les Etats signataires s'engagent à s'abstenir de toute action qui pourrait constituer une menace d'agression contre un autre Etat.

Dans le cas où un des Etats signataires estime qu'un autre Etat procède à des préparatifs de guerre, il a le droit d'en saisir le Conseil.

Celui-ci, après avoir vérifié les faits, opère comme il est dit à l'article 7, alinéas 2, 4 et 5.

ARTICLE 9.

L'existence de zones démilitarisées étant de nature à prévenir les agressions et à en faciliter la détermination sans équivoque conformément à l'article 10 ci-dessous, l'établissement de pareilles zones est recommandé entre les Etats qui y seraient également consentants, comme un moyen d'éviter une violation du présent Protocole.

Les zones démilitarisées déjà existantes en vertu de certains Traités ou Conventions, ou qui seraient établies à l'avenir entre Etats également consentants, pourront faire l'objet d'un contrôle temporaire ou permanent, organisé par le Conseil, à la demande et aux frais d'un ou de plusieurs Etats limitrophes.

out with the utmost possible despatch, and the signatory States undertake to afford every facility for carrying them out.

The sole object of measures taken by the Council as above provided is to facilitate the pacific settlement of disputes and they shall in no way prejudge the actual settlement.

If the result of such enquiries and investigations is to establish an infraction of the provisions of the first paragraph of the present Article, it shall be the duty of the Council to summon the State or States guilty of the infraction to put an end thereto. Should the State or States in question fail to comply with such summons, the Council shall declare them to be guilty of a violation of the Covenant or of the present Protocol, and shall decide upon the measures to be taken with a view to end as soon as possible a situation of a nature to threaten the peace of the world.

For the purposes of the present Article decisions of the Council may be taken by a two-thirds majority.

ARTICLE 8.

The signatory States undertake to abstain from any act which might constitute a threat of aggression against another State.

If one of the signatory States is of opinion that another State is making preparations for war, it shall have the right to bring the matter to the notice of the Council.

The Council, if it ascertains that the facts are as alleged, shall proceed as provided in paragraphs 2, 4, and 5 of Article 7.

ARTICLE 9.

The existence of demilitarised zones being calculated to prevent aggression and to facilitate a definite finding of the nature provided for in Article 10 below, the establishment of such zones between States mutually consenting thereto is recommended as a means of avoiding violations of the present Protocol.

The demilitarised zones already existing under the terms of certain treaties or conventions, or which may be established in future between States mutually consenting thereto, may at the request and at the expense of one or more of the conterminous States, be placed under a temporary or permanent system of supervision to be organised by the Council.

Article 10.

Est agresseur tout Etat qui recourt à la guerre en violation des engagements prévus au Pacte ou au présent Protocole. Est assimilée au recours à la guerre la violation du statut d'une zone démilitarisée.

Dans le cas d'hostilités engagées, est présumé agresseur, sauf décision contraire du Conseil prise à l'unanimité:

1° Tout Etat qui aura refusé de soumettre le différend à la procédure pour règlement pacifique prévue aux articles 13 et 15 du Pacte, complétés par le présent Protocole—ou qui aura refusé de se conformer, soit à une décision judiciaire ou arbitrale, soit à une recommandation unanime du Conseil—ou qui aura passé outre à un rapport unanime du Conseil, à une décision judiciaire ou arbitrale reconnaissant que le différend qui s'est élevé entre lui et l'autre Etat belligérant porte sur une question que le Droit international laisse à la compétence exclusive de cet Etat; toutefois, dans ce dernier cas, l'Etat ne sera présumé agresseur que s'il n'a pas soumis auparavant la question au Conseil ou à l'Assemblée, conformément à l'article 11 du Pacte.

2° Tout Etat qui aura violé une des mesures provisoires prescrites par le Conseil pendant la période de procédure, visées à l'article 7 du présent Protocole.

Hors les hypothèses visées aux numéros 1 et 2 du présent article, si le Conseil n'a pu déterminer dans le plus bref délai l'agresseur, il aura l'obligation de prescrire aux belligérants un armistice dont il fixera les conditions à la majorité des deux tiers et dont il surveillera l'observation.

Tout belligérant ayant refusé l'armistice ou en ayant violé les conditions, sera réputé agresseur.

Le Conseil enjoindra aux Etats signataires d'appliquer sans retard contre l'agresseur les sanctions visées à l'article 11 du présent Protocole, et tout Etat signataire, ainsi requis, sera dès lors fondé à exercer les droits d'un belligérant.

ARTICLE 10.

Every State which resorts to war in violation of the undertakings contained in the Covenant or in the present Protocol is an aggressor. Violation of the rules laid down for a demilitarised zone shall be held equivalent to resort to war.

In the event of hostilities having broken out, any State shall be presumed to be an aggressor, unless a decision of the Council, which must be taken unanimously, shall otherwise declare:

1. If it has refused to submit the dispute to the procedure of pacific settlement provided by Articles 13 and 15 of the Covenant as amplified by the present Protocol, or to comply with a judicial sentence or arbitral award or with a unanimous recommendation of the Council, or has disregarded a unanimous report of the Council, a judicial sentence or an arbitral award recognising that the dispute between it and the other belligerent State arises out of a matter whch by international law is solely within the domestic jurisdiction of the latter State; nevertheless, in the last case the State shall only be presumed to be an aggressor if it has not previously submitted the question to the Council or the Assembly, in accordance with Article 11 of the Covenant.

2. If it has violated provisional measures enjoined by the Council for the period while the proceedings are in progress as contemplated by Article 7 of the present Protocol.

Apart from the cases dealt with in paragraphs 1 and 2 of the present Article, if the Council does not at once succeed in determining the aggressor, it shall be bound to enjoin upon the belligerents an armistice, and shall fix the terms, acting, if need be, by a two-thirds majority and shall supervise its execution.

Any belligerent which has refused to accept the armistice or has violated its terms shall be deemed an aggressor.

The Council shall call upon the signatory States to apply forthwith against the aggressor the sanctions provided by Article 11 of the present Protocol, and any signatory State thus called upon shall thereupon be entitled to exercise the rights of a belligerent.

ARTICLE 11.

Dès que le Conseil a fait aux Etats signataires l'injonction prévue au dernier alinéa de l'article 10 du présent Protocole, les obligations desdits Etats en ce qui concerne les sanctions de toute nature visées aux alinéas 1 et 2 de l'article 16 du Pacte, deviennent immédiatement opérantes afin que ces sanctions puissent porter leurs effets contre l'agresseur sans aucun retard.

Ces obligations doivent être interprétées en ce sens que chacun des Etats signataires est tenu de collaborer loyalement et effectivement pour faire respecter le Pacte de la Société des Nations et pour s'opposer à tout acte d'agression dans la mesure que lui permettent sa situation géographique et les conditions spéciales de ses armements.

Conformément à l'alinéa 3 de l'article 16 du Pacte, les Etats signataires prennent l'engagement, individuel et collectif, de venir à l'aide de l'Etat attaqué ou menacé, et de se prêter un mutuel appui, grâce à des facilités et à des échanges réciproques en ce qui concerne le ravitaillement en matières premières et denrées de toute nature, les ouvertures de crédit, les transports et le transit et, à cet effet, de prendre toutes mesures en leur pouvoir pour maintenir la sécurité des communications terrestres et maritimes de l'Etat attaqué ou menacé.

Si les deux Parties au différend sont agresseurs au sens de l'article 10, les sanctions économiques et financières s'appliquent à l'une et à l'autre.

ARTICLE 12.

En raison de la complexité des conditions dans lesquelles le Conseil pourrait être appelé à remplir les fonctions visées à l'article 11 ci-dessus concernant les sanctions économiques et financières et pour préciser les garanties qui sont offertes par le présent Protocole aux Etats signataires, le Conseil invitera immédiatement les organisations économiques et financières de la Société des Nations à procéder à une étude et à sou-

Article 11.

As soon as the Council has called upon the signatory States to apply sanctions, as provided in the last paragraph of Article 10 of the present Protocol, the obligations of the said States, in regard to the sanctions of all kinds mentioned in paragraphs 1 and 2 of Article 16 of the Covenant, will immediately become operative in order that such sanctions may forthwith be employed against the aggressor.

Those obligations shall be interpreted as obliging each of the signatory States to co-operate loyally and effectively in support of the Covenant of the League of Nations, and in resistance to any act of aggression, in the degree which its geographical position and its particular situation as regards armaments allow.

In accordance with paragraph 3 of Article 16 of the Covenant the signatory States give a joint and several undertaking to come to the assistance of the State attacked or threatened, and to give each other mutual support by means of facilities and reciprocal exchanges as regards the provision of raw materials and supplies of every kind, openings of credits, transport and transit, and for this purpose to take all measures in their power to preserve the safety of communications by land and by sea of the attacked or threatened State.

If both parties to the dispute are aggressors within the meaning of Article 10, the economic and financial sanctions shall be applied to both of them.

Article 12.

In view of the complexity of the conditions in which the Council may be called upon to exercise the functions mentioned in Article 11 of the present Protocol concerning economic and financial sanctions, and in order to determine more exactly the guarantees afforded by the present Protocol to the signatory States, the Council shall forthwith invite the economic and financial organisations of the League of Nations to consider and report

mettre un rapport sur la nature des dispositions à prendre pour
mettre en vigueur les sanctions et mesures de coopération économique et financière, visées à l'article 16 du Pacte et à l'article
11 du présent Protocole.

En possession de ces informations, le Conseil établira par ses
organismes compétents:

> 1° les plans d'action destinés à faire jouer les sanctions
> économiques et financières contre un Etat agresseur;
> 2° les plans de coopération économique et financière entre
> un Etat attaqué et les divers Etats lui portant assistance,

et il communiquera ces plans aux Membres de la Société et
aux autres Etats signataires.

ARTICLE 13.

Eu égard aux sanctions militaires, navales et aériennes dont
l'application éventuelle est prévue à l'article 16 du Pacte et à
l'article 11 du présent Protocole, le Conseil aura qualité pour
recevoir les engagements d'Etats déterminant par avance les
forces militaires, navales et aériennes que ces Etats pourraient
faire intervenir immédiatement afin d'assurer l'exécution des
obligations dérivant à ce sujet du Pacte et du présent Protocole.

Dès que le Conseil a fait aux Etats signataires l'injonction prévue au dernier alinéa de l'article 10 ci-dessus, ces Etats peuvent
en outre faire entrer en ligne, suivant les accords antérieurement
faits, leurs forces militaires, navales et aériennes au secours d'un
Etat particulier, victime de l'agression.

Les accords visés au précédent alinéa sont enregistrés et pu-
bliés par le Secrétariat de la Société des Nations; ils restent
ouverts à tout Etat Membre de la Société, qui voudrait y accéder.

ARTICLE 14.

Le Conseil a seul qualité pour déclarer qui'l y a lieu de faire
cesser l'application des sanctions et de rétablir les conditions
normales.

as to the nature of the steps to be taken to give effect to the financial and economic sanctions and measures of co-operation contemplated in Article 16 of the Covenant and in Article 11 of this Protocol.

When in possession of this information, the Council shall draw up through its competent organs:

1. Plans of action for the application of the economic and financial sanctions against an aggressor State;
2. Plans of economic and financial co-operation between a State attacked and the different States assisting it;

and shall communicate these plans to the Members of the League and to the other signatory States.

ARTICLE 13.

In view of the contingent military, naval and air sanctions provided for by Article 16 of the Covenant and by Article 11 of the present Protocol, the Council shall be entitled to receive undertakings from States determining in advance the military, naval and air forces which they would be able to bring into action immediately to ensure the fulfilment of the obligations in regard to sanctions which result from the Covenant and the present Protocol.

Furthermore, as soon as the Council has called upon the signatory States to apply sanctions, as provided in the last paragraph of Article 10 above, the said States may, in accordance with any agreements which they may previously have concluded, bring to the assistance of a particular State, which is the victim of aggression, their military, naval and air forces.

The agreements mentioned in the preceding paragraph shall be registered and published by the Secretariat of the League of Nations. They shall remain open to all States Members of the League which may desire to accede thereto.

ARTICLE 14.

The Council shall alone be competent to declare that the application of sanctions shall cease and normal conditions be re-established.

ARTICLE 15.

Pour répondre à l'esprit du présent Protocole, les Etats signataires conviennent que la totalité des frais de toute opération d'ordre militaire, naval ou aérien, entreprise pour la répression d'une agression, conformément aux termes de ce Protocole, ainsi que la réparation de tous dommages subis par les personnes civiles ou militaires, et de tous dommages matériels occasionnés par les opérations de part et d'autre, seront supportés par l'Etat agresseur jusqu'à l'extrême limite de sa capacité.

Toutefois, vu l'article 10 du Pacte, il ne pourra, comme suite à l'application des sanctions visées au présent Protocole, être porté atteinte en aucun cas à l'intégrité territoriale ou à l'indépendance politique de l'Etat agresseur.

ARTICLE 16.

Les Etats signataires conviennent qu'en cas de différend entre un ou plusieurs parmi eux et un ou plusieurs Etats non signataires du présent Protocole értangers à la Société des Nations, ces Etats étrangers seront invités, aux conditions prévues à l'article 17 du Pacte, à se soumettre aux obligations acceptées par les signataires du présent Protocole aux fins de règlement pacifique.

Si l'Etat invité, refusant d'accepter les dites conditions et obligations, recourt à la guerre contre un Etat signataire, les dispositions de l'article 16 du Pacte, telles qu'elles sont précisées par le présent Protocole, lui sont applicables.

ARTICLE 17.

Les Etats signataires s'engagent à prendre part à une Conférence internationale pour la réduction des armements qui devra être convoquée par le Conseil et qui se réunira à Genève le lundi 15 juin 1925. Tous autres Etats, Membres ou non de la Société, seront invités à cette Conférence.

En vue de la convocation de la Conférence, le Conseil pré-

ARTICLE 15.

In conformity with the spirit of the present Protocol, the signatory States agree that the whole cost of any military, naval or air operations undertaken for the repression of an aggression under the terms of the Protocol, and reparation for all losses suffered by individuals, whether civilians or combatants, and for all material damage caused by the operations of both sides, shall be borne by the aggressor State up to the extreme limit of its capacity.

Nevertheless, in view of Article 10 of the Covenant, neither the territorial integrity nor the political independence of the aggressor State shall in any case be affected as the result of the application of the sanctions mentioned in the present Protocol.

ARTICLE 16.

The signatory States agree that in the event of a dispute between one or more of them and one or more States which have not signed the present Protocol and are not Members of the League of Nations, such non-Member States shall be invited, on the conditions contemplated in Article 17 of the Covenant, to submit, for the purpose of a pacific settlement, to the obligations accepted by the States signatories of the present Protocol.

If the State so invited, having refused to accept the said conditions and obligations, resorts to war against a signatory State, the provisions of Article 16 of the Covenant, as defined by the present Protocol, shall be applicable against it.

ARTICLE 17.

The signatory States undertake to participate in an International Conference for the Reduction of Armaments which shall be convened by the Council and shall meet at Geneva on Monday, June 15th, 1925. All other States, whether Members of the League or not, shall be invited to this Conference.

In preparation for the convening of the Conference, the Coun-

parera, en tenant compte des engagements prévus aux articles
11 et 13 du présent Protocole, un programme général pour la
reduction et la limitation des armements qui sera mis à la disposition de cette Conférence et communiqué aux gouvernements
le plus tôt possible, et au plus tard trois mois avant la réunion.

Si au moins la majorité des Membres représentés en permanence au Conseil et dix autres Membres de la Société n'ont pas
déposé leur ratification pour le 1er mai 1925, le Secrétaire général
de la Société devra prendre immédiatement l'avis du Conseil
pour savoir s'il doit annuler les invitations ou simplement ajour-
ner la Conférence à une date ultérieure, qui sera fixée par le
Conseil pour permettre la réunion du nombre nécessaire de ratifications.

ARTICLE 18.

Toutes les fois que, dans l'article 10 ou dans toutes autres
dispositions du présent Protocole, il est fait mention d'une décision du Conseil, elle s'entend dans le sens de l'article 15 du
Pacte, à savoir que le vote des représentants des Parties au différend ne compte pas dans le calcul de l'unanimité ou de la majorité requise.

ARTICLE 19.

A défaut de stipulations expresses, le présent Protocole n'af-
fecte pas les droits et les obligations des Membres de la Société
des Nations, tels qu'ils résultent du Pacte.

ARTICLE 20.

Tout différend relatif à l'interprétation du présent Protocole
sera soumis à la Cour permanente de Justice internationale.

ARTICLE 21.

Le présent Protocole, dont les textes français et anglais feront
foi, sera ratifié.

cil shall draw up with due regard to the undertakings contained in Articles 11 and 13 of the present Protocol a general programme for the reduction and limitation of armaments, which shall be laid before the Conference and which shall be communicated to the Governments at the earliest possible date, and at the latest three months before the Conference meets.

If by May 1st, 1925, ratifications have not been deposited by at least a majority of the permanent Members of the Council and ten other Members of the League, the Secretary-General of the League shall immediately consult the Council as to whether he shall cancel the invitations or merely adjourn the Conference to a subsequent date to be fixed by the Council so as to permit the necessary number of ratifications to be obtained.

ARTICLE 18.

Wherever mention is made in Article 10, or in any other provision of the present Protocol, of a decision of the Council, this shall be understood in the sense of Article 15 of the Covenant, namely that the votes of the representatives of the parties to the dispute shall not be counted when reckoning unanimity or the necessary majority.

ARTICLE 19.

Except as expressly provided by its terms, the present Protocol shall not affect in any way the rights and obligations of Members of the League as determined by the Covenant.

ARTICLE 20.

Any dispute as to the interpretation of the present Protocol shall be submitted to the Permanent Court of International Justice.

ARTICLE 21.

The present Protocol, of which the French and English texts are both authentic, shall be ratified.

Le dépôt des ratifications sera effectué au Secrétariat de la Société des Nations le plus tôt qu'il sera possible.

Les Etats dont le gouvernement a son siège hors d'Europe auront la faculté de se borner à faire connaître au Secrétariat de la Société des Nations que leur ratification a été donnée et, dans ce cas, ils devront en transmettre l'instrument aussitôt que faire se pourra.

Dès que la majorité des Membres représentés en permanence au Conseil et dix autres Membres de la Société auront déposé ou effectué leur ratification, un procès-verbal sera dressé par le Secrétariat pour le constater.

La mise en vigueur du Protocole aura lieu après que ce procès-verbal aura été dressé et dès que le plan de réduction des armements aura été adopté par la Conférence prévue à l'article 17.

Si, dans un délai, à fixer par ladite Conférence après l'adoption du plan de réduction des armements, ce plan n'a pas été exécuté, il appartiendra au Conseil de le constater; par l'effet de cette constatation le présent Protocole deviendra caduc.

Les conditions en vertu desquelles le Conseil pourra constater que le plan établi par la Conférence internationale pour la réduction des armements n'a pas été exécuté et que, par conséquent, le présent Protocole est devenu caduc, seront définies par la Conférence elle-même.

Tout Etat signataire qui ne se conformerait pas, après l'expiration du délai fixé par la Conférence, au plan adopté par elle, ne pourra bénéficier des dispositions du présent Protocole.

En foi de quoi les Soussignés, dûment autorisés à cet effet, ont signé le présent Protocole.

Fait à Genève, le deux octobre, mil neuf cent vingt-quatre, en un seul exemplaire qui restera déposé dans les archives du Secrétariat de la Société des Nations et qui sera enregistré par lui à la date de son entrée en vigueur.

The deposit of ratifications shall be made at the Secretariat of the League of Nations as soon as possible.

States of which the seat of government is outside Europe will be entitled merely to inform the Secretariat of the League of Nations that their ratification has been given; in that case, they must transmit the instrument of ratification as soon as possible.

So soon as the majority of the permanent Members of the Council and ten other Members of the League have deposited or have effected their ratifications, a *procès-verbal* to that effect shall be drawn up by the Secretariat.

After the said *procès-verbal* has been drawn up, the Protocol shall come into force as soon as the plan for the reduction of armaments has been adopted by the Conference provided for in Article 17.

If within such period after the adoption of the plan for the reduction of armaments as shall be fixed by the said Conference, the plan has not been carried out, the Council shall make a declaration to that effect; this declaration shall render the present Protocol null and void.

The grounds on which the Council may declare that the plan drawn up by the International Conference for the Reduction of Armaments has not been carried out, and that in consequence the present Protocol has been rendered null and void, shall be laid down by the Conference itself.

A signatory State which, after the expiration of the period fixed by the Conference, fails to comply with the plan adopted by the Conference, shall not be admitted to benefit by the provisions of the present Protocol.

In faith whereof the Undersigned, duly authorised for this purpose, have signed the present Protocol.

Done at Geneva, on the second day of October, nineteen hundred and twenty-four, in a single copy, which will be kept in the archives of the Secretariat of the League and registered by it on the date of its coming into force.

GENERAL REPORT SUBMITTED TO THE FIFTH ASSEMBLY
ON BEHALF OF THE FIRST AND THIRD COMMITTEES
BY M. POLITIS (GREECE) AND M. BENES
(CZECHOSLOVAKIA).

I

INTRODUCTION.

After being examined for several years by the Third Committee, the problem of the reduction of armaments has this year suddenly assumed a different, a wider and even an unexpected form.

Last year a draft Treaty of Mutual Assistance was prepared, which the Assembly sent to the Members of the League for their consideration. The replies from the Governments were to be examined by the Fifth Assembly.

At the very beginning of its work, however, after a memorable debate, the Assembly indicated to the Third Committee a new path. On September 6th, 1924, on the proposal of the Prime Ministers of France and Great Britain, M. Edouard Herriot and Mr. Ramsay MacDonald, the Assembly adopted the following resolution:

"The Assembly,

"Noting the declarations of the Governments represented, observes with satisfaction that they contain the basis of an understanding tending to establish a secure peace,

"Decides as follows:

"With a view to reconciling in the new proposals the divergences between certain points of view which have been expressed and, when agreement has been reached, to enable an international conference upon armaments to be summoned by the League of Nations at the earliest possible moment:

"(1) The Third Committee is requested to consider the

material dealing with security and the reduction of armaments, particularly the observations of the Governments on the draft Treaty of Mutual Assistance, prepared in pursuance of Resolution XIV of the Third Assembly and other plans prepared and presented to the Secretary-General since the publication of the draft Treaty, and to examine the obligations contained in the Covenant of the League in relation to the guarantees of security which a resort to arbitration and a reduction of armaments may require:

"(2) The First Committee is requested:

"(*a*) To consider, in view of possible amendments, the articles in the Covenant relating to the settlement of disputes;

"(*b*) To examine within what limits the terms of Article 36, paragraph 2, of the Statute establishing the Permanent Court of International Justice might be rendered more precise and thereby facilitate the more general acceptance of the clause;

and thus strengthen the solidarity and the security of the nations of the world by settling by pacific means all disputes which may arise between States."

This resolution had two merits, first, that of briefly summarising all the investigations made in the last four years by the different organisations of the League in their efforts to establish peace and bring about the reduction of armaments, and, secondly, that of indicating the programme of work of the Committees in the hope that, with the aid of past experience, they would at last attain the end in view.

The Assembly had assigned to each Committee a distinct and separate task; to the First Committee, the examination of the pacific settlement of disputes by methods capable of being applied in every case; to the Third Committee, the question of the security of nations considered as a necessary preliminary condition for the reduction of their armaments.

Each Committee, after a general discussion which served to

detach the essential elements from the rest of the problem, referred the examination of its programme to a Sub-Committee, which devoted a large number of meetings to this purpose.

The proposals of the Sub-Committees then led to very full debates by the Committees, which terminated in the texts analysed below.

As, however, the questions submitted respectively to the two Committees form part of an indivisible whole, contact and collaboration had to be established between the Committees by means of a Mixed Committee of nine members and finally by a joint Drafting Committee of four members.

For the same reason, the work of the Committees has resulted in a single draft protocol accompanied by two draft resolutions for which the Committees are jointly responsible.

Upon these various texts, separate reports were submitted, which, being approved by the Committees respectively responsible for them, may be considered as an official commentary by the Committees.

These separate reports have here been combined in order to present as a whole the work accomplishd by the two Committees and to facilitate explanation.

Before entering upon an analysis of the proposed texts, it is expedient to recall, in a brief historical summary, the efforts of the last four years, of which the texts are the logical conclusion.

Historical Statement.

The problem of the reduction of armaments is presented in Article 8 of the Covenant in 'terms which reveal at the outset the complexity of the question and which explain the tentative manner in which the subject has been treated by the League of Nations in the last few years.

"The Members of the League recognise that the maintenance of peace requires the reduction of national armaments to the lowest point consistent with national safety and the enforcement by common action of international obligations."

Here we see clearly expressed the need of reducing the burden which armaments imposed upon the nations immediately after the war and of putting a stop to the competition in armaments, which was, in itself, a threat to the peace of the world. But, at the same time, there is recognised the duty of safeguarding the national security of the Members of the League and of safeguarding it, not only by the maintenance of a necessary minimum of troops, but also by the co-operation of all the nations, by a vast organisation for peace.

Such is the meaning of the Covenant, which, while providing for reduction of armaments properly so called, recognises at the same time the need of *common action,* by all the Members of the League, with a view to compelling a possible disturber of the peace to respect his *international obligations.*

Thus, in this first paragraph of Article 8, which is so short but so pregnant, mention is made of all the problems which have engaged the attention of our predecessors and ourselves and which the present Assembly has specially instructed us to solve, the problems of *collective security* and the *reduction of armaments.*

Taking up Article 8 of the Covenant, the First Assembly had already outlined a programme. At its head it placed a pronouncement of the Supreme Council:

"In order to diminish the economic difficulties of Europe, armies should everywhere be reduced to a peace footing. Armaments should be limited to the lowest possible figure compatible with national security."

The Assembly also called attention to a resolution of the International Financial Conference of Brussels held a short time before:

"Recommending to the Council of the League of Nations the desirability of conferring at once with the several Governments concerned with a view to securing a general reduction of the crushing burdens which, on their existing scale, armaments still impose on the impoverished peoples of the world, sapping their resources and imperilling their recovery from the ravages of war."

It also requested its two Advisory Commissions to set to work at once to collect the necessary information regarding the problem referred to in Article 8 of the Covenant.

From the beginning the work of the Temporary Mixed Commission and of the Permanent Advisory Commission revealed the infinite complexity of the question.

The Second Assembly limited its resolutions to the important, but none the less (if one may say so) secondary, questions of traffic in arms and their manufacture by private enterprise. It only touched upon the questions of military expenditure and budgets in the form of recommendations and, as regards the main question of reduction of armaments, it confined itself to asking the Temporary Mixed Commission to formulate a definite scheme.

It was between the Second and Third Assemblies that the latter Commission, which was beginning to get to grips with the various problems, revealed their constitutent elements. In its report it placed on record that:

"The memory of the world war was still maintaining in many countries a feeling of insecurity, which was represented in the candid statements in which, at the request of the Assembly, several of them had put forward the requirements of their national security, and the geographical and political considerations which contributed to shape their policy in the matter of armaments."

At the same time, however, the Commission stated:

"Consideration of these statements as a whole has clearly revealed not only the sincere desire of the Governments to reduce national armaments and the corresponding expenditure to a minimum, but also the importance of the results achieved. These facts"—according to the Commission—"are indisputable, and are confirmed, moreover, by the replies received from Governments to the Recommendation of the Assembly regarding the limitation of military expenditure."

That is the point we had reached *two years ago;* there was a *unanimous desire to reduce armaments.* Reductions, though as yet inadequate, had been begun, and there was a *still stronger desire to ensure the security of the world* by a stable and permanent organisation for peace.

That was the position which, after long discussions, gave rise *at the Third Assembly to the famous Resolution XIV* and at the Fourth Assembly *to the draft Treaty of Mutual Assistance,* for which we are now substituting the Protocol submitted to the Fifth Assembly.

What progress has been made during these four years?

Although the Treaty of Mutual Assistance was approved in principle by eighteen Governments, it gave rise to certain misgivings. We need only recall the most important of these, hoping that a comparison between them and an analysis of the new scheme will demonstrate that the First and Third Committees have endeavoured, with a large measure of success, to dispose of the objections raised and that the present scheme consequently represents an immense advance on anything that has hitherto been done.

In the first place, a number of Governments or delegates to the Assembly argued that the guarantees provided by the draft Treaty of Mutual Assistance did not imply with sufficient definiteness the reduction of armaments which is the ultimate object of our work.

The idea of the Treaty was to give effect to Article 8 of the Covenant, but many persons considered that it did not, in fact, secure the automatic execution of that article. Even if a reduction of armaments was achieved by its means, the amount of the reduction was left, so the opponents of the Treaty urged, to the estimation of each Government, and there was nothing to show that it would be considerable.

With equal force many States complained that no provision had been made for the development of the *juridicial and moral elements of the Covenant* by the side of material guarantees. The novel character of the charter given to the nations in 1919 lay essentially in the advent of a moral solidarity which foreshadowed the coming of a new era. That principle ought to have, as its natural consequence, *the extension of arbitration and international jurisdiction,* without which no human society can be solidly grounded. A considerable portion of the Assembly asked that efforts should also be made in this direction. The draft Treaty seemed from this point of view to be insufficient and ill-balanced.

Finally, the articles relating to partial treaties gave rise, as you are aware, to certain objections. Several Governments considered that they would lead to the establishment of groups of Powers animated by hostility towards other Powers or groups of Powers and that they would cause political tension. The absence of the barriers of compulsory arbitration and judicial intervention was evident here as everywhere else.

Thus, by a logical and gradual process, there was elaborated the system at which we have now arrived.

The reduction of armaments required by the Covenant and demanded by the general situation of the world to-day led us to consider the question of security as a necessary complement to disarmament.

The support demanded from different States by other States less favourably situated had placed the former under the obligation of asking for a sort of moral and legal guarantee that the States which have to be supported would act in perfect good faith and would always endeavor to settle their disputes by pacific means.

It became evident, however, with greater clearness and force than ever before, that if the security and effective assistance demanded in the event of aggression was the condition *sine quâ non* of the reduction of armaments, it was at the same time the necessary complement of the pacific settlement of international disputes, since the non-execution of a sentence obtained by pacific methods of settlement would necessarily drive the world back to the system of armed force. Sentences imperatively required sanctions or the whole system would fall to the ground.

Arbitration was therefore considered by the Fifth Assembly to be the necessary third factor, the complement of the two others with which it must be combined in order to build up the new system set forth in the Protocol.

Thus, after five years' hard work, we have decided to propose to the Members of the League *the present system of arbitration, security and reduction of armaments*—a system which we regard as being complete and sound.

That is the position with which the Fifth Assembly has to deal to-day. The desire to arrive at a successful issue is unanimous. A great number of the decisions adopted in the past years have met with general approval. There has arisen a thoroughly clear appreciation of the undoubted gaps which have to be filled and of the reasonable apprehensions which have to be dissipated. Conditions have therefore become favourable for arriving at an agreement.

An agreement has been arrived at on the basis of the draft Protocol which is now submitted to you for consideration.

II

ANALYSIS OF THE SCHEME.

1.—Work of the First Committee.

(*Rapporteur:* M. Politis)

DRAFT PROTOCOL FOR THE PACIFIC SETTLEMENT OF INTERNATIONAL DISPUTES.

Preamble.

The object of the Protocol, which is based upon the resolution of September 6th, 1924, is to facilitate the reduction and limitation of armaments provided for in Article 8 of the Covenant of the League of Nations by guaranteeing the security of States through the development of methods for the pacific settlement of all international disputes and the effective condemnation of aggressive war.

These general ideas are summarised in the preamble of the Protocol.

COMPULSORY ARBITRATION.

(*Articles 1 to 6, 10, 16, 18 and 19 of the Protocol*)

1.—Introduction.

Compulsory arbitration is the fundamental basis of the proposed system. It has seemed to be the only means of attaining the ultimate aim pursued by the League of Nations, viz. the establishment of a pacific and legal order in the relations between peoples.

The realisation of this great ideal, to which humanity aspires with a will which has never been more strongly affirmed, presupposes, as an indispensable condition, the elimination of war, the extension of the rule of law and the strengthening of the sentiment of justice.

The Covenant of the League of Nations erected a wall of protection around the peace of the world, but it was a first attempt at international organisation and it did not succeed in closing the circle sufficiently thoroughly to leave no opening for war. It reduced the number of possible wars. It did not condemn them all. There were some which it was forced to tolerate. Consequently, there remained, in the system which it established, numerous fissures, which constituted a grave danger to peace.

The new system of the Protocol goes further. It closes the circle drawn by the Covenant; it prohibits all wars of aggression. Henceforth no purely private war between nations will be tolerated.

This result is obtained by strengthening the pacific methods of procedure laid down in the Covenant. The Protocol completes them and extends them to all international disputes without exception, by making arbitration compulsory.

In reality, the word "arbitration" is used here in a somewhat different sense from that which it has generally had up to now. It does not exactly correspond with the definition given by the Hague Conferences which, codifying a century-old custom, saw in it "the settlement of disputes between States by judges of their own choice and on the basis of respect for law" (Article 37 of the Convention of October 18th, 1907, for the Pacific Settlement of International Disputes).

The arbitration which is now contemplated differs from this classic arbitration in various respects:

(a) It is only part of a great machinery of pacific settlement. It is set up under the auspices and direction of the Council of the League of Nations.

(b) It is not only an instrument for the administration of justice. It is, in addition and above all, an instrument of peace. The arbitrators must no doubt seek in the first place to apply the rules and principles of international law. This is the reason why, as will be seen below, they are bound to consult the Permanent Court of International Justice if one of the parties so requests. But if international law furnishes no rule or principle applicable to the particular case, they cannot, like ordinary arbitrators, refuse to give a decision. They are bound to proceed on grounds of equity, for in our system arbitration is always of necessity to lead to a definitive solution of the dispute. This is not to be regretted, for to ensure the respect of law by nations it is neccessary first that they should be assured of peace,

(c) It does not rest solely upon the loyalty and good faith of the parties. To the moral and legal force of an ordinary arbitration is added the actual force derived from the international organisation of which the kind of arbitration in question forms one of the principal elements; the absence of a sanction which has impeded the development of compulsory arbitration is done away with under our system.

In the system of the Protocol, the obligation to submit disputes to arbitration is sound and practical because it has always a sanction. Its application is automaticaly ensured, by means of the intervention of the Council; in no case can it be thrown on one side through the ill-will of one of the disputant States. The awards to which it leads are always accompanied by a sanction, adapted to the circumstances of the case and more or less severe according to the degree of resistance offered to the execution of the sentence.

2.—NATURE OF THE RULES OF THE PROTOCOL.

Article 1.

The rules laid down in the Protocol do not all have the same scope or value for the future.

As soon as the Protocol comes into force, its provisions will become compulsory as between the signatory States, and in its dealings with them the Council of the League of Nations will at once be able to exercise all the rights and fulfil all the duties conferred upon it.

As between the States Members of the League of Nations, the Protocol may in the first instance create a dual régime, for, if it is not immediately accepted by them all, the relations between signatories and non-signatories will still be governed by the Covenant alone while the relations between signatories will be governed by the Protocol as well.

But this situation cannot last. Apart from the fact that it may be hoped that all Members of the League will adhere to it, the Protocol is in no sense designed to create among the States which accept it a restricted League capable of competing with or opposing in any way the existing League. On the contrary, such of its provisions as relate to articles of the Covenant will, as soon as possible, be made part of the general law by amendment of the Covenant effected in accordance with the procedure for revision laid down in Article 26 thereof. The signatory States which are Members of the League of Nations undertake to make every effort to this end.

When the Covenant has been amended in this way, some parts of the Protocol will lose their value as between the said States: some of them will have enriched the Covenant, while others, being temporary in character, will have lost their object.

The whole Protocol will remain applicable to relations between signatory States which are Members of the League of Nations and signatory States outside the League, or between States coming within the latter category.

It should be added that, as the League realises its aim of universality, the amended Covenant will take the place, as regards all States, of the separate régime of the Protocol.

3.—CONDEMNATION OF AGGRESSIVE WAR.

Article 2.

The general principle of the Protocol is the prohibition of aggressive war.

Under the Covenant, while the old unlimited right of States to make war is restricted, it is not abolished. There are cases in which the exercise of this right is tolerated; some wars are prohibited and others are legitimate.

In future the position will be different. In no case is any State signatory of the Protocol entitled to undertake on its own sole initiative an offensive war against another signatory State or against any non-signatory State which accepts all the obligations assumed by the signatories under the Protocol.

The prohibition affects only aggressive war. It does not, of course, extend to defensive war. The right of legitimate self-defence continues, as it must, to be respected. The State attacked retains complete liberty to resist by all means in its power any acts of aggression of which it may be the victim. Without waiting for the assistance which it is entitled to receive from the international community, it may and should at once defend itself with its own force. Its interests are identified with the general interest. This is a point on which there can be no doubt.

The same applies when a country employs force with the consent of the Council or the Assembly of the League of Nations under the provisions of the Covenant and the Protocol. This eventuality may arise in two classes of cases: either a State may take part in the collective measures of force decided upon by the League of Nations in aid of one of its Members which is the victim of aggression; or a State may employ force with the authorisation of the Council or the Assembly in order to enforce a decision given in its favour. In the former case, the assistance given to the victim of aggression is indirectly an act of legitimate self-defence. In the latter, force is used in the service of the general interest, which would be threatened if decisions reached by a pacific procedure could be violated with impunity. In all these cases the country resorting to war is not acting on its private initiative but is in a sense the agent and the organ of the community.

It is for this reason that we have not hesitated to speak of the exceptional authorisation of war. It has been proposed that the word "force" should be used in order to avoid any mention of "war"—in order to spare the public that disappointment which it might feel when it found that, notwithstanding the solemn condemnation of war, war was still authorised in exceptional cases. We preferred, however, to recognise the position frankly by retaining the expression "resort to war" which is used in the Covenant. If we said "force" instead of "war," we should not be altering the facts in any way. Moreover, the confession that war is still possible in specific cases has a certain value, because the term describes a definite and well-understood situation, whereas the expression "resort to force" would be liable to be misunderstood, and also because it emphasises the value of the sanctions at the disposal of the community of States bound by the Protocol.

4.—COMPULSORY JURISDICTION OF THE PERMANENT COURT OF INTERNATIONAL JUSTICE.

Article 3.

The general principle of the Protocol could not be accepted unless the pacific settlement of all international disputes without distinction were made possible.

This solution has been found, in the first place, in the extension of the compulsory jurisdiction of the Permanent Court of International Justice.

According to its Statute, the jurisdiction of the Court is, in principle, optional. On the other hand, Article 36, paragraph 2, of the Statute, offers States the opportunity of making the jurisdiction compulsory in respect of all or any of the classes of legal disputes affecting: (*a*) the interpretation of a Treaty; (*b*) any question of international law; (*c*) the existence of any fact which, if established, would constitute a breach of an international obligation; (*d*) the nature or extent of the reparation to be made for the breach of an international obligation. States have only to declare their intention through the special Protocol annexed to the Statute. The undertaking then holds good in respect of any other State which assumes the same obligation. It may be given either unconditionally or on condition of reciprocity on the part of several or certain other States; either permanently or for a fixed period.

So far such compulsory jurisdiction has only been accepted by a small number of countries. The majority of States have abstained because they did not see their way to accept compulsory jurisdiction by the Court in certain cases falling within one or another of the classes of dispute enumerated above, and because they were not sure whether, in accepting, they could make reservations to that effect.

It was for this reason that the Assembly in its resolution of September 6th, requested the First Committee to render more precise the terms of Article 36, paragraph 2, in order to facilitate its acceptance.

Careful consideration of the article has shown that it is sufficiently elastic to allow of all kinds of reservations. Since it is open to the States to accept compulsory jurisdiction by the Court in respect of certain of the classes of dispute mentioned and not to accept it in respect of the rest, it is also open to them only to accept it in respect of a portion of one of those classes; rights need not be exercised in their full extent. In giving the undertaking in question, therefore, States are free to declare that it will not be regarded as operative in those cases in which they consider it to be inadmissible.

We can imagine possible and therefore legitimate, reservations either in connection with a certain class of dispute or, generally speaking, in regard to the precise stage at which the dispute may be laid before the Court. While we cannot here enumerate all the conceivable reservations, it may be worth while to mention merely as examples those to which we referred in the course of our discussions.

From the class of disputes relating to "the interpretation of a treaty" there may be excluded, for example, disputes as to the interpretation of certain specified classes of treaty such as political treaties, peace treaties, etc.

From the class of disputes relating to "any point of international law" there may be excluded, for example, disputes as to the application of a political treaty, a peace treaty, etc., or as to any specified question or disputes which might arise as the outcome of hostilities initiated by one of the signatory States in agreement with the Council or the Assembly of the League of Nations.

Again, there are many possible reservations as to the precise stage at which a dispute may be laid before the Court. The most far-reaching of these would be to make the resort to the Court in connection with every dispute in respect of which its compulsory jurisdiction is recognised contingent upon the establishment of an agreement for submission of the case which, failing agreement between the parties, would be drawn up by the Court itself, the analogy of the provisions of the Hague Convention of 1907 dealing with the Permanent Court of Arbitration being thus followed.

It might also be stated that the recognition of the compulsory jurisdiction of the Court does not prevent the parties to the dispute from agreeing to resort to a preliminary conciliation procedure before the Council of the League of Nations or any other body selected by them, or to submit their disputes to arbitration in preference to going before the Court.

A State might also, while accepting compulsory jurisdiction by the Court, reserve the right of laying disputes before the Council of the League with a view to conciliation in accordance with paragraphs 1-3 of Article 15 of the Covenant, with the proviso that neither party might, during the proceedings before the Council, take proceedings against the other in the Court.

It will be seen, therefore, that there is a very wide range of reservations which may be made in connection with the undertaking referred to in Article 36, paragraph 2. It is possible that apprehensions may arise lest the right to make reservations should destroy the practical value of the undertaking. There seems, however, to be no justification for such misgivings. In the first place, it is to be hoped that every Government will confine its reservations to what is absolutely essential. Secondly, it must be recognised that, however restrictive the scope of the undertaking may be, it will always be better than no undertaking at all.

The fact that the signatory States undertake to accede, even though it be with reservations, to paragraph 2 of Article 36 may therefore be held to constitute a great advance.

Such accession must take place at latest within the month following upon the coming into force or subsequent acceptance of the Protocol.

It goes without saying that such accession in no way restricts the liberty which States possess, under the ordinary law, of concluding special agreements for arbitration. It is entirely open to any two countries signatory of the Protocol which have acceded to paragraph 2 of Article 36 to extend still further, as between themselves, the compulsory jurisdiction of the Court, or to stipulate that before having recourse to its jurisdiction they will submit their disputes to a special procedure of conciliation or even to stipulate, either before or after a dispute has arisen, that it shall be brought before a special tribunal of arbitrators or before the Council of the League of Nations rather than to the Court.

It is also certain that up to the time of the coming into force or acceptance of the Protocol accession to paragraph 2 of Article 36, which will thenceforth become compulsory, will remain optional, and that if such accession has already taken place it will continue to be valid in accordance with the terms under which it was made.

The only point which may cause difficulty is the question what is the effect of accessions given to the Protocol if the latter becomes null and void. It may be asked whether such accessions are to be regarded as so intimately bound up with the Protocol that they must disappear with it. The reply must be in the negative. The sound rule of interpretation of international treaties is that, unless there is express provision to the contrary, effects already produced survive the act from which they sprang.

The natural corollary is that any State which wishes to make the duration of its accession to Article 36 dependent on the duration of the Protocol must make an express stipulation to this effect. As Article 36 permits acceptance of the engagement in question for a specified term only, a State may, when acceding, stipulate that it only undertakes to be bound during such time as the Protocol shall remain in force.

5.—Strengthening of Pacific Methods of Procedure.

Article 4.

We have, in the second place, succeeded in making possible the pacific settlement of all disputes by strengthening the procedure laid down in the Covenant.

Article 4, paragraph 1.

Action by the Council with a view to reconciliation.—If a dispute does not come within the compulsory jurisdiction of the

Permanent Court of International Justice and if the Parties have been unable to come to an agreement to refer it to the Court or to submit it to arbitration, it should, under the terms of Article 15 of the Covenant, be submitted to the Council, which will endeavour to secure a settlement by reconciling the parties. If the Council's efforts are successful, it must, so far as it considers it advisable, make public a statement giving such facts and explanations regarding the dispute and the terms of settlement thereof as it may deem appropriate.

In this connection no change has been made in the procedure laid down by the Covenant. It appeared unnecessary to specify what particular procedure should be followed. The Council is given the utmost latitude in choosing the means most appropriate for the reconciliation of the parties. It may take advice in various quarters; it may hear expert opinions; it may proceed to investigations or expert enquiries, whether by itself or through the intermediary of experts chosen by it; it may even, upon application by one of the parties, constitute a special conciliation committee. The essential point is to secure, if possible, a friendly settlement of the dispute; the actual methods to be employed are of small importance. It is imperative that nothing should in any way hamper the Council's work in the interests of peace. It is for the Council to examine the question whether it would be expedient to draw up for its own use and bring to the notice of the Governments of the signatory States general regulations of procedure applicable to cases brought before it and designed to test the good-will of the parties with a view to persuading them more easily to reach a settlement under its auspices.

Experience alone can show whether it will be necessary to develop the rules laid down in the first three paragraphs of Article 15 of the Covenant.

For the moment it would appear to be expedient to make no addition and to have full confidence in the wisdom of the Council, it being understood that, whether at the moment in question or at any other stage of the procedure, it will be open to the parties to come to an agreement for some different method of settlement: by way of direct understanding, constitution of a special committee of mediators or conciliators, appeal to arbitration or to the Permanent Court of International Justice.

The new procedure set up by the Protocol will be applicable only in the event of the Council's failing in its efforts at reconciliation and of the parties failing to come to an understanding in regard to the method of settlement to be adopted.

In such case, before going further, the Council must call upon the parties to submit their dispute to judicial settlement or to arbitration.

It is only in the case where this appeal—which the Council will make in the manner which appears to it most likely to secure a favourable hearing—is not listened to that the procedure will acquire the compulsory character which is necessary to make certain the final settlement of all disputes.

There are three alternatives:

> (*a*) Compulsory arbitration at the request of one of the parties;
>
> (*b*) A unanimous decision by the Council;
>
> (*c*) Compulsory arbitration enjoined by the Council.

Appropriate methods are laid down for all three cases.

Article 4, paragraph 2.

First case of Compulsory Arbitration.—If the parties, being called upon by the Council to submit their dispute to a judicial or arbitral settlement, do not succeed in coming to an agreement on the subject, there is no question of optional arbitration, but if a single party desires arbitration, arbitration immediately becomes compulsory.

The dispute is then *ipso facto* referred to a Committee of Arbitrators, which must be constituted within such time limit as the Council shall fix.

Full liberty is left to the parties themselves to constitute this Committee of Arbitrators. They may agree between themselves in regard to the number, names and powers of the arbitrators and the procedure. It is to be understood that the word "powers" is to be taken in the widest sense, including, *inter alia,* the questions to be put.

It was not considered desirable to develop this idea further. It appeared to be sufficient to state that any result which could be obtained by means of an agreement between the parties was preferable to any other solution.

It also appeared inexpedient to define precisely the powers which should be conferred upon the arbitrators. This is a matter which depends upon the circumstances of each particular case. According to the case, the arbitrators, as is said above, may fill the rôle of judges giving decisions of pure law or may have the function of arranging an amicable settlement with power to take account of considerations of equity.

It has not been thought necessary to lay this down in the form of a rule. It has appeared preferable to leave it in each case to the parties to agree between themselves to decide the matter according to the circumstances of the case.

Nevertheless, consideration has been given to the possibility that the arbitrators need not necessarily be jurists. It has therefore been decided that, when called upon to deal with points of law, they shall, if one of the parties so desires, request, through the medium of the Council, the advisory opinion of the Permanent Court of International Justice, which must, in such a case, meet with the utmost possible despatch. The opinion of the Court is obtained for the assistance of the arbitrators; it is not legally binding upon them, although its scientific authority must, in all cases, exercise a strong influence upon their judgment. With a view to preventing abusively frequent consultations of this kind, it is understood that the opinion of the Court in regard to disputed points of law can only be asked on a single occasion in the course of each case.

The extension which, in the new system of pacific settlement of disputes, has been given to the advisory procedure of the Court has suggested the idea that it might be desirable to examine whether, even in such cases, it might not be well to adopt the system of adding national judges which at present only obtains in litigious proceedings, and also that of applying to the advisory procedure the provisions of Article 24 of the Statute of the Court relating to withdrawal of judges.

If the parties have not been able to come to an understanding on all or on some of the points necessary to enable the arbitration to be carried out, it lies with the Council to settle the unsettled points, with the exception of the formulation of the questions to be answered, which the arbitrators must seek in the claims set out by the parties or by one of them if the others make default.

In cases where the selection of arbitrators thus falls upon the Council, it has appeared necessary—however much confidence may be felt in the Council's wisdom—to lay down for the selection of the arbitrators certain rules calculated to give the arbitration the necessary moral authority to ensure that it will in practice be respected.

The first rule is that the Council shall, before proceeding to the selection of arbitrators, have regard to the wishes of the parties. It was suggested that this idea should be developed by conferring on the parties the right to indicate their preferences and to challenge a certain number of the arbitrators proposed by the Council.

This proposal was set aside on account of the difficulty of laying down detailed regulations for the exercise of this double right. But it is understood that the Council will have no motive for failing to accept candidates proposed to it by the different parties nor for imposing upon them arbitrators whom they might wish to reject, nor, finally, for failing to take into account any other suggestion which the parties might wish to make. It is indeed evident that the Council will always be desirous of acting in the manner best calculated to increase to the utmost degree the confidence which the Committee of Arbitrators should inspire in the parties.

The second rule is based on the same point of view. It lays down the right of the Council to select the arbitrators and their president from among persons who, by their nationality, their personal character and their experience, appear to furnish the highest guarantees of competence and impartiality.

Here, too, experience will show whether it would be well for the Council to draw up general regulations for the composition and functioning of the compulsory arbitration now in question and of that above referred to, and for the conciliation procedure in the Council itself. Such regulations would be made for the Council's own use but would be communicated to the Governments of the signatory States.

Article 4, paragraph 3.

Unanimous decision by the Council.—If arbitration is refused by both parties the case will be referred back to the Council, but this time it will acquire a special character. Refusal of arbitration implies the consent of both parties to a final settlement of the dispute by the Council. It implies recognition of an exceptional jurisdiction of the Council. It denotes that the parties prefer the Council's decision to an arbitral award.

Resuming the examination of the question, the Council has not only the latitude which it customarily possesses. It is armed with full powers to settle the question finally and irrevocably if it is unanimous. Its decision, given unanimously by all the members other than those representing parties to the dispute, is imposed upon the parties with the same weight and the same force as the arbitration award which it replaces.

Article 4, paragraph 4.

Second case of Compulsory Arbitration.—If the Council does not arrive at a unanimous decision, it has to submit the dispute to the judgment of a Committee of Arbitrators, but this time, owing to the parties being deemed to have handed their case over to the Council, the organisation of the arbitration procedure is taken entirely out of their hands. It will be for the Council to settle all the details, the composition, the powers and the procedure of the Committee of Arbitrators. The Council is of course at liberty to hear the parties and even to invite suggestions from them, but it is under no obligation to do so. The only regulation with which it must comply is that, in the choice of arbitrators, it must bear in mind the guarantees of competence and impartiality which, by their nationality, their personal character and their experience, these arbitrators must always furnish.

Article 4, paragraph 6.

Effect of, and Sanction enforcing, Decisions.—Failing a friendly arrangement, we are, thanks to the system adopted, in all cases certain of arriving at a final solution of a dispute, whether in the form of a decree of the Permanent Court of International Justice or in the form of an arbitral award or, lastly, in the form of a unanimous decision of the Council.

To this solution the parties are compelled to submit. They must put it into execution or comply with it in good faith.

If they do not do so, they are breaking an engagement entered into towards the other signatories of the Protocol, and this breach involves consequences and sanctions according to the degree of gravity of the case.

If the recalcitrant party confines itself to offering passive resistance to the solution arrived at, it will first be the object of pacific pressure from the Council, which must exercise all its influence to persuade it to respect its engagements. If the Council is unsuccessful, it must propose measures calculated to ensure effect being given to the decision.

On this point the Protocol has been guided solely by the regulation contained at the end of Article 13 of the Covenant. The

Council may thus institute against the recalcitrant party collective sanctions of an economic and financial order. It is to be supposed that such sanctions will prove sufficient. It has not appeared possible to go further and to employ force against a State which is not itself resorting to force. The party in favour of which the decision has been given might, however, employ force against the recalcitrant party if authorised to do so by the Council.

But if the State against which the decision has been given takes up arms in resistance thereto, thereby becoming an aggressor against the combined signatories, it deserves even the severe sanctions provided in Article 16 of the Covenant, interpreted in the manner indicated in the present Protocol.

Sphere of Application of Methods of Pacific Procedure.— Necessary as the system which we have laid down is for the purpose of ensuring settlement of all disputes, in applying it, the pacific aim which underlies it must be the only guide. It must not be diverted to other purposes and used as an occasion for chicanery and tendencious proceedings by which the cause of peace would lose rather than gain.

A few exceptions to the rule have also had to be made in order to preserve the elasticity of the system. These are cases in which the claimant must be nonsuited, the claim being one which has to be rejected *in limine* by the Council, the Permanent Court of International Justice or the arbitrators, as the case may be.

The disputes to which the system will not apply are of three kinds:

Article 4, paragraph 5.

1. The first concerns disputes relating to questions which, at some time prior to the entry into force of the Protocol, have been the subject of a unanimous recommendation by the Council accepted by one of the parties concerned. It is essential to

international order and to the prestige of the Council that its unanimous recommendations, which confer a right upon the State accepting them, shall not be called into question again by means of a procedure based upon compulsory arbitration. Failing a friendly arrangement, the only way which lies open for the settlement of disputes to which these recommendations may give rise is recourse to the Council in accordance with the procedure at present laid down in the Covenant.

Article 4, paragraph 7.

2. The same applies to disputes which arise as the result of measures of war taken by one or more signatory States in agreement with the Council or the Assembly of the League of Nations. It would certainly not be admissible that compulsory arbitration should become a weapon in the hands of an enemy to the community to be used against the freedom of action of those who, in the general interest, seek to impose upon that enemy respect for his engagements.

In order to avoid all difficulty of interpretation, these first two classes of exceptions have been formally stated in the Protocol.

3. There is a third class of disputes to which the new system of pacific settlement can also not be applied. These are disputes which aim at revising treaties and international acts in force, or which seek to jeopardise the existing territorial integrity of signatory States. The proposal was made to include these exceptions in the Protocol, but the two Committees were unanimous in considering that, both from the legal and from the political point of view, the impossibility of applying compulsory arbitration to such cases was so obvious that it was quite superfluous to make them the subject of a special provision. It was thought sufficient to mention them in this report.

6.—Role of the Assembly Under the System Set Up by the Protocol.

Article 6.

The new procedure should be adapted to the old one, which gave the Assembly the same powers as the Council when a dispute is brought before it, either by the Council itself or at the request of one of the parties.

The question has arisen whether the system of maintaining in the new procedure this equality of powers between the two organs of the League of Nations is a practical one. Some were of opinion that it would be better to exclude intervention by the Assembly. Finally, however, the opposite opinion prevailed; an appeal to the Assembly may, indeed, have an important influence from the point of view of public opinion. Without going so far as to assign to the Assembly the same rôle as to the Council, it has been decided to adopt a mixed system by which the Assembly is, in principle, substituted for the Council in order that, when a dispute is referred to it in conformity with paragraph 9 of Article 15 of the Covenant, it may undertake, in the place of the Council, the various duties provided for in Article 4 of the present Protocol with the exception of purely executive acts which will always devolve upon the Council. For example, the organisation and management of compulsory arbitration, or the transmission of a question to the Permanent Court of International Justice, must always be entrusted to the Council, because, in practice, the latter is the only body qualified for such purposes.

The possible intervention of the Assembly does not affect in any way the final result of the new procedure. If the Assembly does not succeed in conciliating the parties and if one of them so requests, compulsory arbitration will be arranged by the Council in accordance with the rules laid down beforehand.

If none of the parties asks for arbitration, the matter is referred back to the Assembly, and if the solution recommended by the Assembly obtains the majority required under paragraph 10 of Article 15 of the Covenant, it has the same value as a unanimous decision of the Council.

Lastly, if the necessary majority is not obtained, the dispute is submitted to a compulsory arbitration organised by the Council.

In any event, as in the case where the Council alone intervenes, a definitive and binding solution of the dispute is reached.

7.—DOMESTIC JURISDICTION OF STATES.

Article 5.

The present Protocol in no way derogates from the rule of Article 15, paragraph 8, of the Covenant, which protects national sovereignty.

In order that there might be no doubt on this point, it appeared advisable to say so expressly.

Before the Council, whatever be the stage in the procedure set up by the Protocol at which the Council intervenes, the provision referred to applies without any modification.

The rule is applied also to both cases of compulsory arbitration. If one of the States parties to the dispute claims that the dispute or part thereof arises out of a matter which by international law is solely within its jurisdiction, the arbitrators must on this point take the advice of the Permanent Court of International Justice through the medium of the Council, for the question thus put in issue is a legal question upon which a judicial opinion should be obtained.

The Court will thus have to give a decision as to whether the question in dispute is governed by international law or whether it falls within the domestic jurisdiction of the State concerned. Its functions will be limited to this point and the question will in any event be referred back to the arbitrators. But, unlike other opinions requested of the Court in the course of a compulsory arbitration—opinions which for the arbitrators are purely advisory—in the present case the opinion of the Court is compulsory in the sense that, if the Court has recognised that the question in dispute falls entirely within the domestic jurisdiction of the State concerned, the arbitrators will simply have to register this conclusion in their award. It is only if the Court holds that the question in dispute is governed by international law that the arbitrators will again take the case under consideration in order to give a decision upon its substance.

The compulsory character of the Court's opinion, in this case, increases the importance of the double question referred to above, in connection with Article 4, relating to the calling-in of national judges, and the application of Article 24 of the Statute of the Court in matters of advisory procedure.

While the principle of Article 15, paragraph 8, of the Covenant is maintained, it has been necessary, in order to make its application more flexible, to call in aid the rule contained in Article 11 of the Covenant, which makes it the duty of the League of Nations, in the event of war or a threat of war, to "take any action that may be deemed wise and effective to safeguard the peace of nations," and obliges the Secretary-General to summon forthwith a meeting of the Council on the request of any Member of the League. It is in this way understood that when it has been recognised that a dispute arises out of a matter which is solely within the domestic jurisdiction of one of the parties, that party or its opponent will be fully entitled to call upon the Council or the Assembly to act.

There is nothing new in this simple reference to Article 11. It leaves unimpaired the right of the Council to take such action as it may deem wise and effectual to safeguard the peace of nations. It does not confer new powers of functions on either the Council or the Assembly. Both these organs of the League simply retain the powers now conferred upon them by the Covenant.

In order to dispel any doubt which may arise from the

parallel which has been drawn between Article 15, paragraph 8, and Article 11 of the Covenant, a very clear explanation was given in the course of the discussion in the First Committee.

Where a dispute is submitted to the Council under Article 15 and it is claimed by one party that the dispute arises out of a matter left exclusively within its domestic jurisdiction by international law, paragraph 8 prevents the Council from making any recommendations upon the subject if it holds that the contention raised by the party is correct and that the dispute does in fact arise out of a matter exclusively within that State's jurisdiction.

The effect of this paragraph is that the Council cannot make any recommendation in the technical sense in which that term is used in Article 15, that is to say, it cannot make, even by unanimous report, recommendations which become binding on the parties in virtue of paragraph 6.

Unanimity for the purpose of Article 15 implies a report concurred in by all the members of the Council other than the parties to the dispute. Only a report so concurred in is one which the parties to the dispute are bound to observe, in the sense that, if they resort to war with any party which complies with the recommendations, it will constitute a breach of Article 16 of the Covenant and will set in play the sanctions which are there referred to.

On the other hand, Article 11 is of different scope: first, it operates only in time of war or threat of war; secondly, it confers no right on the Council or on the Assembly to impose any solution of a dispute without the consent of the parties. Action taken by the Council or the Assembly under this article cannot become binding on the parties to the dispute in the sense in which recommendations under Article 15 become binding, unless they have themselves concurred in it.

One last point should be made clear. The reference which is made to Article 11 of the Covenant holds good only in the eventuality contemplated in Article 15, paragraph 8, of the Covenant. It is obvious that when a unanimous decision of the

Council or an arbitral award has been given upon the substance of a dispute, that dispute is finally settled and cannot again be brought either directly or indirectly under discussion. Article 11 of the Covenant does not deal with situations which are covered by rules of law capable of application by a judge. It applies only to cases which are not yet regulated by international law. In fact, it demonstrates the existence of loop-holes in the law.

The reference to Article 11 in two of the articles of the Protocol (Articles 5 and 10) has advantages beyond those to which attention is drawn in the commentary on the text of those articles. It will be an incitement to science to clear the ground for the work which the League of Nations will one day have to undertake with a view to bringing about, through the development of the rules of international law, a closer reconciliation between the individual interests of its Members and the universal interests which it is designed to serve.

8.—DETERMINATION OF THE AGGRESSOR.

Article 10.

In order that the procedure of pacific settlement may be accompanied by the necessary sanctions, it has been necessary to provide for determining exactly the State guilty of aggression to which sanctions are to be applied.

This question is a very complex one, and in the earlier work of the League the military experts and jurists who had had to deal with it found it extremely difficult.

There are two aspects to the problem: first, aggression has to be defined, and, secondly, its existence has to be ascertained.

The definition of aggression is a relatively easy matter, for it is sufficient to say that any State is the aggressor which resorts in any shape or form to force in violation of the engagements contracted by it either under the Covenant (if, for instance, being a Member of the League of Nations, it has not respected the territorial integrity or political independence of another Member of the League) or under the present Protocol (if, for instance, being a signatory of the Protocol, it has refused to conform to an arbitral award or to a unanimous decision of the Council). This is the effect of Article 10, which also adds that the violation of the rules laid down for a demilitarised zone is to be regarded as equivalent to resort to war. The text refers to resort to war, but it was understood during the discussion that, while mention was made of the most serious and striking instance, it was in accordance with the spirit of the Protocol that acts of violence and force, which possibly may not constitute an actual state of war, should nevertheless be taken into consideration by the Council.

On the contrary, to ascertain the existence of aggression is a very difficult matter, for although the first of the two elements which together constitute aggression, namely, the violation of an engagement, is easy to verify, the second, namely, resort to force, is not an easy matter to ascertain. When one country attacks another, the latter necessarily defends itself, and when hostilities are in progress on both sides, the question arises which party began them.

This is a question of fact concerning which opinions may differ.

The first idea which occurs to the mind is to make it the duty of the Council to determine who is the aggressor. But, immediately, the question arises whether the Council must decide this question unanimously, or whether a majority vote would suffice. There are serious disadvantages in both solutions and they are therefore unacceptable.

To insist upon a unanimous decision of the Council exposes the State attacked to the loss of those definite guarantees to which it is entitled, if one single Member of the Council—be it in good faith or otherwise—insists on adhering to an interpretation of the facts different from that of all his colleagues. It is impossible to admit that the very existence of a nation should be subject to such a hazard. It is not sufficient to point out that the Council would be bound to declare the existence of aggression in an obvious case and that it could not fail to carry out its duty. The duty would be a duty without a sanction and if by any chance the Council were not to do its duty, the State attacked would be deprived of all guarantees.

But it would also be dangerous to rely on a majority vote of the Council. In that case, the danger would be incurred by the State called upon to furnish assistance and to support the heavy burden of common action, if it still entertained some doubt as to the guilt of the country against which it had to take action. Such a country would run the risk of having to conform to a decision with which it did not agree.

The only escape from this dilemma appeared to lie in some automatic procedure which would not necessarily be based on a decision of the Council. After examining the difficulty and discussing it in all its aspects, the First Committee believes that it has found the solution in the idea of a presumption which shall hold good until the contrary has been established by a unanimous decision of the Council.

The Committee is of opinion that this presumption arises in three cases, namely, when a resort to war is accompanied:

> By a refusal to accept the procedure of pacific settlement or to submit to the decision resulting therefrom;
> By violation of provisional measures enjoined by the Council as contemplated by Article 7 of the Protocol;
> Or by disregard of a decision recognising that the dispute arises out of a matter which lies exclusively within the domestic jurisdiction of the other party and by failure or by refusal to submit the question first to the Council or the Assembly.

In these cases, even if there is not absolute certainty, there exists at any rate a very strong presumption which should suffice for the application of sanctions unless proof to the contrary has been furnished by a unanimous decision of the Council.

It will be noticed that there is a characteristic difference between the first two cases and the third.

In the first two cases the presumption exists when, in addition to a state of war, the special condition referred to is also fulfilled.

In the third case, however, the presumption is dependent upon three conditions: disobedience to a decision, wilful failure to take advantage of the remedy provided in Article 11 of the Covenant, and the existence of a state of war.

This difference is due to the necessity of taking into account the provisions of Article 5 analysed above, which, by its reference to Article 11 of the Covenant, renders the application of paragraph 8 of Article 15 of the Covenant more flexible. After very careful consideration it appeared that it would be unreasonable and unjust to regard as *ipso facto* an aggressor a State which, being prevented through the operation of paragraph 8 of Article 15 from urging its claims by pacific methods and being thus left to its own resources, is in despair driven to war.

It was considered to be more in harmony with the requirements of justice and peace to give such a State which has been non-suited on the preliminary question of the domestic jurisdiction of its adversary, a last chance of arriving at an amicable agreement by offering it the final method of conciliation prescribed in Article 11 of the Covenant. It is only if, after rejecting this method, it has recourse to war that it will be presumed to be an aggressor.

This mitigation of the rigid character of paragraph 8 of Article 15 has been accepted, not only because it is just, but also because it opens no breach in the barrier set up by the Protocol against aggressive war: it in no way infringes the principle—which remains unshaken—that a war undertaken against a State whose exclusive jurisdiction has been formally recognised is an international crime to be avenged collectively by the signatories of the Protocol.

When a State whose demands have been met with the plea of the domestic jurisdiction of its adversary has employed the resource provided for in Article 11 of the Covenant, the presumption of aggression falls to the ground. The aggression itself remains. It will be for the Council to decide who is responsible for the aggression in accordance with the procedure which will be described below.

Apart from the above cases, there exists no presumption which can make it possible automatically to determine who is the aggressor. But this fact must be determined, and, if no other solution can be found, the decision must be left to the Council. The same principle applies where one of the parties is a State which is not a signatory of the Protocol and not a Member of the League.

If the Council is unanimous, no difficulty arises. If, however, the Council is not unanimous, the difficulty is to be overcome by directing that the Council must enjoin upon the belligerents an armistice the terms of which it will fix if need be by a two-thirds majority and the party which rejects the armistice or violates it is to be held to be an aggressor.

The system is therefore complete and is as automatic as it can be made.

Where a presumption has arisen and is not rejected by a unanimous decision of the Council, the facts themselves decide who is an aggressor; no further decision by the Council is needed and the question of unanimity or majority does not present itself; the facts once established, the Council is bound to act accordingly.

Where there is no presumption, the Council has to declare the fact of aggression; a decision is necessary and must be taken unanimously. If unanimity is not obtained, the Council is bound to enjoin an armistice, and for this purpose no decision properly speaking has to be taken: there exists an obligation which the Council must fulfil; it is only the fixing of the terms of the armistice which necessitates a decision, and for this purpose a two-thirds majority suffices.

It was proposed to declare that, in cases of extreme urgency, the Council might determine the aggressor, or fix the conditions of an armistice, without waiting for the arrival of the representative which a party not represented among its members has been invited to send under the terms of paragraph 5 of Article 4 of the Covenant.

It seemed preferable, however, not to lay down any rule on this matter at present but to ask the special Committee which the Council is to appoint for the drafting of amendments to the Covenant on the lines of the Protocol, to consider whether such a rule is really necessary.

It may in fact be thought that the Council already possesses all the necessary powers in this matter and that, in cases of extreme urgency, if the State invited to send a representative is too far distant from the seat of the Council, that body may decide that the representative shall be chosen from persons near at hand and shall attend the meeting within a prescribed period, on the expiry of which the matter may be considered in his absence.

The fact of aggression having been established by presumption or by unanimous decision of the Council or by refusal to accept or violation of the armistice, it will only remain to apply the sanctions and bring into play the obligations of the guarantor States. The Council will merely call upon them to fulfil their duty; here, again, there is no decision to be taken but an obligation to be fulfilled, and the question of majority or unanimous vote does not arise.

It is not, indeed, a matter of voting at all.

In order to leave no room for doubt, it has been formally laid down that a State which, at the invitation of the Council, engages in acts of violence against an aggressor is in the legal position of a belligerent and may consequently exercise the rights inherent in that character.

It was pointed out in the course of the discussion that such a State does not possess entire freedom of action. The force employed by it must be proportionate to the object in view and must be exercised within the limits and under the conditions recommended by the Council.

Article 18.

Likewise, in order to avoid any misunderstanding, it has been stipulated, in a special Article, that unanimity or the necessary majority in the Council is always calculated according to the rule referred to on several occasions in Article 15 of the Covenant and repeated in Article 16 of the Covenant for the case of expulsion of a Member from the League, viz., without counting the votes of the representatives of the parties to the dispute.

9.—DISPUTES BETWEEN STATES SIGNATORY AND STATES NON-SIGNATORY OF THE PROTOCOL.

Article 16.

As regards the settlement of disputes arising between a State signatory and one or more States non-signatory and non-Members of the League of Nations, the new system has had to be adapted to the former system.

In order that States signatory might enjoy the essential advantages offered by the Protocol, which forbids all wars of aggression, it has been necessary to bring the rule laid down in Article 17 of the Covenant into harmony with the provisions of the Protocol. It has therefore been decided that States non-signatory and non-Members of the League of Nations in conflict with a State signatory shall be invited to conform to the new procedure of pacific settlement and that, if they refuse to do so and resort to war against a State signatory, they shall be amenable to the sanctions provided by Article 16 of the Covenant as defined by the Protocol.

There is no change in the arrangements laid down in the Covenant for the settlement of disputes arising between States Members of the League of Nations of which one is a signatory of the Protocol and the other is not. The legal nexus established by the Covenant between two such parties does not allow the signatory States to apply as of right the new procedure of pacific settlement to non-signatory but Member States. All that signatory States are entitled to expect as regards such other States is that the Council should provide the latter with an opportunity to follow this procedure and it is to be hoped that they will do so. But such States can only be offered an opportunity to follow the new procedure; they cannot be obliged to follow it. If they refuse, preferring to adhere to the procedure laid down in the Covenant, no sanctions could possibly be applied to them.

The above indicated solution of the case of States non-signatory but Members of the League of Nations appears to be so obvious as to require no special mention in the Protocol. A proposal to make a special mention of the matter was made, but after explanations had been given, the authors withdrew their suggestion, declaring that they would be satisfied with the above reference to the subject.

At first sight the difference in the way it is proposed to treat non-signatories non-Members of the League of Nations and non-signatories Members of the League may cause some surprise, for it would seem that the signatory States impose greater obligations on the first category than on the second. This, however, is only an appearance. In reality, the signatory States impose no obligations on either category. They cannot do so because the present Protocol is *res inter alios acta* for all non-signatory States, whether they are Members of the League of Nations or not. The signatories merely undertake obligations as between themselves as to the manner in which they will behave if one of them becomes involved in a conflict with a third State. But whereas, in possible conflicts with a State non-signatory and non-Member of the League, they are entirely free to take such action as they choose, in conflicts which may arise between them and States non-signatory but Members, like themselves, of the League of Nations, their freedom of action is to some extent circumscribed because both parties are bound by legal obligations arising under the Covenant.

2.—WORK OF THE THIRD COMMITTEE.

(Rapporteur: M. BENES)

SECURITY AND REDUCTION OF ARMAMENTS.

(Articles 7 to 9, 11 to 15, 17 and 21 of the Protocol)

1.—INTRODUCTION.

The special work of the Third Committee was to deal with the problem of security (sanctions) and the reduction of armaments.

The work required, above all, important political negotiations. While the question of arbitration only required one political decision of principle, namely, the acceptance of compulsory arbitration, and the remainder was principally a matter of drafting—without question an extremely difficult task—of a scheme for the application of such arbitration, the questions of security and disarmament necessitated long and laborious political negotiations; for they involved fundamental interests, questions of vital importance to the States, engagements so far-reaching as radically to change the general situation of the various countries.

Although in the work of the First Committee the Assembly had distinctly indicated in its resolution of September 6th that there was a likelihood—indeed, a necessity—of amending the Covenant, the work of the Third Committee as regards questions of security and reduction of armaments had, in conformity with the debates of the Assembly, to remain within the framework of the Covenant. Above all, it was a question of developing and rendering more precise what is already laid down in the Covenant. All our discussions, all our labours, were guided by these principles, and a delicate task was thus imposed upon us. But the spirit of conciliation which pervaded all the discussions has permitted us to resolve the two problems which were placed before us. This is, indeed, an important result, and if the solution of the problem of arbitration which has been so happily arrived at by the First Committee be also taken into consideration, we are in the presence of a system the adoption of which may entirely modify our present political life.

This is the real import of the articles of the Protocol concerning the questions of security and reduction of armaments.

2.—THREAT OF AGGRESSION: PREVENTIVE MEASURES.

Article 7.

The pacific settlement of disputes being provided for in the present Protocol, the signatory States undertake, should any conflict arise between them, not to resort to preparations for the settlement of such dispute by war and, in general, to abstain from any act calculated to aggravate or extend the said dispute. This principle applies both to the period preceding the submission of the dispute to arbitration or conciliation and to the period in which the case is pending.

This provision is not unaccompanied by sanctions. Any appeal against the violation of the aforesaid undertakings may, in conformity with Article 11 of the Covenant, be brought before the Council. One might say that, in addition to such primary dispute as is or might be submitted to the Council or to some other competent organ, a second dispute arises, caused by the violation of the undertakings provided for in the first paragraph.

The Council, unless it be of opinion that the appeal is not worthy of consideration, will proceed with the necessary enquiries and investigations. Should it be established that an offence has been committed against the provisions of the first paragraph, it will be the duty of the Council, in the light of the results of such enquiries and investigations, to call upon any State guilty of the offence to put an end thereto. Any such State failing to comply will be declared by the Council to be guilty of violation of the Covenant (Article 11) or the Protocol.

The Council must, further, take the necessary measures to put an end, as soon as possible, to a situation calculated to threaten the peace of the world. The text does not define the nature of these preventive measures. Its elasticity permits the Council to take such measures as may be appropriate in each concrete case, as, for example, the evacuation of territories.

Any decisions which may be taken by the Council in virtue of this Article may be taken by a two-thirds majority, except in the case of decisions dealing with questions of procedure which still come under the general rule of Article 5, paragraph 2, of the Covenant. The following decisions, therefore, can be taken by a two-thirds majority:

> The decision as to whether there has or has not been an offence against the first paragraph;
> The decision calling upon the guilty State to remedy the offence;
> The decision as to whether there has or has not been refusal to remedy the offence;
> Lastly, the decision as to the measures calculated to put an end, as soon as possible, to a situation calculated to threaten the peace of the world.

The original text of Article 7 provided that, in the case of enquiries and investigations, the Council should avail itself of the organisation to be set up by the Conference for the Reduction of Armaments in order to ensure respect for the decisions of that Conference. There is no longer any mention of this organisation, but this omission does not prejudice any decisions which the Conference may be called upon to take regarding the matter. It will be entirely free to set up an organisation, if it judges this necessary, and the Council's right to make use of this body for the enquiries and investigations contemplated will, *a fortiori*, remain intact.

Article 8.

Article 8 must be considered in relation to Article 2. Article 2 establishes the obligation not to resort to war, while Article 8, giving effect to Article 10 of the Covenant, goes further. The signatories undertake to abstain from any act which might constitute a threat of aggression against any other State. Thus, every act which comes within the scope of this idea of a threat of war—and its scope is sufficiently elastic—constitutes a breach of the Protocol, and therefore a dispute with which the Council is competent to deal.

If, for example, one State alleges that another State is engaged in preparations which are nothing less than a particular form of threat of war (such as any kind of secret mobilisation, concentration of troops, formation of armed bodies with the connivance of the Government, etc.), the Council, having established that there is a case for consideration, will apply the procedure which may be defined as the procedure of preventive measures; it will arrange for suitable enquiries and investigations, and, in the event of any breach of the provisions of paragraph 1 being established, will take the steps described in Article 7, paragraph 4.

3.—SECURITY—SANCTIONS.

Article 11.

(Article 11, paragraphs 1 and 2, of the Protocol in its relation to Articles 10 and 16 of the Covenant)

According to Article 10 of the Covenant, Members of the League undertake to preserve as against external aggression the territorial integrity and existing political independence of all Members of the League. In case of aggression, the Council shall advise upon the means by which this obligation shall be fulfilled.

According to Article 16, should any Member of the League resort to war in disregard of its engagements under Articles 12, 13 or 15, all other Members of the League undertake immediately to apply economic sanctions; furthermore, it shall be the duty of the Council to recommend to the several Governments concerned what effective military, naval or air forces the Members of the League shall severally contribute to the armed forces to be used to protect the engagements of the League.

At the time when they were drafted at the Peace Conference in Paris in 1919, these articles gave rise to keen controversy as to the exact scope of the engagements entered into in these provisions, that is to say, as to the nature and extent of the obligations referred to in Article 10, the exact moment at which such obligations arose, and the legal consequences of the Council recommendations referred to in Article 16, paragraph 2. This controversy continued, as is well known, in the debates here in Geneva, where the question has been discussed in previous years.

Article 11 is intended to settle this controversy. The signatories of the present Protocol accept the obligation to apply against the aggressor the various sanctions laid down in the Covenant, as interpreted in Article 11 of the Protocol, when an act of aggression has been established and the Council has called upon the signatory States immediately to apply such sanctions (Article 10, last paragraph). Should they fail so to do, they will not be fulfilling their obligations.

The nature and extent of this obligation is clearly defined in paragraph 2 of Article 11. According to this paragraph, the reply to the question whether a signatory to the Protocol has or has not fulfilled its obligation depends on whether it has loyally and effectively co-operated in resisting the act of aggression to an extent consistent with its geographical position and its particular situation as regards armaments.

The State remains in control of its forces, and itself, and not the Council, directs them, but paragraph 2 of Article 11 gives us positive material upon which to form a judgment as to whether or not the obligation has been carried out in any concrete case. This criterion is supplied by the term: *loyally and effectively.*

In answering the question whether a State has or has not fulfilled its obligations in regard to sanctions, a certain elasticity in the obligations laid down in Article 11 allows of the possibility of *taking into account, from every point of view, the position of each State which is a signatory to the present Protocol.* The signatory States are not all in possession of equal facilities for acting when the time comes to apply the sanctions. This depends upon the geographical position and economic and social condition of the State, the nature of its population, internal institutions, etc.

Indeed, during the discussion as to the system of sanctions, certain delegations declared that their countries were in a special situation by reason of their geographical position or the state of their armaments. These countries desired to co-operate to the fullest extent of their resources in resistance to every act of aggression, but they drew attention to their special conditions. In order to take account of this situation, an addition has been made to paragraph 2 of Article 11 pointing out this state of affairs and laying stress on the particular situation of the countries in question. Moreover, Article 13 of the Protocol allows such countries to inform the Council of these matters beforehand.

I would further add that the obligations I refer to are imperfect obligations in the sense that no sanctions are provided for against any party which shall have failed loyally and effectively to co-operate in protecting the Covenant and resisting every act of aggression. It should, however, be emphasised that such a State would have failed in the fulfilment of its duties and would be guilty of a violation of engagements entered into.

In view of the foregoing, the gist of Article 11, paragraphs 1 and 2, might be expressed as follows: Each State is the judge of the manner in which it shall carry out its obligations but not of the existence of those obligations, that is to say, each State remains the judge of what it will do but no longer remains the judge of what it should do.

Now that the present Protocol has defined more precisely the origin, nature and extent of the obligations arising out of the Covenant, *the functions of the Council, as provided in Articles 10 and 16, have become clearer and more definite.*

Directly the Council has called upon the signatories to the Protocol to apply without delay the sanctions provided in Article 11, it becomes a regulating, or rather an advisory, body, but not an executive body. The nature of the acts of aggression may vary considerably; the means for their suppression will also vary. It would frequently be unnecessary to make use of all the means which, according to paragraphs 1 and 2 of Article 11, are, so to speak, available for resisting an act of aggression. It might even be dangerous if, from fear of failing in their duties, States made superfluous efforts. It will devolve upon the Council, which, under Article 13 can be put in possession of the necessary data, to give *its opinion*, should need occur, as to the best means of executing the obligations which arise directly it enjoins the application of sanctions, especially as to the sequence in which the sanctions must be applied.

The practical application of the sanctions would, however, always devolve upon the Governments; the real co-operation would ensue upon their getting into touch, through diplomatic channels—perhaps by conferences—and by direct relations between different General Staffs, as in the last war. The Council would, of course, be aware of all these negotiations, would be consulted and make recommendations.

The difference between the former state of affairs and the new will therefore be as follows:

According to the system laid down by the Covenant:

1. The dispute arises.

2. In cases where neither the arbitral procedure nor the judicial settlement provided for in Article 13 of the Covenant is applied, the Council meets and discusses the dispute, attempts to effect conciliation, mediation, etc.

3. If it be unsuccessful and war breaks out, the Council, if unanimous, has to express an opinion as to which party is guilty. The Members of the League then decide for themselves whether this opinion is justified and whether their obligations to apply economic sanctions become operative.

4. It then has, *by a unanimous decision, to recommend* military sanctions.

5. If unanimity cannot be obtained, the Council ceasing to take action, each party is practically free to act as it chooses.

According to the new system defined in the Protocol, the situation is as follows:

1. The dispute arises.

2. The system of peaceful settlement provided for by the Protocol comes into play.

3. The Council intervenes, and if, after arbitration has been refused, war is resorted to, if the provisional preventive measures are not observed, etc., the Council decides which party is the aggressor and calls upon the signatory States to apply the sanctions.

4. This decision implies that such sanctions as the case requires—economic, financial, military, naval and air—shall be applied forthwith, and without further recommendations or decisions.

We have therefore the following new elements:

(*a*) The obligation to apply the necessary sanctions of every kind as a direct result of the decision of the Council.

(*b*) The elimination of the case in which all parties would be practically free to abtain from any action. The introduction of a system of arbitration and of provisional measures which permits of the determination in every case of the aggressor.

(*c*) No decision is taken as to the strength of the military, naval and air forces, and no details are given as to the measures which are to be adopted in a particular case. None the less, objective criteria are supplied which define the obligation of each signatory; it is bound, in resistance to an act of aggression, to collaborate *loyally and effectively* in applying the sanctions in accordance with its geographical situation and its particular situation as regards armaments.

That is why I said that *the great omission in the Covenant has been made good.*

It is true that no burden has been imposed on States beyond the sanctions already provided for in the Covenant. But, at present, a State seeking to elude the obligations of the Covenant can reckon on two means of escape:

(1) The Council's recommendations need not be followed.

(2) The Council may fail to obtain unanimity, making impossible any declaration of aggression, so that no obligation to apply military sanctions will be imposed and everyone will remain free to act as he chooses.

We have abandoned the above system and both these loopholes are now closed.

Article 11, paragraphs 3 and 4.

Paragraph 3 of Article 11 has been drafted with a view to giving greater precision to certain provisions of Article 11, paragraph 3, of the Covenant. Article 16, paragraph 3, refers to mutual support in the application of financial and economic measures. Article 11, paragraph 3, of the present Protocol establishes real economic and financial co-operation between a State which has been attacked and the various States which come to its assistance.

As, under Article 10 of the Protocol, it may happen that both States involved in a dispute are declared to be aggressors, the question arose as to what would be the best method of settling this problem. There were three alternatives: to apply the principle contained in paragraph 1, which is practically equivalent to making a sort of police war on both parties—or to leave the matter to pursue its course, or, finally, to compel States which disturb the peace of the world to desist from acts of war by the employment of means less severe than those indicated in paragraph 1. It is the last method which has been chosen. Only economic measures will be taken against such States, and naturally they will not be entitled to receive the assistance referred to in Article 11, paragraph 3.

Article 12.

Article 16, paragraph 1, of the Covenant provides for the immediate severance of all trade or financial relations with the aggressor State, and paragraph 3 of the same Article provides, *inter alia,* for economic and financial co-operation between the State attacked and the various States coming to its assistance.

As has already been pointed out, these engagements have been confirmed and made more definite in Article 11 of the Protocol.

But the severance of relations and the co-operation referred to necessarily involve measures so complex that, when the moment arises, doubts may well occur as to what measures are necessary and appropriate to give effect to the obligations assumed under the above provisions. These problems require full consideration in order that States may know beforehand what their attitude should be.

Article 12 defines the conditions of such investigation.

It is not expressly stated that the problem will be examined by the Council in collaboration with the various Governments, but the Council will naturally, if it deems it necessary, invite the Governments to furnish such information as it may require for the purpose of carrying out the task entrusted to it under Article 12.

Article 13, paragraph 1.

The above explanation of Article 11, paragraphs 1 and 2, contains many references to Article 13.

As I have already pointed out, in case sanctions have to be applied, it is highly important that there should exist some organ competent to express an opinion as to the best way in which their obligations could be carried out by the signatories. As you are aware, this organ, according to the Covenant, is the Council. In order that the Council may effectively fulfil this duty, Article 13 empowers it to receive undertakings from States, determining *in advance* the military, naval and air forces which they would be able to bring into action immediately in order to ensure the fulfilment of the obligations in regard to sanctions arising, out of the Covenant and the present Protocol.

It is also necessary to emphasise the fact that the means which the States signatories to the present Protocol have at their disposal for the fulfilment of the obligations arising out of Article 11 vary considerably owing to the differences in the geographical, economic, financial, political and social condition of different States. Information as to the means at the disposal of each State is therefore indispensable in order that the Council may in full understanding give its opinion as to the best method by which such obligations may best be carried out.

Finally, as regards the question of the reduction of armaments, which is the final goal to which our efforts are tending, the information thus furnished to the Council may be of very great importance, as every State, knowing what forces will be available for its assistance in case it is attacked, will be able to judge to what extent it may reduce its armaments without compromising its existence as a State, and every State will thus be able to provide the International Conference for the Reduction of Armaments with very valuable data. I should add, moreover, that Article 13, paragraph 1, does not render it compulsory for States to furnish this information. It is desirable that States should furnish the Council with this information, but they are at liberty not to do so.

Article 13, paragraphs 2 and 3.

The provisions of Article 13, paragraphs 2 and 3, refer to the special agreements which were discussed at such length last year. In view of the fact that, according to paragraph 2, such agreements can only come into force when the Council has invited the signatory States to apply the sanctions, the nature of these agreements may be defined as follows:

Special agreements must be regarded as the means for the rapid application of sanctions of every kind in a particular case of aggression. They are additional guarantees which give weaker States an absolute assurance that the system of sanctions will never fail. They guarantee that there will always be States prepared immediately to carry out the obligations provided for in Article 11 of the Protocol.

In accordance with Article 18 of the Covenant, it is expressly stated that these agreements will be registered and published by the Secretariat, and it has also been decided that they will remain open for signature to any State Member of the League of Nations which may desire to accede to them.

4.—ENDING OF SANCTIONS: PUNISHMENT OF THE AGGRESSOR.

Article 14.

Article 14 is in perfect keeping with the last paragraphs of Articles 10 and 11. In the paragraphs in question, the coming into operation of the sanctions depends upon an injunction by the Council; it therefore also devolves upon the Council to declare that the object for which the sanctions were applied has been attained. Just as the application of the sanctions is a matter for the States, so it rests with them to liquidate the operations undertaken with a view to resisting the act of aggression.

Article 15.

Paragraph 1 is similar to Article 10 of the Draft Treaty of Mutual Assistance drawn up last year.

Paragraph 2 is designed to prevent the sanctions provided for in Article 11 from undergoing any change in character during the process of execution and developing into a war of annexation.

In view of the observations of various delegations regarding the punishment of the aggressor, it should be added that it would be incorrect to interpret this article as meaning that the only penalties to be apprehended by the aggressor as the result of his act shall be the burdens referred to in paragraph 1. If necessary, securities against fresh aggression, or pledges guaranteeing the fulfilment of the obligations imposed in accordance with paragraph 1, might be required. Only annexation of territory and measures involving the loss of political independence are declared inadmissible.

"Territory" is to be taken to mean the whole territory of a State, no distinction being made between the mother-country and the colonies.

5.—REDUCTION OF ARMAMENTS.

Articles 17 and 21.

Although it has not been possible to solve the problem of the reduction of armaments in the clauses of the document submitted to the Assembly for approval, our work paves the way to it and makes it possible.

The reduction of armaments will result, in the first place, from the general security created by a diminution of the dangers of war arising from the compulsory pacific settlement of all disputes.

It will also ensue from the certainty which any State attacked will have of obtaining the economic and financial support of all the signatory States, and such support would be especially important should the aggressor be a great Power, capable of carrying on a long war.

Nevertheless, for States which, owing to their geographical position, are especially liable to attack, and for States whose most important centres are adjacent to their frontiers, the dangers of a sudden attack are so great that it will not be possible for them to base any plan for the reduction of their armaments simply upon the political and economic factors referred to above, no matter what the importance of such factors may be.

It has also been repeatedly declared that many States would require to know what military support they could count on, before the convening of the Conference, if they are to submit to the Conference proposals for large reductions of armaments; this might necessitate negotiations between the Governments and with the Council before the meeting of the Conference for the reduction of armaments provided for in Article 17. The undertakings referred to in Article 13 of the Protocol should be interpreted in the light of the above.

In drawing up the general programme of the Conference, it will also be necessary, as stated in paragraph 2 of Article 17, for the Council, apart from other criteria "to take into account the undertakings mentioned."

In view of the close interdependence of the three great problems involved, namely, the pacific settlement of disputes, sanctions against those who disturb the peace of the world, and reduction of armaments, the Protocol provides for the convening by the Council of a general Conference for the Reduction of Armaments and for the preparation of the work of such a Conference. Furthermore, the application of the clauses concerning arbitration and sanctions will be conditional on the adoption by the said Conference of a plan for the reduction and limitation of armaments.

Moreover, in order to preserve the connection between the three big problems referred to above, it is provided that the whole Protocol will lapse in the event of the non-execution of the scheme adopted by the Conference. It devolves upon the Council to declare this under conditions to be determined by the Conference itself.

The last paragraph of Article 21 provides for the case of the partial lapsing of the Protocol after it has been put into force. Should the plan adopted by the Conference be regarded as having been put into effect, any State which fails to execute it, so far as it is concerned, will not benefit by the provisions of the Protocol.

6.—The Covenant and the Protocol.

Article 19.

The present Protocol emphasises and defines certain obligations arising out of the Covenant. Those of which the present Protocol makes no mention are not affected in any manner. They still exist. Examples which might be quoted are those laid down in Article 16, paragraph 3, of the Covenant, namely, the obligation of the States to give one another mutual support in order to minimise the loss and inconvenience resulting from the application of the economic and financial sanctions or the obligation of the States to take the necessary steps to afford passage through their territory to forces which are co-operating to protect the covenants of the League.

Moreover, as the Swiss Delegation suggests, attention should be directed to the fact that the present Protocol does not in any way affect the special position of Switzerland arising out of the Declaration of the Council at London on February 13th, 1920. As the special position of Switzerland is in accordance with the Covenant, it will also be in accordance with the Protocol.

III

CONCLUSION.

No further explanations need be added to these comments on the articles. The main principles of the Protocol are clear, as are the detailed provisions.

Our purpose was to make war impossible, to kill it, to annihilate it. To do this, we had to create a system for the pacific settlement of *all disputes* which might arise. In other words, it meant the creation of a system of arbitration from which no international dispute, whether legal or political, could escape. The plan drawn up leaves no loophole; it prohibits wars of every description and lays down that all disputes shall be settled by pacific means.

But this absolute character which has been given to the system of arbitration should also belong to the whole of the scheme, to the treatment of every question of principle. If there were one single gap in the system, if the smallest opening were left for any measure of force, the whole system would collapse.

To this end arbitration is provided for every kind of dispute, and aggression is defined in such a way as to give no cause for hesitation when the Council has to take a decision.

These reasons led us to fill in the gaps in the Covenant and to define the sanctions in such a way that no possible means could be found of evading them, and that there should be a sound and definite basis for the feeling of security.

Finally, the Conference for the Reduction of Armaments is indissolubly bound up with this whole system: *there can be no arbitration or security without disarmament, nor can there be disarmament without arbitration and security.*

The peace of the world is at stake.

The Fifth Assembly has undertaken a work of worldwide political importance which, if it succeeds, is destined profoundly to modify present political conditions. This year great progress in this direction has been made in our work. If we succeed, the League of Nations will have rendered an inestimable service to the whole modern world. Such success depends partly upon the Assembly itself and partly upon individual Governments. We submit to the Assembly the fruit of our labours: a work charged with the highest hopes. We beg the Assembly to examine our proposals with care, and to recommend them to the various Governments for acceptance.

In this spirit and with such hopes do we request the Assembly to vote the draft resolutions 1 and 2 that are presented with this Report.

ANNEX D.

RESOLUTIONS.

Resolution of the Assembly, September 6th, 1924.

The Assembly,

Noting the declarations of the Governments represented, observes with satisfaction that they contain the basis of an understanding tending to establish a secure peace,

Decides as follows:

With a view to reconciling in the new proposals the divergences between certain points of view which have been expressed and, when agreements have been reached, to enable an International Conference upon Armaments to be summoned by the League of Nations at the earliest possible moment:

(1) The Third Committee is requested to consider the material dealing with security and the reduction of armaments, particularly the observations of the Governments on the draft Treaty of Mutual Assistance prepared in pursuance of Resolution XIV of the Third Assembly and other plans prepared and presented to the Secretary-General, since the publication of the draft Treaty, and to examine the obligations contained in the Covenant of the League in relation to the guarantees of security which a resort to arbitration and a reduction of armaments may require:

(2) The First Committee is requested:

(*a*) To consider, in view of possible amendments, the articles in the Covenant relating to the settlement of disputes;

(*b*) To examine within what limits the terms of Article 36, paragraph 2, of the statute establishing the Permanent Court of International Justice might be rendered more precise and thereby facilitate the more general acceptance of the clause;

and thus strengthen the solidarity and the security of the nations of the world by settling by pacific means all disputes which may arise between States.

RESOLUTION OF THE ASSEMBLY, SEPTEMBER 27TH, 1924.

Whereas the work of the League of Nations in connection with the reduction of armaments is entering this year upon a period of re-organisation which requires the direct attention of the Council,

The Assembly entrusts to the Council the question of the co-ordination of the work of its Commissions for the Reduction of Armaments.

The Assembly recommends the Council to re-organise the Temporary Mixed Commission in conformity with the following principles:

(1) The Commission shall include the representatives of a certain number of Governments;

(2) The Commission shall include qualified delegates of the Technical Organisation of the League of Nations, that is to say:

Representatives of the Economic Committee,
"   " " Financial Committee,
"   " " Transit Committee,
"   " " Permanent Advisory Commission,
"   " " Employers' and Labour Groups of the International Labour Office,
Experts, jurists or others elected by the Council.

(3) Delegates of States not represented on the Commission may be invited to attend whenever the Commission thinks fit.

(4) The Council may invite any States not Members of the League of Nations which may have notified their intention of taking part in the International Conference for the Reduction of Armaments to appoint representatives to participate in the work of the Commission.

RESOLUTION OF THE ASSEMBLY, OCTOBER 2ND, 1924.

I. The Assembly,

Having taken note of the reports of the First and Third Committees on the questions referred to them by the Assembly resolution of September 6th, 1924,

Welcomes warmly the draft Protocol on the Pacific Settlement of International Disputes proposed by the two Committees, of which the text is annexed to this resolution, and

Decides

(1) To recommend to the earnest attention of all the Members of the League the acceptance of the said draft Protocol;

(2) To open immediately the said Protocol in the terms proposed for signature by those representatives of Members of the League who are already in a position to sign it and to hold it open for signature by all other States;

(3) To request the Council forthwith to appoint a Committee to draft the amendments to the Covenant contemplated by the terms of the said Protocol;

(4) To request the Council to convene an International Conference for the Reduction of Armaments, which shall meet at Geneva as provided by the following stipulations of Article 17 of the draft Protocol:

> "In preparation for the convening of the Conference, the Council shall draw up, with due regard to the undertakings contained in Articles 11 and 13 of the present Protocol, a general programme for the reduction and limitation of armaments which shall be laid before the Conference and be communicated to the Governments at the earliest possible date, and at the latest, three months before the Conference meets.
>
> "If by May 1st, 1925, ratifications have not been deposited by at least a majority of the permanent Members of the Council and ten other Members of the League, the Secretary-General of the League shall immediately consult the Council as to whether he shall cancel the invitations or merely adjourn the Conference to a subsequent date to be fixed by the Council so as to permit the necessary number of ratifications to be obtained."

(5) To request the Council to put into immediate execution the provisions of Article 12 of the draft Protocol.

RECOMMENDATION OF THE ASSEMBLY, OCTOBER 2ND, 1924.

II. The Assembly,

Having taken cognisance of the report of the First Committee upon the terms of Article 36, paragraph 2, of the Statute of the Permanent Court of International Justice;

Considering that the study of the said terms shows them to be sufficiently wide to permit States to adhere to the special Protocol, opened for signature in virtue of Article 36, paragraph 2, with the reservations which they regard as indispensable;

Convinced that it is in the interest of the progress of international justice, and consistent with the expectations of the opinion of the world, that the greatest possible number of States should, to the widest possible extent, accept as compulsory the jurisdiction of the Court.

Recommends:

States to accede at the earliest possible date to the special Protocol opened for signature in virtue of Article 36, paragraph 2, of the Statute of the Permanent Court of International Justice.

RESOLUTION OF THE ASSEMBLY, OCTOBER 2ND, 1924.

I. The Assembly recommends the Council to place the question of Regional Agreements for the Reduction of Armaments on the agenda of the International Conference for the Reduction of Armaments.

II. Whereas the majority of the States which have replied have stated that, with certain exceptions, they have not exceeded the expenditure on armaments shown in their last budgets, and whereas the recommendation addressed to the Governments relates to the period which must elapse before the meeting of the International Conference for the Reduction of Armaments, which is to take place next year:

The Assembly does not consider it necessary to repeat the recommendation regarding the limitation of expenditure on armaments, as this question is to be placed upon the agenda of the International Conference for the Reduction of Armaments.

III. The Assembly is of the opinion:

1. That another technical conference on naval disarmament is unnecessary.

2. That the question of naval disarmament should be discussed as part of the general question of disarmament dealt with by the International Conference proposed in the resolution of September 6th, 1924, adopted by the Fifth Assembly, and that it rests with the Council to settle the programme.

IV. The Assembly requests the Council, in preparing the general programme of the Conference for the Reduction of Armaments provided for in Article 17 of the Protocol, to consider the advisability of including in that programme the following points:

1. General plan for a reduction of armaments in accordance with Article 8 of the Covenant, in particular:

(*a*) Basis and methods of reduction (budget, peace-time effectives, tonnage of naval and air fleets, population, configuration of frontiers, etc.);

(*b*) Preparation of a typical budget for expenditure on armaments.

2. Special position of certain States in relation to the reduction of armaments:

(*a*) Temporary reservations by countries exposed to special risks;

(*b*) Recommendation of regional agreements for the reduction (or limitation) of armaments,

3. Recommendation of the establishment of demilitarised zones (Article 9).

4. Control and investigation of armaments in the contracting States.

The Assembly also requests the Council to instruct the competent organisations of the League to examine the schemes relating to the above questions which have already been submitted to the Third Committee, or which may subsequently be received by the Secretariat, and to take them into consideration in preparing the programme of the Conference.

RESOLUTION OF THE COUNCIL, OCTOBER 3RD, 1924.

1. With a view to the preparation of the Conference for the Reduction of Armaments, the Council decides to form itself into a Committee. The representatives on the Council who consider that it will not be possible to attend the Committee in person will, as soon as possible, send to the Secretary-General the names of their substitutes on this Committee.

The Committee will hold its first meeting on November 17th, in order to draw up a general programme of the work connected with the application of Article 12 of the Protocol and with the reduction of armaments.

The Governments of the States represented on the Council are requested to give their representatives on the Committee the necessary instructions in order that the general lines of the programme may be laid down during its meeting of November 17th.[a]

----

a. The Council, at its 31st Session at Brussels, October 28th, 1924, "decided itself to undertake at its session in Rome (December, 1924) the work of preparing for the Conference on the Reduction of Armaments," instructing the Council Committee to continue and complete this work and report to the Council at its session in March, 1925.

The work of either the Council or its Committee was dependent to a large extent upon the receipt of suggestions from Members of the League which had been requested from them in a circular letter of the Secretary-General, October 11, 1924.

Various items regarding the Protocol of Geneva were on the Agenda of the Council for its December, 1924, meeting at Rome. Preparatory work regarding "the general program" under the second paragraph of Article 17 of the Protocol was the most important. Two other relevant items were (1) the reorganization of the Temporary Mixed Commission and the Permanent Advisory Commission into a single coordinated Commission; and (2) the date of the meeting of the Commission of Jurists (appointed at the Brussels session of the Council in October, 1924) to draft the amendments to the Covenant contemplated by the Protocol.

A Conservative Government came into power in Great Britain early in November, 1924, Mr. Austen Chamberlain becoming Foreign Secretary. At the request of the British Government, the agenda items for the December, 1924 meeting of the Council at Rome relating to the Protocol of Geneva were postponed until the March meeting. In the meantime, the British Government has suggested to the Dominions a meeting of the Imperial Conference for the purpose of adopting a policy of the British Commonwealth of Nations regarding the Protocol of Geneva. Whether such a meeting will be held, or whether the general British policy will be decided on as a result of correspondence, is not at this writing certain.

The Secretary-General will invite the Governments of the States Members of the League not represented on the Council to forward through him to the Committee any suggestions which they may think useful with a view to the preparation of this programme.

2. The Secretariat is requested to collect the data necessary for the economic and financial investigations relative to the application of Article 12 of the Protocol, and is authorised to distribute these data to the competent organs of the League (Economic and Financial Organisation and Transit Organisation) with a view to the work which will subsequently be required of them by the Committee.

The Secretariat will obtain information from the official documents at the disposal of the League or from documents which might, if necessary, be furnished by the Governments.

3. In conformity with the Assembly resolution, and in order to assist the Committee in co-ordinating the preparatory work for the Conference, the Temporary Mixed Commission shall be re-organised and shall take the name of the Co-ordination Commission, and be composed as follows:

(a) The Committee of the Council (ten members) assisted by:

(b) The President and one member or two members of each of the three Organisations, Economic, Financial and Transit (six members);

(c) Six members appointed by the Permanent Advisory Commission (six members);

(d) Two members of the Employers' Group and two members of the Workers' Group of the Governing Body of the International Labour Office, appointed by the latter (four members);

(e) If considered advisable, a certain number of experts—jurists and others—appointed by the Council.

The Secretary-General is requested to invite at a suitable moment the above-mentioned organisations to appoint their representatives.

ANNEX E.

REPORT OF THE BRITISH DELEGATES RELATING TO THE PROTOCOL FOR THE PEACEFUL SETTLEMENT OF INTERNATIONAL DISPUTES.

Sir,   *London, November* 1, 1924.

WE have the honour to submit herewith a report on the proceedings at the Fifth Assembly of the League of Nations at Geneva this year in connection with the Draft Protocol for the Pacific Settlement of International Disputes.

I.—INTRODUCTION.

The First Assembly of the League of Nations in 1920 prepared to give effect to article 8 of the Covenant, the first two paragraphs of which read: "The Members of the League recognise that the maintenance of peace requires the reduction of national armaments to the lowest point consistent with national safety and the enforcement by common action of International obligations. The Council .... shall formulate plans for such reduction for the consideration and action of the several Governments." That Assembly decided "to instruct a Temporary Commission to prepare reports and proposals for the reduction of armaments as provided for by article 8 of the Covenant." In the following year the Second Assembly defined the task more clearly in a resolution instructing the Temporary Mixed Commission to make proposals for the reduction of armaments which, in order to secure precision, "should be in the form of a draft Treaty or other equally defined plan, to be presented to the Council, if possible, before the Assembly next year" (1922). In the course of the ensuing year the Temporary Mixed Commission was able to formulate certain principles which, in its opinion, might serve as a basis for the draft Treaty which it had been instructed to draw up. After discussion of these principles the Third Assembly passed a resolution—the famous Resolution 14—recognising that in existing circumstances many Governments would be unable to accept responsibility for a serious reduction of armaments unless they received in exchange a satisfactory guarantee of the safety of their country, and suggesting that such guarantee could be found in a defensive agreement binding them to provide immediate and effective assistance, in accordance with a pre-arranged plan, in the event of one of them being attacked. The Temporary Mixed Commission were instructed to prepare a draft Treaty on these lines. The result of their labours was submitted to the Fourth Assembly last year in the form of the Draft Treaty of Mutual Assistance, which was referred by the Assembly to the Governments for their observations.

2. Certain Governments accepted the draft Treaty in principle: very few intimated their readiness to adhere to its actual terms. His Majesty's Government, in a note which has already been made public,* explained the reasons which would render it impossible for them to subscribe to the Treaty.

3. When, therefore, the Fifth Assembly met on the 1st September of this year, the labours of four years, which had been devoted to the preparation of a scheme for giving effect to the obligation undertaken by all signatories in article 8 of the Covenant, had not succeeded in establishing agreement, and there seemed no prospect of making any further advance along the path which had hitherto been followed.

4. Some new direction would have to be given, and the presence in Geneva of the British and French Prime Ministers gave a special importance to the meeting.

5. It was realised that the problem was not merely to find a general scheme of disarmament and security, but that the particular question of French security was of immediate political importance, and would shortly require a solution. The question of "security" had already been raised in conversations between Mr. MacDonald and M. Herriot in July last, at Chequers

---

* Miscellaneous No. 13 (1924), Cmd. 2200.

and in Paris. During the latter meeting, the subject was discussed at some length, and the position as it was then left by the two Prime Ministers was set out in the Franco-British memorandum of the 9th July concerning the application of the Dawes plan. The relevant paragraph read as follows: "The two Governments have likewise proceeded to a preliminary exchange of views on the question of security. They are aware that public opinion requires pacification: they agree to co-operate in devising through the League of Nations or otherwise, as opportunity presents itself, means of securing this, and to continue the consideration of the question until the problem of general security can be finally solved." In a declaration made in the Chamber on the 21st August, reporting on the results of the London Conference, M. Herriot said "security must be the object of another Conference. He did not see why France should not take the initiative .... For the rest, the security question would be dealt with at Geneva."

6. The debate in the League Assembly was opened by the British Prime Minister on the 4th September. Mr. Ramsay MacDonald began by explaining that it was not because they were indifferent to the problem of national security that His Majesty's Government had given an adverse opinion on the Draft Treaty of Mutual Assistance. They believed that security could not be based on military alliances, and they hesitated to become involved in any agreements which committed them to vague and indefinite obligations. In this respect the Treaty of Mutual Assistance was open to criticism, especially in its article 3 and in its definition of aggression. Mr. Ramsay MacDonald emphasised that the main problem was the problem of national security in relation to national armaments, and the initial difficulty was encountered in the definition of such terms as "security" and "aggression." In regard to the latter, he said, "the one method by which we can approximate to an accurate attribution of responsibility for aggression is arbitration," and he proposed that the article of the Statute of the Permanent Court dealing with ar-

bitration should be carefully examined by a Commission, with a view to its being placed before the Assembly in a somewhat more precise, expanded and definite form than it now had. Such a step would be necessary as a preliminary to the discussion of disarmament, which could produce no good result unless an atmosphere of confidence were previously created. To summon a Conference on disarmament without such a preparation of the ground would be to court immediate and disastrous failure. Such a Conference must be the ultimate aim, and it must include all the nations and must be held in Europe. In his view the Covenant already contained ample provisions for starting arbitration, for the sanctions that were necessary and for all other eventualities that might arise: what was now required was that the Covenant should be elaborated. "The British Government thinks that the matter should now be explored, beginning with the Covenant, applying the Covenant to our present circumstances, and, in the spirit of the League of Nations, developing a policy that will give security and reduce armaments. The British Government stands by the Covenant. The British Government has no wish to reduce the authority of the Council. It rather wishes to extend the authority of the Council consistently with the continued existence and prosperity of the League. Articles 10, 12, 13, 15 and 16 of the Covenant might well form themselves into a charter of peace if we would only apply them and fill them out."

7. Speaking on the following day, the French Prime Minister expressed a similar view: "It is in the development and the fullest possible application of the articles of this solemn instrument (the Covenant) that France seeks for the rules which are to guide her future action and her foreign policy." M. Herriot welcomed Mr. Ramsay MacDonald's suggestion that arbitration should be the test of aggression, and he expressed the hope that the Fifth Assembly would be able to accept the principle of arbitration, which would solve the difficulties, as henceforth the aggressor would be the party which refused arbitration. M. Her-

riot added: "Arbitration is essential, but it is not sufficient. It is a means, but not an end. It does not entirely fulfil the intentions of article 8 of the Covenant, which are security and disarmament. We in France regard three three terms—arbitration, security and disarmament—as inseparable." A nation which accepted arbitration had a right to security. "Justice without might is impotent. Might without justice is tyranny." In conclusion: "We stand by the Covenant, but we wish to make it a living Covenant. We simply claim for each nation the rights conferred upon it by the Covenant, no more and no less."

8. It is unnecessary to indicate in detail the views expressed by other speakers who participated in this opening debate, from which it was evident that there was general agreement on a number of points:—

(*a.*) That as a preliminary to disarmament there must be provided an inclusive scheme for the pacific settlement of international disputes of all kinds.

(*b.*) That the Covenant of the League itself provided the basis of such a scheme, but that it required elaboration, precision and extension in certain directions.

(*c.*) That to give effect to such a scheme States should develop the principle of compulsory arbitration.

(*d.*) That a State, having accepted this principle, would, if it resorted to force in disregard of its obligation to submit to arbitration, be automatically declared an aggressor, and outlawed.

(*e.*) That some form of co-operation must be devised for effective resistance to aggression, both as a deterrent to any possible aggressor and as a guarantee of security to all States enabling them to contemplate a reduction of their own armed forces, whch at present constituted their sole guarantee of safety.

9. In order to give effect to these ideas, a resolution was submitted to the Assembly on the 6th September by the British and French delegations in the following terms:—

"The Assembly,

"Noting the declarations of the Governments represented, observes with satisfaction that they contain the basis of an understanding tending to establish a secure peace,

"Decides as follows:—

"With a view to reconciling in the new proposals the divergencies between certain points of view which have been expressed, and when agreement has been reached, to enable an international conference upon armaments to be summoned by the League of Nations at the earliest possible moment—

"(1.) The Third Committee is requested to consider the material dealing with security and reduction of armaments, particularly the observations of the Governments on the draft Treaty of Mutual Assistance prepared in pursuance of Resolution 14 of the Third Assembly, and other plans prepared and presented to the Secretary-General since the publication of the draft Treaty, and to examine the obligations contained in the Covenant of the League in relation to the guarantees of security which a resort to arbitration and a reduction of armaments may require;

"(2.) The First Committee is requested—

"(a.) To consider, in view of possible amendments, the articles in the Covenant relating to the settlement of disputes;

"(b.) To examine within what limits the terms of article 36, paragraph 2, of the Statute establishing the Permanent Court of International Justice might be rendered more precise, and thereby facilitate the more general acceptance of the clause;

"And thus strengthen the solidarity and the security of the nations of the world by settling, by pacific means, all disputes which may arise between States."

10. This resolution was carried unanimously by the Assembly, which thus deputed the preparatory work to its First Committee (dealing with legal and constitutional questions) and its Third Committee (dealing with reduction of armaments).

11.   It will be more convenient at once to consider the final results of the labours of the two Committees, leaving for the moment any detailed account of the progress of their work, in order to see how the draft Protocol which they submitted to the Full Assembly on the 1st October gave effect to the ideas which had been proclaimed in the course of the earlier debate.

12.   In the first place it was necessary to complete the scheme of arbitration and conciliation provided in the Covenant.   The Covenant itself did not provide for every eventuality, and by failing to offer pacific means of settlement of all disputes, it left open, or seemed to leave open, in certain circumstances resort to force.   Especially was this so in article 12 of the Covenant, whereby the Members of the League agreed "in no case to resort to war until three months after the award by the arbitrators or the report by the Council."   Further, paragraph 7 of article 15 of the Covenant laid down that "if the Council fails to reach a report which is unanimously agreed to by the Members thereof, other than the representatives of one or more of the parties to the dispute, the Members of the League reserve to themselves the right to take such action as they shall consider necessary for the maintenance of right and justice."   Under article 2 of the Protocol "the signatory States *agree* in no case to resort to war either with one another or against a State which, if the occasion arises, accepts all the obligations hereinafter set out, except in case of resistance to acts of aggression or when acting in agreement with the Council or the Assembly of the League of Nations in accordance with the provisions of the Covenant and of the present Protocol."   The signatory States having agreed in no case to resort to war, the Protocol proceeds to prohibit the arbitrament of force and to provide a complete system for the pacific settlement of disputes.   As regards cases covered by paragraph 2 of article 36 of the statute of the Permanent Court of International Justice, the signatory States bind themselves to recognize as obligatory the jurisdiction of that Court, "but without prejudice to the right of any State, when

acceding to the special Protocol provided for in the said article and opened for signature on the 16th December, 1920, to make reservations compatible with the said clause" (article 3). As regards other subjects of dispute, the Protocol provides a procedure (article 4) which supplements and completes that defined in article 15 of the Covenant. Briefly, under this procedure, if the Council is at the outset unable to effect a settlement, it persuades the parties to submit to arbitration. If neither party should be willing to go to arbitration, the Council again takes the matter into consideration: If it reaches a unanimous decision, the parties are bound to accept that decision: if it fails to achieve unanimity, the Council itself refers to arbitrators, whose award is final and binding on the parties to the dispute.

13. Thus for every dispute that may arise there is a procedure of pacific settlement, and provision has been made in the Protocol for meeting points (*a*), (*b*) and (*c*) in paragraph 8 above.

14. The establishment of a complete and comprehensive system for the pacific settlement of all disputes that might arise rendered it easier to approach the problem of the definition of "aggression." As the Prime Minister had said, "the one method by which we can approximate to an accurate attribution of responsibility for aggression is arbitration." In other words, any State which refused to avail itself of the means at hand for a peaceful settlement of a dispute, or which refused to accept the award given by the arbitral body or bodies now provided, and proceeded to an act of war, would brand itself as the aggressor. This principle is embodied in article 10 of the Protocol, which thus gives effect to the idea indicated in paragraph 8 (*d*) above. The definition of aggression is extended by articles 7 and 8 of the Protocol to apply to military measures taken before or during proceedings for a pacific settlement, and to acts constituting a threat of aggression against another State.

15. The point raised in paragraph 8 (*e*) above is dealt with in article 11 of the Protocol. Directly aggression takes place,

the Council calls upon the signatory States to apply sanctions against the aggressor (article 10). As soon as the Council has thus called upon the signatory States, "the obligations of the said States, in regard to the sanctions of all kinds mentioned in paragraphs 1 and 2 of article 16 of the Covenant, will immediately become operative in order that such sanctions may forthwith be employed against the aggressor. Those obligations shall be interpreted as obliging each of the signatory States to co-operate loyally and effectively in support of the Covenant of the League of Nations, and in resistance to any act of aggression, in the degree which its geographical position and its particular situation as regards armaments allow." Article 12 of the Protocol provides for the establishment of plans for putting into effect economic and financial sanctions, and article 13, "in view of the contingent military, naval and air sanctions provided for by article 16 of the Covenant," empowers the Council "to receive undertakings from States determining in advance the military, naval and air forces which they would be able to bring into action immediately to ensure the fulfilment of the obligations in regard to sanctions which result from the Covenant and the present Protocol."

16. Article 11—the "sanctions" article—has been more closely scrutinized and has been the subject of more criticism than any other article of the draft Protocol, and a hasty examination of it by some critics has led them to object that it goes beyond article 16 of the Covenant and imposes fresh obligations on the signatory States. In reply to such critics, it may be best to quote the words used by the British delegate in his speech to the Third Committee on the 22nd September:—

> "It cannot be too strongly emphasized that everything in this article is already stated or implied in article 16 of the Covenant. We are remaining within the terms of the Covenant and we are undertaking no new obligations .... Surely loyal and effective co-operation in support of the Covenant is what may confidently be expected from every Member of the League of Nations ....

The extent of the co-operation must depend on the actual circumstances not only as regards the aggression but also as regards the geographical position and the resources of all kinds of individual States. It would be no use to bind oneself to do a variety of things which may not be required. We must and we can rely on the good faith of the Members of the League to decide themselves how their effective co-operation can best be given if and when the necessity arises."

17. In order to complete the fulfilment of the task assigned to the committees by the Assembly's resolution of the 6th September, the Protocol finally provides (article 17) for the summoning in June next year of an International Conference for the reduction of armaments, to meet in Geneva and to include representatives of all states whether Members of the League or not. M. Herriot first, and other speakers after him, had emphasised the interdependence of the three great problems of arbitration, security and disarmament, and the framers of the Protocol, bearing this in mind, have been careful to preserve this interdependence in the document itself. Thus if sufficient ratifications of the Protocol have not been received by a certain date, the Conference on Disarmament is to be postponed. In any case, the Protocol does not come into force until that Conference shall have adopted a plan for the reduction of armaments. And if within a further period, that plan has not been carried out, the Protocol becomes null and void.

18. The above brief summary indicates how in the Protocol the committees of the Assembly have sought to embody, in concrete form, the proposals made to the Assembly itself by the British and French Prime Ministers. The Protocol is an attempt to complete the Covenant, to facilitate and develop the procedure of pacific settlement provided therein, and to define more clearly the obligations imposed by it on States Members of the League. The Protocol is based on the Covenant and keeps within its terms except in so far that it extends the Covenant procedure to give an alternative procedure by peaceful settle-

ment, even in those cases for which the framers of the Covenant in 1919 were unable to find a remedy. So far as it contains anything new, it is to be found in the definition of aggression which follows as a necessary corollary to the limitations inserted in the establishment of a universal system of peaceful settlement. But even here the principle is not new. Article 16 of the Covenant decreed that sanctions should be applied against any Member of the League that might "resort to war in disregard of its Covenants under articles 12, 13 or 15." Article 10 of the Protocol decrees sanctions against any State resorting to war without availing itself or in defiance of, the procedure of pacific settlement provided in the Covenant as amplified by the Protocol itself. The amplification of that procedure to cover all cases, so as to remove all excuse for resort to war, has enabled the framers of the Protocol to give a more exact definition of aggression, and to make that definition more certain and more automatic. The Protocol is thus free from the reproach that had been levelled against the Draft Treaty of Mutual Assistance, which left a wide and dangerous discretion to the Council in determining which party to a dispute was the aggressor. It further discards the system proposed in the draft Treaty, whereby power was given to the Council to decide on and to direct the military sanctions required. The draft Treaty tended towards the realisation of the idea of the League as a "super-State": the Protocol respects the principle of national sovereignty. Every State retains its own liberty of action: it is still free to choose what it will do. The Protocol has stated in clearer terms what is expected of those who signed the Covenant in 1919, and it is to be hoped that this more explicit declaration may serve to deter those who would contemplate a violation of the spirit of the Covenant, whilst reassuring those who have hitherto sought safety in their own armed strength, by giving them confidence in the solidarity of the civilised nations and in their determination to resist all unscrupulous attempts to plunge the world again into the disaster of war.

19. It remains only to say a few words as to the actual procedure adopted by the Assembly for putting into effect the
scheme thus elaborated. It was generally agreed that mere resolutions of the Assembly would not give sufficient assurance of
progress. The famous Resolution 14 of the Third Assembly had
been discussed and debated and had seemed to lead to an *im-
passe* with the rejection of the Treaty of Mutual Assistance. The
Prime Minister, in his speech to the Assembly, had said: "Let
us see to it that even before we rise, before the Assembly breaks
up, some substantial progress shall be made in co-ordinating
these ideas and in producing from their apparent diversities
some measure of agreement and consent." It was therefore decided that the scheme should be embodied in the form of a
Protocol, ready for signature, and that the Assembly should pass
a resolution endorsing the principles contained therein, recommending the Protocol to the Governments for their acceptance,
and directing that it should be opened immediately for signature.
The terms of this Resolution, which was carried unanimously,
have already been published.

20. The Protocol itself was signed in Geneva by Delegates
of the Governments of Albania, Bulgaria, Esthonia, France,
Greece, Latvia, Poland, Portugal, the Serb-Croat-Slovene State
and Czechoslovakia. The Delegate of France at the same time
signed on behalf of his Government the special Protocol opened
for signature in virtue of article 36, paragraph 2, of the Statute
of the Permanent Court of International Justice, making the
following declaration:—

> "I hereby declare that, subject to ratification, the
> French Government gives its adhesion to the optional
> clause of article 36, paragraph 2, of the Statute of the
> Court, on the condition of reciprocity, for a period of fif-
> teen years, with power of denunciation, should the Proto-
> col of Arbitration, Security and the Reduction of Arma-
> ments, signed this day, lapse, and further, subject to the
> observations made at the First Committee of the Fifth
> Assembly, according to the terms of which 'one of the

parties to the dispute may bring the said dispute before the Council of the League of Nations for the purposes of the pacific settlement laid down in paragraph 3 of article 15 of the Covenant, and during such proceedings neither party may take proceedings against the other in the Court.' "

21.   Having briefly summarized the discussion which gave rise to the elaboration of the draft Protocol, and having examined in what way that instrument embodies the ideas expressed in that discussion, it may be of interest to review summarily the progress of the work of the two Committees of the Assembly that were charged with the drafting of the scheme, and to show how the various articles were evolved.

22.   It will be seen from the terms of the resolution of the 6th September that the scheme of "arbitration, security and disarmament," though forming one indivisible whole, would require the deliberation of two of the regular Committees of the Assembly. The First Committee, dealing with the legal questions, would have to develop the principle of arbitration, while the Third Committee, dealing with the reduction of armaments, would have to consider the problems of security and disarmament.

23.   It was realised that the work would overlap at many points, and the two Committees kept in constant touch throughout, the result of their labours being finally co-ordinated by a joint drafting sub-Committee.

24.   During the whole period of discussion the British Delegation kept in close touch with the Dominion and Indian Delegations, who were consulted on all points of difficulty, and who were given every opportunity of expressing their views. This was done, not only by means of private consultation, but also at fourteen formal meetings of the Delegations.

25.   In the following sections an attempt is made to trace the evolution of the Protocol through its various stages in the First and Third Committees.

II.—Work of the First Committee.

26. The first plenary meeting of the First Committee was held on the 2nd September, when Sir Littleton Groom (Australia) was elected Chairman, and M. Limburg (Netherlands) Vice-Chairman. Sir C. Hurst represented the British Empire.

27. On the 9th September the Committee began its deliberations on the Assembly resolution of the 6th September regarding arbitration, security and disarmament. The Assembly, by this resolution, instructed the First Committee:—

"(a.)To consider, in view of possible amendments, the articles in the Covenant relating to the settlement of disputes;

"(b.) To examine within what limits the terms of article 36, paragraph 2, of the Statute establishing the Permanent Court of International Justice might be rendered more precise, and thereby facilitate the more general acceptance of the clause;

"and thus strengthen the solidarity and security of the nations of the world by settling by pacific means all disputes which may arise between States."

28. The British Delegation commenced their labours by considering the second of these two tasks, as it was a British suggestion emanating from the Prime Minister himself. The question of the acceptance by His Majesty's Government of the principle of compulsory arbitration for legal disputes, as provided in the optional clause referred to in article 36, paragraph 2, of the Statute establishing the Permanent Court of International Justice, had been examined in London before the meeting of the Assembly. This examination had shown so clearly the difficulties which might arise in connection with disputes with neutral Powers arising out of British naval action in time of war, that the limitation of the acceptance by his Majesty's Government of the optional clause by the exclusion of disputes arising out of British belligerent action at sea was suggested. To achieve this it was proposed that His Majesty's Government

should make a reservation as to disputes arising out of action taken in conformity with the Covenant, or at the request, or with the approval, of the Council of the League.

29. The suggestion was accepted by the British Delegation. As, however, the question was clearly one which affected the Empire as a whole, the Dominion and Indian Delegations were especially consulted in regard to it. The position as it appeared to the British Delegation was fully explained to them, and it was understood that they would telegraph to their respective Governments, making clear the nature of the reservation proposed.

30. The general discussion by the First Committee of the subject of the acceptance of the compulsory jurisdiction of the Permanent Court of International Justice took place at the third plenary meeting on the 11th September. The British Delegate reminded the Committee that the views of His Majesty's Government had already been explained in the Assembly in regard to the optional clause. The Prime Minister had then stated that the British Government wished to sign a clause of this kind, subject to its being clearly drafted. The British Delegate proceeded to discuss the position of the British Empire supposing that it accepted the compulsory jurisdiction of the Court, and was then forced, in support of the Covenant, to go to war at sea. Sea warfare, he said, inevitably brought a belligerent into sharp conflict with the nationals of foreign Powers carrying on trade with the enemy State. The British Empire might therefore find itself forced to support before the International Court the legality of action taken at the request of the League itself. The British Delegation therefore asked the Committee to consider whether it would be possible, either by amendment of article 36, paragraph 2, of the Statute of the Court or by the admission of a reservation acceptable to other Members of the League, to exclude from the acceptance of that clause disputes which arose out of action taken, either in accordance with the Covenant, or at the request, or with the sanction, of the Council of the League.

31. The French Delegation were content with the idea of such a reservation, and both the Belgian and Brazilian Delegations stated that they had no objection to it. The delegate of Brazil, however, said he would prefer to proceed by way of a reservation rather than by any modification of the text. Though the representatives of the Netherlands and of Sweden were slightly more critical, it became apparent that no real objection would be raised to the British reservation.

32. The Belgian Delegate suggested even going further still and excluding, when accepting the optional clause, the whole of sub-heading (*b*), which relates to questions of international law. The effect of this would be to exclude all questions of international law where that law has not yet been codified, as where it has been codified the dispute becomes one of the interpretation of a Treaty. This, the British Delegation thought, would be going to far. It would deprive the International Court of the power to build up a case law in the international field. It would, moreover, have gone further than the Delegation felt necessary, because it was only in the field of established international law, where there are two distinct schools of thought— the continental and the Anglo-Saxon—that the difficulties referred to by the British Delegate would arise.

33. As regards the question of amendments to the Covenant, the French representative did not, during the general discussion in a plenary meeting of the First Committee, specify the nature of the amendments suggested by the French Delegation. He contented himself with drawing attention to three points. The first was the last sentence of article 13 of the Covenant, which provides that in the event of any failure to carry out an arbitration award, the Council shall propose what steps shall be taken to give effect thereto. This the French Delegation regarded as inadequate. The second was the provision of article 15 by which, if the Council cannot reach a unanimous decision, the parties to a dispute which is submitted to the Council recover their liberty of action. Here, he said, was a gap in the

Covenant which must be filled. Was the position to be perpetuated, he asked, by which any one member of the Council could completely prevent a peaceful settlement of a dispute? The third was paragraph 8 of article 15, which provides that in matters within the domestic jurisdiction of a State the Council can make no recommendation. The French Delegation asked the Committee to consider whether it would not be possible to discover a method of friendly conciliation over matters relating to domestic jurisdiction.

34. After the general discussion had been declared closed, the First Committee adjourned for a week and entrusted to a sub-committee, known as the Fifth Sub-Committee, the ask of formulating concrete proposals. The work done by this sub-committee was of such importance that it is considered desirable to indicate its composition, which was as follows:

> Mr. Adatci (Japan).
> Count Albert Apponyi (Hungary).
> M. Loucheur (France).
> Mr. John O'Byrne (Irish Free State).
> M. Erich (Finland).
> M. Raul Fernandez (Brazil).
> Sir Cecil Hurst (British Empire).
> M. Nicolas Politis (Greece).
> M. Rolin (Belgium).
> M. Vittorio Scialoja (Italy).
> M. Nicolas Titulesco (Roumania).
> M. Torriente (Cuba).
> M. Limburg (Netherlands).
> M. Unden (Sweden).

35. The discussion was taken up on the 12th September in the sub-committee on the lines of the general debate in the full Committee. The meetings were not open to the public. As regards the proposed British reservation to the acceptance of the obligatory jurisdiction of the Permanent Court of International Justice, by signing the optional clause in the Statute of the Court, some opposition developed at first from two quarters. Subsequently, however, it waned and did not reappear.

36.   As regards the extension of the principle of arbitration by amendments to the Covenant, it at once became clear that there were many conflicting views as to the best system to adopt. The days were spent mainly in ascertaining, inside and outside the sub-committee, the extent and the nature of the different points of view.

37.   The work on which the sub-committee was engaged was intimately related to the questions of security and disarmament with which the Third Committee was dealing. On the 16th September, Dr. Benes, chairman of the sub-committee of the Third Committee, who had been in close touch with the British and French Delegations, produced a draft Protocol covering the whole ground, in which he had attempted to reconcile opposing points of view and which was intended to serve as a basis for discussion. Articles 1, 2, 3 and 5 of this draft Protocol concerned the First Committee and were referred to the sub-committee. They may be summarised as follows:—

38.   *Article* 1.—The signatories recognise the jurisdiction of the Permanent Court of International Justice as compulsory, "subject to the following reserves":—

39.   *Article* 2.—The signatories undertake to submit all disputes, not covered by articles 12, 13 and 15 of the Covenant, to the Council of the League, subject to an express reserve as to the right given exclusively to the Assembly in article 19 of the Covenant, whereby the Assembly alone is entitled to advise the reconsideration of existing treaties. The Council in such cases to act as an arbitration tribunal and to decide by a majority vote. Pending an examination of the dispute the Council may, by a majority, define measures to be taken by the parties to avert or put an end to armed conflict. Similarly, the Council may, in case of imminent danger, call upon the parties to discontinue any measure likely to cause the dispute to become more acute.

40.   *Article* 3.—The procedure laid down in article 2 to apply to the Permanent Court in cases concerning the competence of that Court.

41. *Article* 5.—Any signatory which does not submit its disputes to the methods of pacific settlement indicated above, or which does not comply with the provisional measures referred to in article 2, or which does not carry out an award of a duly qualified arbitral body, shall, if these acts of non-compliance are likely to disturb the peace of the world, be declared to be an aggressor and outlawed, the declaration to be made by the Permanent Court or by the Council acting, if need be, by a majority. When this declaration has been made, the Council is to call on Members of the League to put into operation the sanctions contained in article 7.

42. Consideration of these proposals and of those contained in two other schemes submitted led to long discussions in the Committee. These discussions served mainly to bring into relief the different schools of thought. One favoured the widest possible extension of the jurisdiction of the Permanent Court, even into the field of disputes of a political nature; the other held that the Court's jurisdiction should be rigidly limited to disputes of a legal character, while a far-reaching system of arbitration should be established to deal with political disputes. Strong disinclination was shown towards any increase in the existing powers of the Council. On the other hand, it was made clear that no decrease of those powers would be tolerated. On one side it was urged that the Council, when acting as an arbitral body, should make its decisions by a majority vote; on the other, strong exception was taken to any departure from the unanimity rule. As regards the application of sanctions, one group held that mere refusal to arbitrate or failure to carry out an award should justify their application. Another contended equally strongly that sanctions should only be applied when such refusal or failure was accompanied by a resort to war. The extent to which war was legitimate under the Covenant in cases relating to domestic jurisdiction was very fully discussed. The net result was a unanimous agreement to leave paragraph 8 of article 15 untouched.

43. As regards the filling of the gap in article 15 of the Covenant, little progress was made. On the 19th September, therefore, the British representative submitted a scheme to the sub-committee, in which he had endeavoured to meet the differences of opinion which had been expressed. This scheme provided for the acceptance as compulsory of the jurisdiction of the Permanent Court in the cases covered by article 36, paragraph 2, of the Statute of the Court, with such reserves as may be consistent therewith. Its main object was, however, the amendment of the Covenant on the lines of the following text:—

"The undersigned will support the introduction of amendments to article 15 of the Covenant for the purpose of amplifying paragraphs 4, 5, 6 and 7 of that article on the following lines:—

"If the dispute submitted to the Council is not settled by it as provided in paragraph 3, the Council shall endeavour to persuade the parties to submit the dispute to judicial settlement or arbitration.

"If the parties cannot agree to do so, the Council shall again take the dispute under consideration, and, if it reaches a report which is unanimously agreed to by the Members thereof other than the representatives of the parties to the dispute, the Members of the League agree to accept the recommendations contained in the report.

"If the Council fails to reach a report which is concurred in by all the members other than the representatives of the parties to the dispute, and if the parties are still unable to agree to refer the dispute to arbitration, the Council is empowered to refer the dispute to arbitration on their behalf. One-half of the members of the tribunal, excluding the president, shall be appointed by the Council, after consultation with one party to the dispute, and the other half after consultation with the other party to the dispute. The president shall be appointed by the Council after consultation with the Permanent Court of International Justice if in session, or, if not in session, with the members of its chamber of summary jurisdiction.

"The Members of the League agree that they will comply with the recommendations contained in any award of the Arbitration Tribunal set up by the Council as above.

"In the event of any failure to comply with the recommendations of a report concurred in by all the Members of the Council other than the parties to the dispute, or in any award of an arbitration tribunal set up by the Council as above, the Council shall exert all its influence to secure compliance therewith. If such failure to carry out the recommendations is accompanied by any resort to war, the sanctions provided for in article 16, interpreted as provided in this Protocol, shall be applied."

44. The British Delegate explained that the willingness of Governments to amend the Covenant must be clearly expressed in the Protocol. In no other way could the danger of creating within the League an inner ring of Powers, bound towards each other by ties and obligations more close than those binding the ordinary members of the League, be avoided. The drafting of amendments to the Covenant was, however, a technical matter, and time was short. He therefore suggested that the Council should be asked to set up a committee of experts to draft the amendments to the Covenant contemplated by the Protocol.

45. These proposals provided the bases of articles 1, 3 and 4 of the Protocol and of paragraph 3 of the Assembly Resolution of the 2nd October. The bases of articles 2 and 5 had already been established. Article 10 was beginning to take shape in new drafts in substitution for Dr. Benes's definition of an aggressor. On the 21st September these articles were provisionally adopted by the joint drafting committee of the First and Third Committees. At this stage, therefore, for the first time, the substance of a workable text on the subjects referred to the First Committee began to emerge from the shadow of discussion.

46. Throughout this period, however, the negotiations had been carried on entirely in the sub-committee in secret sessions. Although the closest possible touch had been kept by the British Delegation with the Dominion and Indian Delegations, the British representative felt himself to be in a position

of great responsibility in carrying on the work in the sub-committee. He felt that a stage had been reached where a wider consultation was necessary, as, with the exception of the Attorney-General of the Irish Free State, who was unfortunately obliged to return to Ireland about this date, he was the only British member. He proposed, therefore, that the work of the sub-committee should be reported to the full Committee on which all the Dominion and Indian Delegations were represented. The full Committee thereupon met on the 24th September, and then and at further meetings held on the 25th, 26th, 27th and 28th September, the articles of the Protocol were fully discussed in public sessions. The articles of the Protocol under consideration thus took their shape in the sub-committee, they were then submitted to the Joint Drafting Committee representing the First and Third Committees, and were then finally approved after public discussions in Committee No. 1. Here, then, it will be convenient to deal with the purpose and evolution of each article separately.

The Preamble.

47. The draft of the Preamble, as revised by the Joint Drafting Committee of the First and Third Committees, was adopted at a plenary session of the First Committee on the 27th September. The Lithuanian Delegate made a reservation that the reference to territorial security in no way prejudiced existing disputes between States signing the Protocol. The Portuguese Delegate proposed an amendment to substitute for the word "territories" in the first sentence, the phrase "territories under the sovereignty of States." The object was to make it clear that oversea territories under the sovereignty of a State were not excluded, but the British representative reminded the committee of the nature of the varied character of the territories of the British Empire, and said that if one class of oversea territories were mentioned, all must be mentioned. The amendment was rejected.

Article 1.

48.   Article 1 was designed to ensure that the universality of
the League should be maintained even if the Protocol comes into
force.   For a while there must no doubt be a dual régime.   States
signatory to the Protocol will be bound by its terms, and the
régime of the Covenant will continue to exist and to be binding
upon States members of the League.   This will, however, not
last, as the principal provisions of the Protocol will be transformed into amendments to the Covenant.

Article 2.

49.   Article 2 was intended to make all aggressive war il-
legal.   Exceptions were, however, made to safeguard (1) the
right of a State to fight in self-defence, and (2) the position of
a State acting in accordance with the provisions of the Covenant or the Protocol.   A proposal, strongly urged, to substitute
the words "resort to force" for the words "resort to war" was
rejected.

Article 3.

50.   Article 3 provides for the compulsory recognition of the
jurisdiction of the Permanent Court.   The Joint Drafting Committee proposed to remove this article from the Protocol, as
certain Delegations felt it went beyond the Assembly Resolution.
The British Empire Delegation feared that this might result in
the separation of the three principles—arbitration, security and
disarmament.   At the suggestion of the British representative,
therefore, the article was retained.   As a result of the discussions on this matter, it was generally agreed that the power to
make reservations to article 36 of the Permanent Court Statute
was much wider than had been at first believed.   It was understood that the proposed British reservation was within the limits
admissible.

Article 4.

51.   Article 4 was designed to extend the system of arbitra-

tion contained in the Covenant and to fill the existing gap in article 15 of the Covenant, by which the parties to a dispute recover their liberty of action and are entitled to resort to war if the Members of the Council are unable to agree upon a unanimous report. In the sub-committee a strong feeling manifested itself against unanimous decisions of the Council being binding in cases where one party to a dispute, but not both, desired arbitration. Certain of the smaller States, in particular, felt that such a system gave too much power to the Council, which was already regarded as a body which expressed only the will of the great Powers.

52. Paragraphs 2 (*a*) and (*b*) of article 4 were drafted to avoid this difficulty. Arbitration is to be compulsory at the request of one of the parties, and the Council is given power to appoint the arbitral body if the parties cannot agree as to its constitution. A unanimous decision of the Council is only to be binding where none of the parties ask for arbitration. If, therefore, any party wishes to avoid a decision by the Council, it has only to ask for arbitration. For similar reasons, the words "accepted by one of the parties" were added after the words "decision of the Council" in paragraph 5.

53. Discussions in the sub-committee revealed a divergence of view as to whether or not sanctions should be applied in the event of passive resistance to the award of the Arbitral Commission. It was finally agreed that the provision contained at the end of article 13 of the Covenant would be sufficient to meet a case of passive resistance and that the sanctions of article 16 should only be applied when such resistance was accompanied by a resort to war (*vide* paragraph 6 of article 4).

54. At the request of the British representative, paragraph 7 was added to ensure that reservations, similar to that which the British Delegation considered that it would be obliged to make if the British Empire accepted article 36 of the Statute of the Permanent Court, would also exist in the case of the new system of compulsory arbitration.

Article 5.

55.   Article 5 was inserted as the result of a unanimous decision of the sub-committee to leave untouched paragraph 8 of article 15 of the Covenant, which safeguards the rights of States Members in regard to matters of domestic jurisdiction. The whole British Empire Delegation held the view that when the Arbitration Commissions were faced with such questions, they should be bound to refer them to the Permanent Court, and that the opinion of the Court should be binding.   As the Permanent Court itself is bound to apply international law, and paragraph 8 of article 15 refers to questions which by *international law* are solely within the domestic jurisdiction of the State concerned, this provision ensures that a uniform rule will be applied by the Council, the Permanent Court and the arbitral bodies to be set up under the new system.

56.   The last sentence of article 5 was added to meet certain difficulties raised by the Japanese Delegation.   They pointed out that the second gap in the Covenant, referred to by the French Delegation during the general discussion, had not been filled. On the 24th September, they accordingly proposed an amendment to article 5, which appeared to have the effect of giving the Council power, in cases relating to domestic jurisdiction, to recommend the parties to adopt some solution which would ensure a pacific settlement of the dispute.   After the discussion in the sub-committee, the Japanese Delegation modified this proposal and suggested that the following words be added as the final paragraph of article 5:—

> "The above provisions do not prejudice the duty of the Council to endeavour to bring the parties to an agreement so as to ensure the maintenance of peace and a good understanding between nations."

This proposal came up before the plenary session of the First Committee on the 25th September.   The British Delegation asked for a postponement of the discussion.   Immediate steps were taken to consult the Dominion and Indian Delegations, and in the subsequent negotiations the closest co-operation with them was maintained.

57. It transpired that the Japanese Delegation, if they failed to secure acceptance of this amendment to article 5, intended to press for the exclusion from article 10 of the sentence at the end of paragraph 2 (1), which included in the definition of an "aggressor" a State which resorted to war and disregarded a unanimous report of the Council or a judicial sentence or an arbitral award recognising that the dispute arose out of a matter within the domestic jurisdiction of the other State concerned. They pointed out that it was unjust that in such cases the League, while refusing pacific means of settlement to an injured State, should denounce that State as an aggressor if it took steps to defend its legitimate interests by force.

58. The possible effect of this alternative amendment was regarded by many Delegations with great concern. It would have suggested the legitimacy of a resort to war in connection with a dispute arising out of some domestic matter as to which the Council could give no help and make no recommendation for its solution.

59. In these circumstances the British Empire Delegation was agreed that the best course was to endeavour to find a solution by enlarging article 19 of the Protocol, so as to make it clear that the existing power of the Council, under article 11 of the Covenant, of endeavouring to achieve a pacific settlement in any case where the peace of the world was endangered, was not prejudiced by the provisions of the Protocol. Though the discussions of the matter remained very friendly in tone this proposal did not prove acceptable to the Japanese Delegation. Accordingly, when the amendment came before the plenary meeting of the First Committee on the 28th September, the Japanese Delegation withdrew their amendment to article 5 and proposed the amendment to article 10. At the suggestion of the French Delegate the question was referred back to the sub-committee.

60. Late on the 29th September the basis of solution was found. It was immediately submitted to the representatives of the Dominions and India, and was fully considered by them at two further meetings on the following day. After slight modifications the text of two amendments proved acceptable to the British Empire Delegation, and after being accepted by the Japanese and French Delegations, these amendments were adopted by the First Committee. They involved the addition to the last sentence of article 5 of the words "this decision shall not prevent consideration of the situation by the Council or the Assembly under article 11 of the Covenant," and the addition at the end of paragraph 2 (1) of article 10 of the words "nevertheless in the last case the State shall only be presumed to be an aggressor if it has not previously submitted the question to the Council or the Assembly in accordance with article 11 of the Covenant."

61. In the opinion of the British Empire Delegation these amendments conferred no new powers or functions on either the Council or the Assembly. They merely served to make clear the relationship between paragraph 8 of article 15 and article 11 of the Covenant. Article 11 of the Covenant only operates in time of war or threat of war, and it confers no right on the Council or the Assembly to impose a solution of a dispute without the consent of the parties. The Council or the Assembly may mediate and conciliate, but they cannot make recommendations which are binding under paragraph 6 of article 15 of the Covenant. When these amendments were adopted at the final plenary meeting of the First Committee on the 30th September, the British representative made a statement on the above lines. This interpretation proved generally acceptable, and it was agreed to incorporate it in the report to be submitted to the Assembly.

62. At the final plenary meeting of the First Committee the British representative drew attention to the difficulty in which many Delegations were placed, in that they had had no oppor-

tunity to consult their Governments in regard to these amendments. The Delegations of Australia and several other countries thereupon stated that, though they accepted the texts, they could not commit their Governments in any way.

Article 6.

63. Article 6. When the system of compulsory arbitration, contained in article 4, had been established, the British representative pointed out that under paragraphs 9 and 10 of article 15 of the Covenant a dispute might still be referred to the Assembly. Article 6 was therefore drafted to ensure that the provisions referring to the actions and powers of the Council should apply to the Assembly under the new system. After considerable discussion it was decided to reserve questions of procedure to the Council as being a more suitable body.

Article 10.

64. Article 10, which contains the definition of an aggressor, provided one of the most difficult tasks of the First Committee. By the 23rd September a number of drafts had been considered but no satisfactory text had been found. The original idea was that it should be the duty of the Council to determine the aggressor, but the question then arose as to whether, in making this decision, the Council should act unanimously or by majority vote. Adherence to the unanimity rule would have made it possible for one State to prevent a decision being reached. Procedure by a majority vote might have resulted in a State being obliged to apply sanctions against its own judgment. The only way out of this difficulty was to avoid a decision by the Council at all, and to make the test of aggression automatic, when once certain conditions had been found to obtain. This is achieved by establishing a presumption which is to hold good until the Council has made a unanimous decision to the contrary. If the presumption stands it is considered sufficient to justify the application of sanctions. Even then it was thought that there would have to be something in the nature of a "dec-

laration of aggression" in order to initiate the enforcement of sanctions, and that this declaration would have to be made by unanimity. Objections were raised to this, but these objections were finally satisfied by the insertion of paragraph 3, according to which the Council, if it cannot at once determine the aggressor, is bound, as a matter of course, to enjoin an armistice upon the belligerents.

65. The Japanese Delegation were opposed to any presumption of aggression arising against a state which was involved in a dispute covered by paragraph 8 of article 15 of the Covenant, and found as the result that, though it had submitted the dispute to the Council, the Council were unable to make any recommendations on the subject. To meet this view, the amendment previously referred to was made to article 5, and the words "nevertheless in the last case the State shall only be presumed to be an aggressor if it has not previously submitted the question to the Council or the Assembly in accordance with article 11 of the Covenant" were added to paragraph 2 (1) of article 10. In the opinion of the British Delegation, this amendment does not affect paragraph 3 of article 10. If a resort to war occurs, and the Council cannot determine the aggressor, it is still bound to impose an armistice upon the belligerents.

66. To the final paragraph of article 10 the words "and any signatory State thus called upon shall thereupon be entitled to exercise the rights of a belligerent" were added at the suggestion of the British representative. This addition was made to safeguard the position of a State which, though no party to the dispute, joined in coercive measures to uphold the Covenant of the League and in so doing took forcible measures against the persons or the property of nationals of another State.

Article 16.

67. The relations between States signatory to the Protocol and States non-signatory and non-members of the League presented a problem the solution of which required great care.

The various aspects of the question were thoroughly examined, and it was finally agreed that it would be sufficient to bring the principle contained in article 17 of the Covenant into harmony with the provisions of the Protocol. Sanctions can only be imposed on a State which is not a Member of the League if it refuses to accept the conditions and obligations of the Protocol when invited to do so, and resorts to war against a signatory State.

68. The question was raised of the relationship between States Members of the League signatory to the Protocol and non-signatory States Members. After careful examination, it was generally agreed that no special arrangement was necessary. The Members of the League are bound *inter se* by the Covenant and non-signatory Members are entitled, if they wish, to prefer the procedure laid down in the Covenant to the new procedure of the Protocol.

Article 18.

69. Article 18 was inserted to satisfy apprehensions which had been expressed in certain quarters. The British Delegation were not convinced of its necessity, but saw no reason to object to it.

Article 19.

70. Article 19 was inserted as a saving clause. It emphasises the intention to preserve the Covenant as the principal document governing the relations between States Members of the League. The relations between signatories and non-signatories to the Protocol are still to be governed by the Covenant. The Covenant is to stand, but it is to be enriched by the principal provisions of the Protocol. The amended Covenant is intended ultimately to take the place of the separate régime of the Protocol.

Resolution No. 1.

71. It had been originally suggested that the provisions of

the Protocol should be embodied in the form of resolutions to be submitted for adoption by the Assembly. In view, however, of the fact that adoption of such resolutions by the Assembly might be held to commit the Governments there represented to the acceptance of its provisions, and in view of the difficulty which Delegations found in consulting their Governments, this proposal was found to be impracticable. It was thereupon decided that the Protocol should be drawn up as a separate instrument, and that its acceptance should be recommended by the Assembly to all States Members of the League.

72. The draft of a resolution on these lines, which had been drawn up by the British representative, was discussed by the First Committee on the 27th September. Paragraph 1 recommends the acceptance of the Protocol. Paragraph 2 provides that the Protocol shall be open immediately for signature for those representatives who were already in a position to sign. This was added in view of the fact that the French and several other Delegations had announced their intention to sign the Protocol before leaving Geneva. Paragraph 3 was inserted because it was felt that the drafting of amendments to the Covenant was too technical a matter to be done hastily.

73. The remaining paragraphs of the resolution relate to the proposed Disarmament Conference which was dealt with by the Third Committee. The resolution was unanimously adopted by the Assembly on the 2nd October.

Resolution No. 2.

74. This resolution recommends the acceptance of the obligatory jurisdiction of the Permanent Court of International Justice at The Hague by all Members of the League. The discussions regarding the special Protocol opened for signature in virtue of article 36, paragraph 2, of the Statute of the Permanent Court, had revealed that the power to make reservations was wider than had been at first thought. It was therefore decided that no new Protocol was required, but that the power to make

reservations should be clearly recognised in the resolution of the Assembly.

M. Politis's Report.

75.   M. Politis's draft report on the work of the First Committee was presented to the Committee on the 28th September, and the discussion upon it lasted all day.   This draft, which was very ably drawn up, gave a remarkably clear and adequate account of the achievement of the First Committee.

76.   Some criticism was made by the representative of Hungary and others of a tendency in the report to give peace a secondary position to that of justice in the predominating idea of arbitration. As a result, the offending passages were redrafted.

77.   In its final form M. Politis's report was incorporated in the general report submitted to the Fifth Assembly by the First and Third Committees.   This general report[a] was adopted unanimously by the Assembly on the 2nd October, and it can thus be regarded as the official document containing the views of the Members of the League in regard to the interpretation of the Protocol.

III.—WORK OF THE THIRD COMMITTEE.

78.   The Third Committee began its deliberations on the Assembly resolution on arbitration, security and disarmament on the 9th September, under the presidency of M. Duca (Roumania) (subsequently replaced by M. Politis [Greece]), and the proceedings opened with a general discussion, which was continued until the 13th.   Lord Parmoor and Mr. Henderson represented the British Empire.

79.   After the method of procedure had been settled, a statement was made expressing the standpoint of the British Delegation on the questions of arbitration under the three heads of arbitration, court decisions and conciliation, and the views then expressed were maintained at the subsequent meetings.   A short

---

a.   See Annex C, p. 156.

reference was made to the question of sanctions, but any detail was avoided in order to leave room for free discussion with the members of the French Delegation. The note of the British Government on the Draft Treaty of Mutual Assistance was referred to as expressing the final view and not requiring any further comment.

80.   Most of the speakers devoted some time to a statement of the views of their Governments on the Draft Treaty of Mutual Assistance, against which the main objections urged were the uncertainty in regard to the definition of aggression, the too wide discretion and powers conferred upon the Council and the evils attendant on the system of "complementary agreements" sanctioned by the Treaty. The first defect might now be remedied by the extension of the system of arbitration, which would simplify the definition of aggression. As regards the "complementary agreements," even those who recognized their harmful possibilities were compelled to admit that they could not be abolished or prevented, and that their power for evil might be lessened if they were controlled and brought within a general scheme of mutual assistance under the League.

81.   All the speakers were in substance agreed that the Covenant itself afforded the best basis for any scheme of mutual assistance; that it needed only to be developed and carried to its logical conclusion in order that it might provide an adequate basis of security.

82.   In summing up the debate the President observed that there appeared to be general agreement on the interdependence of the three problems of arbitration, security and disarmament, and on the point that a complete system could be evolved from the Covenant itself. Everyone was prepared to accept the principle of economic and financial sanctions, though some difference might exist on the subject of military sanctions. Little had been said about disarmament, which could only follow as a consequence of the solution of the twin problems of arbitration and security.

83. It was then agreed, on the morning of the 13th September, to appoint a sub-committee of representatives of twelve Delegations to formulate concrete proposals.

84. The sub-committee, known as the Fourth Sub-Committee of the Third Committee, was composed as follows:—

> Lord Parmoor or Mr. Henderson (British Empire).
> M. Paul-Boncour (France).
> M. Schanzer (Italy).
> M. Branting (Sweden).
> M. Benes (Czechoslovakia).
> M. Villegas (Chile).
> M. Kalfov (Bulgaria).
> M. Poullet (Belgium).
> M. Titulesco (Roumania).
> Mr. Matsuda (Japan).
> M. Lange (Norway).
> M. Skrzynski (Poland).

85. The sub-committee met for the first time on the afternoon of the 13th September, under the presidency of Dr. Benes. The first meeting was occupied by a discussion on procedure. In the first instance, it was proposed to appoint a drafting committee of three members to draw up proposals, keeping in close touch with a similar committee to be appointed by the First Committee, but this idea was subsequently abandoned, and the President was requested to draw up the outline of a scheme, to be submitted to the sub-committee, if possible, on the 15th September. This the President undertook to do, but he was only able to submit his proposals for the first time on the 16th September. The delay was due mainly to the necessity of consulting with representatives of the First Committee and with certain Delegations. In particular, meetings were held on the 15th September between representatives of the French and British Delegations who went carefully through the scheme and reached a preliminary agreement on a number of points of principle. This agreement greatly facilitated the eventual completion of the work.

86. These proposals were in the form of a draft Protocol, of which articles 1, 2, 3 and 5 concerned the First Committee, and have already been dealt with in the preceding section of this report. The remaining articles, as originally proposed, may be summarised as follows:—

87. *Article* 4.—The Council or the Permanent Court may appoint International Control Commissions, composed of civilian and military experts, to ensure that during the course of the arbitral procedure none of the parties makes preparations for economic or military mobilisation.

88. *Article* 6 recommends the establishment of demilitarised zones and their control, if desired, by the League of Nations.

89. *Article* 7.—As soon as the declaration of aggression has been made, the obligations of the signatories in regard to the sanctions of all kinds in article 16, paragraphs 1 and 2, of the Covenant will immediately become operative against the aggressor. These obligations to be interpreted as obliging each of the Members of the League to co-operate loyally and effectively in support of the Covenant of the League and in resistance to any act of aggression.

90. In accordance with article 16 of the Covenant the signatories undertake, individually or collectively, to come to the assistance of the State attacked or threatened, and to give each other mutual support by means of facilities and reciprocal exchanges as regards supplies of raw materials and food-stuffs of every kind, openings of credits, transports, transit, and for this purpose to ensure the safety of the land and sea communications of the attacked or threatened State.

91. If both parties to the dispute are declared aggressors according to the above provisions, the economic sanctions to be applied to both of them.

92. *Article* 7A.—The Council of the League of Nations to instruct the Economic and Financial Committees, Temporary Mixed Commission and Permanent Advisory Commission to draw up (1) plans of action for establishing the blockade of

the aggressor State, and (2) plans of economic and financial co-operation between the State attacked and the different States assisting it.

93. *Article 8.*—The Council to be entitled to accept individual or collective undertakings entered into by States, determining in advance the military forces which they would immediately place at the Council's disposal in order to carry out the measures decided upon, in accordance with the preceding articles.

94. When the aggressor has been designated, the signatories may, in accordance with undertakings previously entered into, place in the field the whole, or such proportion as they may consider necessary, of their military forces against the aggressor.

95. *Article 8A.*—In view of article 10 of the Covenant, the above sanctions must not include the violation of the political or territorial independence of the aggressor.

96. *Article 9.*—The signatories to take part as soon as possible in an International Conference for the Reduction of Armaments under the auspices of the League. The Council to draw up the programme for this Conference.

97. If, within a time limit of　　　　　after the coming into force of the Protocol, the Conference has not met, or the scheme for the reduction of armaments drawn up by it has not been adopted and carried out, the Council may record the fact, and each signatory shall regain its freedom of action.

98. If, during the time limit specified above, a dispute arises, the provisions in the Protocol to be applicable in full.

99. *Supplementary Clause* (to be inserted in article 9).—The conditions in which the Council may declare that the scheme of the International Conference has not been carried out, shall be defined by the Conference itself.

100. *Article 10.*—Differences relating to the carrying out or interpretation of the Protocol to be submitted to the Permanent Court of International Justice.

101. *Article 11.*—The Protocol to be open for signature by

all States, to be ratified, and the ratifications to be deposited with the League. The Protocol to come into force between the signatories ratifying it, as from the date of ratification.

102. The sub-committee held eight meetings in all, finishing its work on the 22nd September. The articles were not discussed in their numerical order, and a discussion of one article was often adjourned while the examination of another article was begun. As it is not attempted here to give a full summary of the discussions, it will perhaps be convenient to take the articles in order and show what modifications were introduced.

103. *Article 4.*—Objection was raised to this article, mainly on the ground that it gave the Council or the Permanent Court too wide powers of interference, and introduced the idea of a "super-State." After consultation with other Delegations, the British Delegation produced an alternative draft which was adopted, and which was substantially embodied in the eventual Protocol itself (becoming article 7). The only essential difference betwen this draft and the eventual text was that the former provided, in paragraph 2, that the investigations should be carried out "by the organisation set up by the Conference for the Reduction of Armaments to ensure respect for the decisions of that Conference.

104. *Article 6.*—Words were inserted to the effect that demilitarised zones were recommended "as a means of avoiding violations of the present Protocol." They were to be placed under the supervision of the Council at the request "and at the expense" of one or more of the conterminous States.

105. *Article 7.*—There was considerable discussion on the first paragraph, and some demand for a distinction to be drawn, as in the Covenant, between economic and financial sanctions on the one hand, and military sanctions on the other. It was, however, explained that the proposed definition of the aggressor had produced a clearer situation, in which there was no reason why the application of sanctions of all kinds under article 16 of the Covenant should not be justified. It was pointed out that the

wording of this first paragraph was illogical. The "obligations" could not "become operative against an aggressor." Accordingly, it was agreed to substitute the words "the obligations will immediately come into force in order that the sanctions provided may immediately become operative." The paragraph was then passed with the above amendment.

106. Exception was taken to the words in the third paragraph "undertake individually or collectively to come to the assistance." It might prove difficult to evolve collective plans, and it was agreed, on the proposal of the British Delegate, to substitute the words "give a joint and several undertaking to."

107. In the same paragraph the use of the expression "to ensure the safety of the land and sea communications of the attacked or threatened State" was questioned in the first place, because it seemed that it might imply naval or military operations. In reply, it was pointed out that the words in the same sentence "for this purpose" showed that this paragraph related solely to economic and financial sanctions. In the second place the word "ensure" was objected to, on the score that to undertake to ensure communications might be to undertake an impossibility. Finally, the words "take measures to preserve the safety of communications" were substituted. It was further pointed out that these provisions were to be applied to protect an attacked or threatened State and that a similar distinction was expressly contained in the Covenant.

108. *Article* 7A.—The British Delegation desired a redraft of this article, taking exception in particular to sub-paragraph (1), in which the word "blockade" seemed to suggest belligerent naval action. They at first suggested omitting all words after "Council of the League of Nations" and substituting "shall, as soon as possible after the Protocol has been ratified, take steps to ascertain from each of the signatories what organisation or legislation is necessary to give effect to the economic and financial sanctions." An alternative suggestion from another quarter was to substitute the words "putting into force the economic and

financial sanctions against" for the words "establishing the blockade of" in sub-paragraph (1). It was agreed to combine both amendments—to adopt the British text above, and to begin a second paragraph with the words "When in possession of this information the Council shall draw up, through its competent organs: (1) plans of action for the application of the economic and financial sanctions of article 16 of the Covenant against an aggressor State," &c.

109. Later, the British Delegation proposed to redraft the first paragraph in the form in which it finally appears in the Protocol (having become article 12), to delete the remainder, and to substitute "It shall communicate this report to the members of the League and to the other signatories." The redraft of the first paragraph was accepted, but it was decided to allow the second paragraph to stand, as amended above.

110. *Article 8.*—The British Delegation had objections to raise against both paragraphs of this article. In the first paragraph they objected to the words "place at the Council's disposal," and the second paragraph they regarded as an attempt to revert to what was the operative principle of the Draft Treaty of Mutual Assistance.

111. They suggested as an alternative text:—

"Having regard to the fact that military sanctions are foreseen in article 16 of the Covenant, the Council may receive undertakings from States fixing in advance the military forces which they would be willing to employ against a Member of the League which was declared to be an aggressor.

"In view of the right of Members of the League to enter into such arrangements with the Council, no agreement shall in future be concluded between States Members of the League, providing for military action to be taken by them."

112. It became evident that the sub-committee could not be induced to accept the second paragraph of this alternative text, and it was accordingly withdrawn. Exception was also taken

to the words in the first paragraph, "against a Member of the League," &c., and it was agreed to substitute the words, "to ensure the fulfilment of the obligations in regard to sanctions which result from the Covenant and the present Protocol."

113. The French Delegation then proposed that the article should read:—

> "In view of the contingent military, naval and air sanctions provided for in article 16 of the Covenant, and article 7 of the present Protocol, the Council shall be entitled to receive undertakings entered into by States determining in advance the military, naval and air forces which they would bring into action immediately to ensure the fulfilment of the obligations in regard to sanctions which result from the Covenant and the present Protocol.
>
> "When the aggressor is designated, the signatory States may, moreover, place in the field, in accordance with agreements previously entered into, the whole or such part of their military, naval and air forces as they may consider necessary for the assistance of a State which shall have been the victim of aggression.
>
> "The obligations of the second paragraph shall be duly registered and published by the League of Nations, and shall remain open for adherence by any State Member of the League which so desires."

114. It was the right of States, as the matter then stood, to enter into special agreements with one another for determining in advance the military, naval and air forces which they would bring to the assistance of one another under the conditions indicated. Under the Protocol, these special agreements would only come into force when the Council had decided which State is the aggressor: they would simply provide means for applying rapidly the sanctions prescribed in the Covenant and the Protocol.

115. Before, however, agreeing to this text a statement was made on behalf of the British Delegation, expressing regret that the sub-committee had not seen its way to make the Protocol an instrument whereby the League would only act as a whole. It was, however, recognised that the last paragraph introduced

an improvement, as, if separate agreements must exist, it would be better that they should be registered with the League. "But that does not alter the fact that you are making provision on the face of a new document for that which has been turned down in connection with the Draft Treaty of Mutual Assistance." Further opposition to the draft article was not pressed, but the British Delegation made known their desire that words should be recorded expressing regret that the League was not to act as a whole, and to set its face "like flint against anything like the old balance of power by allowing these regional pacts to go on under this new instrument." The above text was then adopted.

116. *Article* 8A.—The British Delegation proposed that the article should read: "Shall not affect the territorial integrity or political independence of the aggressor State." This was agreed to, and it was also decided to prefix a paragraph relating to the costs of military, naval or air operations, similar to article 10 of the Draft Treaty of Mutual Assistance.

117. *Article* 9.—Objection was raised by the British Delegation to the last paragraph of article 9, and they moved that the following be substituted:—

> "The provisions of the present Protocol in regard to arbitration and sanctions shall come into force when the scheme for the reduction of armaments, drawn up by the International Conference, has been effectively carried out in accordance with the conditions fixed by the Conference itself."

118. The French Delegation maintained strongly that the Protocol must be brought into operation before the International Conference could meet. The British Delegation offered a compromise with the suggestion that their Government might sign the Protocol, and ask Parliament to approve it before the Conference met. But preparatory arrangements for the Conference should go on concurrently. Directly agreement was reached by the Conference, ratifications could be deposited. As this failed to meet the views of the French Delegation, the British

Delegation made a final proposal whereby endeavours should be made to secure ratification and deposit of ratifications before the Conference met, provided the Protocol itself contained a provision to the effect that it should only become operative when the International Conference reached a conclusion. The French Delegation indicated their willingness in principle to accept this, but wished to consider an actual text.

119. At the next meeting the Chairman submitted the following version:—

"The undersigned Members of the League of Nations undertake to participate in an International Conference for the Reduction of Armaments which shall be convened by the Council of the League and shall meet at Geneva on Monday, the 15th June, 1925. States not Members of the League of Nations shall be invited to this Conference.

"The ratifications of the present Protocol shall be deposited with the Secretariat of the League of Nations at the latest by the 1st May, 1925. If at least fifteen Members of the League, of which four are permanently represented on the Council, have not deposited their ratification by the 1st, May 1925, the Secretary-General of the League shall cancel the invitations.

"The entry into force of the present Protocol shall be suspended until a plan for the reduction of armaments has been adopted by the Conference.

"With a view to the summoning of the latter, the Council, taking into account the undertakings contained in articles 7 and 8 of the present Protocol, will prepare a general programme for the reduction of armaments which will be placed at the disposal of the Conference.

"If, within a period of   after the adoption of the plan for the reduction of armaments, that plan has not been carried out, the Council shall make a declaration to that effect; this declaration shall under the present Protocol be null aid void.

"The grounds on which the Council may declare that the plan drawn up by the International Conference for the Reduction of Armaments has not been carried out, and that in consequence the present Protocol has been rendered null and void, shall be laid down by the Conference itself.

"A signatory State which, after the expiration of the period fixed above, fails to comply with the plan adopted by the Conference, shall not be admitted to benefit by the application of sanctions provided in the present Protocol."

120. The sub-committee adopted a proposal to add to the third paragraph "and communicated to Governments two months previously." In view of representations made by the Japanese Delegation, this was subsequently altered to "and communicated to Governments at the earliest possible date, and at the latest three months before the Conference meets."

121. The Swedish Delegation proposed that a clause should be added to the effect that "the present Protocol in no way effects obligations arising out of the Covenant." It was agreed that a clause to this effect could be either added or inserted as a separate article. The latter alternative was eventually adopted (see article 19 of the final Protocol).

122. After some discussion, the number of ratifications required in paragraph 2 of this article was finally fixed as now provided in the Protocol (see paragraph 4 of article 21 of the final Protocol).

(N. B.—The Joint Drafting Committee of the First and Third Committees made a final revise of the whole text, with a view to checking the wording of the various articles, their logical arrangement, &c. In the course of this work they removed paragraphs 3, 5, 6 and 7 of this article and incorporated them in the "ratification" article of the final Protocol—No. 21.)

123. *Article* 10.—The British Delegation proposed the suppression of the words "carrying out." It was decided to consult the First Committee on this point. (The words are omitted in the final Protocol.)

124. *Article* 11.—In view of the new text of article 9, it was decided to omit the second paragraph of this article.

125. This concluded the work of the sub-committee, and

the text of the above articles of the Protocol were submitted to the Third Committee on the 22nd September.

Dr. Benes, as chairman and *rapporteur* of the sub-committee, made a general report on the sub-committee's work, and it was then agreed to discuss the articles seriatim.

126. On *Article* 4 a debate ensued on an objection raised by the Italian Delegation to the proposal that investigations should be carried out by the organisation to be set up by the International Conference. In the first place, they disliked the idea of a permanent organ of investigation—they considered that, if an investigation were necessary, this should be carried out by a special body appointed for the purpose if and when the occasion arose. In the second place, they suggested that it would be improper to anticipate, in the Protocol, any decision that the International Conference might take. The British Delegation explained that this proposal had been inserted in their draft merely as a matter of convenience: thinking that it would be necessary for the Conference to appoint some body to ensure that the decisions of the Conference were carried out, it had seemed to them that it would be only duplicating labour for any other body to be set up by the Council to carry out these special investigations. The Italian Delegation finally suggested that the text should run, "such enquiries and investigations shall be carried out with the utmost possible despatch, and the signatory States undertake to afford every facility for carrying them out." This was accepted, with the consequential amendment to the fourth paragraph, which should now begin: "If, as a result of these enquiries and investigations, any infraction," &c. The article thus adopted became article 7 of the final Protocol.

127.—*Articles* 5 *and* 6 were adopted without modification, becoming articles 10 and 9 respectively of the final Protocol.

128. *Article* 7.—Owing to a change introduced by the First Committee in the text of article 5, in consequence of which it was no longer incumbent on the Council to make a declaration of aggression, it became necessary to alter the wording of the beginning of article 7. It was decided that this should run, "As

soon as the Council has called upon the signatory States to apply sanctions against the aggressor State, in accordance with article 6, the obligations," &c.

129.   In paragraph 2 the words "signatory States" were substituted for "Members of the League."

130.   The article as a whole came in for some criticism, mainly from the Netherlands and Scandinavian Delegations.   Certain remarks made by Dr. Benes in introducing the text to the Third Committee had caused misgivings to those Delegations, who wished to be assured that the obligations in this article did not go beyond those of article 16 of the Covenant.   They observed, as had members of the sub-committee, that the distinction drawn in the Covenant between economic and financial sanctions on the one hand, and military, naval and aerial sanctions on the other, had disappeared from the present text, and they sought a clear declaration that no fresh obligations were incurred in regard to the latter category, and that each Member of the League retained the right to decide its own course of action.   In the course of his reply Dr. Benes said, "the real application of the sanctions will always be within the province of the Government themselves, and true co-operation will always take place by direct contract between the Governments."   The Danish Delegation were not entirely satisfied, and moved to alter the second paragraph so as to make it read, "co-operate loyally and effectively in the carrying out of the obligations provided for in article 16 of the Covenant."   After consultation with the *rapporteur*, they abandoned this amendment, and declared themselves satisfied with the addition to paragraph 2 of the words, "in the degree which its geographical position and its particular situation as regards armaments allow."   As thus amended, the article was adopted, and became article 11 of the final Protocol.

131.   *Article* 7A was adopted without amendment, becoming article 12 of the final Protocol.

132.   *Article* 8.—The change, referred to above, in the text of article 5, rendered necessary an alteration in the wording of the second paragraph of this article, which it was agreed should

begin: "Furthermore, as soon as the Council has called upon the signatory States to apply sanctions, as provided," &c.

133. In the same paragraph it was decided to omit the words, "the whole or such part of," and make it read, "bring to the assistance of a particular State, which is the victim of aggression, their military, naval and air forces." With these modifications, the article was adopted, and become article 13 of the final Protocol.

134. *Article* 8A was adopted, and figures as article 15 in the final Protocol. It was suggested that an addition should be made to this article to the effect that "the Council shall alone be competent to declare that the application of sanctions shall cease and normal conditions be re-established." The Committee decided that this should be inserted as a separate article, and it appears in the final Protocol as article 14.

135. *Articles* 9 *and* 10 were adopted without modification, article 9 being embodied, as explained, in articles 17 and 21 of the final Protocol, and article 10 becoming article 20.

136. The text of an additional article (which became article 19 of the final Protocol) was also approved.

After the work of the First and Third Committees had been concluded, the reports of these Committees were submitted as a whole to the Assembly. The Assembly unanimously, with the assent of every Delegation represented at that time in the Assembly, approved the reports so presented them, and passed the resolutions, the text of which has already been published.[a]

We are,

Sir,

Your obedient servants,

ARTHUR HENDERSON.

PARMOOR.

GILBERT MURRAY.

CECIL J. B. HURST.

The Right. Hon.

    J. RAMSAY MACDONALD, M. P.,

        &c.   &c.   &c.

---

a. See Annex D, p. 210.

ANNEX F.

PROPOSALS OF THE AMERICAN GROUP.[a]

Declaration Outlawing Aggressive War.

CHAPTER I.

Outlawry of Aggressive War.

Article 1.—The High Contracting Parties solemnly declare that aggressive war is an international crime. They severally undertake not to be guilty of its commission.

Article 2.—A State engaging in war for other than purposes of defense commits the international crime describe in Article 1.

Article 3.—The Permanent Court of International Justice shall have jurisdiction, on the complaint of any signatory, to make a judgment to the effect that the international crime described in Article 1 has or has not in any given case been committed.

CHAPTER II.

Acts of Aggression.

Article 4.—The High Contracting Parties solemnly declare that acts of aggression, even when not amounting to a state of war, and preparations for such acts of aggression, are hereafter to be deemed forbidden by international law.

---

a. In their earlier form, as a Draft Treaty of Disarmament and Security, these proposals were circulated to the Members of the Council of the League in June, 1924. For the text, see World Peace Foundation Pamphlets, Vol. VII, No. 8. In the form here printed, the so-called "American Plan" was given out at Geneva on August 29, 1924, with the following note by General Bliss, Professor Shotwell and myself:

"It has been suggested that the proposals of the Draft Treaty of Disarmament and Security prepared by the American Group, of which we are members, might be drawn up in some form other than that of one Treaty.

"In order to facilitate the examination of this suggestion, we have prepared the four draft papers which follow. These papers are a Draft Declaration Outlawing Aggressive War (with a Draft Assembly Resolution regarding the same) and three Draft Resolutions of the Assembly regarding Disarmament.

"Aside from the necessary drafting changes required by the change of form, the text of these papers is substantially, and except in a few instances, literally the same as that of the Draft Treaty of Disarmament and Security above mentioned."

ARTICLE 5.—In the absence of a state of war, measures of force by land, by sea or in the air taken by one State against another and not taken for the purpose of defense against aggression or for the protection of human life shall be deemed to be acts of aggression.

General or partial mobilisation may be deemed to be preparation for an act of aggression.

Any signatory which claims that another signatory has violated any of the terms of this Declaration shall submit its case to the Permanent Court of International Justice.

A signatory refusing to accept the jurisdiction of the Court in any such case shall be deemed an aggressor within the terms of this Declaration.

Failure to accept the jurisdiction of the Court within four days after notification of submission of a claim of violation of this Declaration shall be deemed a refusal to accept the jurisdiction.

ARTICLE 6.—The Court shall also have jurisdiction on the complaint of any signatory to make a judgment to the effect that there has or has not in any given case been committed a violation of international law within the terms of Article 4.

ARTICLE 7.—The Court shall, in any case, have the power to indicate, if it considers that circumstances so require, any provisional measures which ought to be taken to reserve the respective rights of either party.

Pending the final decision, notice of the measures suggested shall forthwith be given to the parties.

CHAPTER III.

SANCTIONS.

ARTICLE 8.—In the event of any H.C.P. having been adjudged an aggressor pursuant to this Declaration, all commercial, trade, financial and property interests of the aggressor shall cease to be entitled, either in the territory of the other signatories or on the high seas, to any privileges, protection, rights or immunities accorded by either international law, national law or treaty.

Any H.C.P. may in such case take such steps towards the severance of trade, financial, commercial and personal intercourse with the aggressor and its nationals as it may deem proper and the H.C.P. may also consult together in this regard.

The period during which any such economic sanction may be continued shall be fixed at any time by the Court at the request of any signatory.

In the matter of measures of force to be taken, each signatory shall consult its own interests and obligations.

ARTICLE 9.—If any H.C.P. shall be adjudged an aggressor by the Permanent Court of International Justice, such Power shall be liable for all damage to all other H.C.P. resulting from its aggression.

CHAPTER IV.

DECREES OF THE PERMANENT COURT.

ARTICLE 10.—The H.C.P. agree to accept the judgment of the Permanent Court of International Justice as to the fulfilment of violation of the contracts of this Declaration.

Any question arising under this Declaration is *ipso facto* within the jurisdiction of the Court.

ARTICLE 11.—If a dispute arising under this Declaration shall be submitted to the Permanent Court of International Justice, it is for the Court to decide as to its jurisdiction and also whether or not its decree has been complied with.

ARTICLE 12.—The High Contracting Parties, recognising that excessive armaments constitute a menace of war, agree to participate in the Permanent Advisory Conference on Disarmament decided upon by the Fifth Assembly of the League of Nations.

ARTICLE 13.—The present Declaration shall be ratified. The ratifications shall be deposited as soon as possible with the Secretary General of the League of Nations.

Any signatory to this Declaration desiring to withdraw therefrom may give notice thereof to the Secretary-General of the League of Nations. Such notice shall take effect one year from the date of deposit thereof and only as to the signatory so withdrawing.

Notice of each ratification and of each withdrawal shall be communicated by the Secretary-General of the League of Nations to each signatory hereto.

RESOLUTION CONCERNING THE DECLARATION OUTLAWING AGGRESSIVE WAR.

1. The Assembly unanimously declares its approval of the Declaration Outlawing Aggressive War which was prepared by the Third Committee of the Assembly and submitted to the Assembly for its approval.

2. The said Declaration shall be submitted within the shortest possible time to the Members of the League of Nations for adoption in the form of a protocol duly ratified and declaring their recognition of this Declaration. It shall be the duty of the Council to submit the Declaration to the Members.

The said protocol shall likewise remain open for signature by States not Members of the League of Nations.

3. As soon as this protocol has been ratified by the majority of the Members of the League the said Declaration shall go into force.

DISARMAMENT RESOLUTION "A."

1. The Assembly, having considered the Report of the Temporary Mixed Commission and having also considered the replies of the various Governments commenting on the proposed Treaty of Mutual Assistance, reaffirms the principles set forth in Resolution 14 of the Third Assembly.

2. Furthermore, the Assembly is of the opinion that all the

Nations of the world, whether or not Members of the League of Nations, should agree

    a. to limit or reduce their armaments to the basis necessary for the maintenance of peace and national security.

    b. to study the ways and means for future reduction of armaments either as between all Nations or as between any two of them.

3. The Assembly is further of the opinion that reciprocal agreements between two or more neighbouring countries for the establishment of demilitarised zones would facilitate the security necessary to progressive disarmament.

4. In order to facilitate the reduction and limitation of armaments, the Assembly requests the Council to call a Permanent Advisory Conference upon disarmament which shall meet periodically at intervals of not less than once every three years.

Invitations to participate in this Permanent Conference shall be sent to all Nations whether Members of the League or not.

The said Conference should from time to time consider the further codifying of the principles of international law particularly in relation to acts of aggression and preparations for such acts.

In this regard the Conference should take into account matters bearing upon the security of the Powers represented and the steps taken toward disarmament.

The recommendations of the Conference shall be submitted to the Powers for their adoption, and shall also be transmitted to the Permanent Court of International Justice.

The said Conference should publish periodical reports concerning the actual conditions of the armaments of the Powers.

The said Conference should advise the Powers concerning measures to be taken to ensure the carrying out of the principles of the present Resolution and it may prepare draft treaties for the establishment of demilitarised zones and for the further promotion of disarmament and peace.

5.   The said Conference should appoint a Permanent Technical Committee.

6.   The said Conference or its Permanent Technical Committee should give advice on technical questions to the Permanent Court of International Justice at the request of said Court.

7.   The expenses of the said Conference and of its agencies should be borne by the Powers in the proportion of their respective budgets for defense.

DISARMAMENT RESOLUTION "B."

1.   Considering that by the terms of Article 8 of the Covenant of the League of Nations

> "The Members of the League undertake to interchange full and frank information as to the scale of their armaments, their military, naval and air programmes and the condition of such of their industries as are adaptable to warlike purposes,"

the Assembly, in order to facilitate the carrying out of the said engagement, requests the Council to set up a Commission charged with the duty of making the necessary official examinations and reports.

2.   The said Commission shall proceed under such regulations as the Council and the Assembly shall from time to time approve.

3.   Subject to such regulations the members of the Commission shall be entitled, when they deem it desirable, to proceed to any point within the territory of any Member of the League or to send sub-commissions or to authorize one or more of their members so to proceed on behalf of the Commission.

4.   The Members of the League will give all necessary facilities to the said Commission in the performance of its duties.

5.   All reports made by the said Commission shall be communicated to the Members of the League.

DISARMAMENT RESOLUTION "C."

The Assembly, taking account of the provisions of the Declaration Outlawing Aggressive War, is of opinion

1. Powers which have ratified the said Declaration may, subject to the following provisions, conclude, either as between two of them or as between a larger number, agreements complementary to the said Declaration, exclusively for the purpose of their mutual defense and intended solely to facilitate the carrying out of the measures prescribed in said Declaration, determining in advance the assistance which they would give to each other in the event of any act of aggression.

Such agreements may, if the H.C.P. interested so desire, be negotiated and concluded under the auspices of the Council.

2. Complementary agreements as defined in the preceding paragraph, shall, before being registered, be examined by the Council with a view to deciding whether they are in accordance with the principles of said Declaration and of the Covenant.

In particular, the Council shall consider if the cases of aggression contemplated in these agreements are of a nature to give rise to an obligation to give assistance on the part of the other H.C.P.

The Council may, if necessary, suggest changes in the texts of the agreements submitted to it.

When recognised, the agreements shall be registered in conformity with Article 16 of the Covenant. They shall be regarded as complementary to the said Declaration and shall in no way limit the general obligations of the H.C.P. nor the sanctions contemplated against an aggressor under the terms of said Declaration.

They will be open to any other H.C.P., Party to said Declaration with the consent of the Signatory States.

3. In all cases of aggression, for which provision is made in the agreement constituting a defensive group, the H. C. P. which are members of such group may undertake to put into operation

automatically the plan of assistance agreed upon between them; and in all other cases of aggression or menace or danger of aggression, directly aimed at them, they will consult each other before taking action, and will inform the Council of the measures which they are contemplating.

4. The Council, taking into account the reports and opinions of the Commission set up under Resolution B of this Assembly, shall at any time when requested, consider summarily whether (a) the armaments of any State are in excess of those fixed under the provisions of any agreement relating to reduction or limitation or armaments; or (b) the military or other preparations of any State are of such a nature as to cause apprehension of aggression or an eventual outbreak of hostilities.

5. If the Council shall upon such request be of the opinion that there is reasonable ground for thinking that a menace of aggression has arisen, the parties to the defensive agreements hereinbefore mentioned may put into immediate execution the plan of assistance which they have agreed upon.

6. If the Council shall, upon such request, not be of the opinion that a menace of aggression has arisen, a public report to the effect shall be made and in such case no State shall be under any obligation to put into execution any plan of assistance to which it is a party; but any Member of the League, believing itself to be threatened with a menace of aggression, notwithstanding the fact that the Council has not been of such opinion, may forthwith notify the Council to that effect, and such Member shall thereupon have full liberty of action in military or other preparations for defense, subject, however, to the limitations as to armament which are imposed by any treaty now in force.

ANNEX G.

THE COVENANT
OF THE LEAGUE OF NATIONS.

INCORPORATING THE PROVISIONS OF THE

PROTOCOL OF GENEVA.[a]

Two clauses added from the Preamble to the Protocol.
Recognising the solidarity of the members of the international community, and

Asserting that a war of aggression constitutes a violation of this solidarity and an international crime,

THE HIGH CONTRACTING PARTIES,

In order to promote international co-operation and to achieve international peace and security
> by the acceptance of obligations not to resort to war,
> by the prescription of open, just and honourable relations between nations,
> by the firm establishment of the understandings of international law as the actual rule of conduct among Governments, and
> by the maintenance of justice and a scrupulous respect for all treaty obligations in the dealings of organised peoples with one another,

Agree to this Covenant of the League of Nations.

Articles 1 to 11, Inclusive.
Unchanged.

Article 11a.

Article 2 of the Protocol with verbal changes.
The Members of the League agree in no case to resort to war either with one another or against a State which, if the occasion arises, accepts all the obligations of the Covenant, except in case of resistance to acts of aggression or when acting in agreement with the Council or the Assembly in accordance with the provisions of the Covenant.

---

a. This is my draft. See *supra,* p. 106. In the text it is called the "amended" Covenant.

Article 12.

Phrase agreeing not to resort to war for three months, omitted as unnecessary.

The Members of the League agree that if there should arise between them any dispute likely to lead to a rupture, they will submit the matter either to arbitration or judicial settlement or to inquiry by the Council.

In any case under this Article the award of the arbitrators or the judicial decision shall be made within a reasonable time, and the report of the Council shall be made within six months after the submission of the dispute.

Article 13.

The Members of the League agree that, whenever any dispute shall arise between them which they recognise to be suitable for submission to arbitration or judicial settlement, and which cannot be satisfactorily settled by diplomacy, they will submit the whole subject-matter to arbitration or judicial settlement.

Disputes as to the interpretation of a treaty, as to any question of international law, was to the existence of any fact which, if established, would constitute a breach of any international obligation, or as to the extent and nature of the reparation to be made for any such breach, are declared to be among those which are generally suitable for submission to arbitration or judicial settlement.

A verbal change in the third paragraph.

For the consideration of any such dispute, the court to which the case is referred shall be the Permanent Court of International Justice, or any tribunal agreed on by the parties to the dispute or stipulated in any convention existing between them.

The Members of the League agree that they will carry out in full good faith any award or decision that may be rendered, and that they will not resort to war against a Member of the League which complies therewith. In the event of any failure to carry out such an award or decision, the Council shall propose what steps should be taken to give effect thereto.

Article 14.

Article 14 of the Covenant, verbally changed.

The Permanent Court of International Justice shall be competent to hear and determine any dispute of an international character which the parties thereto submit to it. The Court may also give an advisory opinion upon any dispute or question referred to it by the Council or by the Assembly.

Article 3 of the Protocol, with some words added.

The Members of the League undertake to recognize as compulsory, *ipso facto* and without special agreement, the jurisdiction of the Permanent Court of International Justice in the cases covered by paragraph 2 of Article 36 of the Statute of the Court, but without prejudice to the right of any Member, when acceding to the special protocol provided for in the said Article and opened for signature on December 16th, 1920, to make reservations compatible with the said clause.

Accession to this special protocol, opened for signature on December 16th, 1920, must be given within a month after the coming into force hereof, and in the case of Members of the League hereafter admitted, within a month after such admission.

Article 20 of the Protocol.

Any dispute as to the interpretation of the Covenant shall be submitted to the Permanent Court of International Justice.

Article 15.

The first three paragraphs of Article 15 of the Covenant, unchanged.

If there should arise between Members of the League any dispute likely to lead to a rupture which is not submitted to arbitration or judicial settlement in accordance with Article 13, the Members of the League agree that they will submit the matter to the Council. Any party to the dispute may effect such submission by giving notice of the existence of the dispute to the Secretary-General, who will make all necessary arrangements for a full investigation and consideration thereof.

For this purpose the parties to the dispute will communicate to the Secretary-General, as promptly as possible, statements of their case with all the relevant facts and papers, and the Council may forthwith direct the publication thereof.

The Council shall endeavour to effect a settlement of the dispute, and, if such efforts are successful, a statement shall be made public giving such facts and explanations regarding the dispute and the terms of settlement thereof as the Council may deem appropriate.

Numbers 1 and 2 of Article 4 of the Protocol, very slightly changed.

If the dispute is not thus settled, the Council shall endeavour to persuade the parties to submit the dispute to judicial settlement or arbitration.

If the parties cannot agree to do so, there shall, at the request of at least one of the parties, be constituted a Committee of Arbitrators. The Committee shall so far as possible be constituted by agreement between the parties.

If within the period fixed by the Council the parties have failed to agree, in whole or in part, upon the number, the names and the powers of the arbitrators and upon the procedure, the Council shall settle the points remaining in suspense. The Council shall with the utmost possible dispatch select in consultation with the parties the arbitrators and their President from among persons who by their nationality, their personal character and their experience, appear to furnish the highest guarantees of competence and impartiality.

After the claims of the parties have been formulated, the Committee of Arbitrators, on the request of any party, shall through the medium of the Council, request an advisory opinion upon any points of law in dispute from the Permanent Court of International Justice, which in such case shall meet with the utmost possible dispatch.

3 of Article 4 of the Protocol. and the fourth, fifth and sixth paragraphs of Article 15 of the Covenant.

If none of the parties asks for arbitration, the Council shall take the dispute under consideration and, either unanimously or by a majority vote, shall make and publish a report containing a statement of the facts of the dispute and the recommendations which are deemed just and proper in regard thereto.

Any Member of the League represented on the Council may make public a statement of the facts of the dispute and of its conclusions regarding the same.

If a report by the Council is unanimously agreed to by the Members thereof, other than the Representatives of any of the parties to the dispute, the Members of the League agree to comply with the recommendations of the report.

5 of Article 4 of the Protocol, with verbal changes.
Eighth paragraph of Article 15 of the Covenant.

In no case may a solution, in accordance with a unanimous recommendation of the Council accepted by one of the parties concerned, be again called in question.

If the dispute between the parties is claimed by one of them, and is found by the Council to arise out of a matter which by international law is solely within the domestic jurisdiction of that party, the Council shall so report and shall make no recommendation as to its settlement.

Seventh paragraph of Article 15 of the Covenant, as modified by 4 of Article 4 of the Protocol.

If the Council fails to reach a report which is unanimously agreed to by the Members thereof, other than the Representatives of any of the parties to the dispute, it shall submit the dispute to arbitration.

The Council shall itself determine the composition, the powers and the procedure of the Committee of Arbitrators and, in the choice of the arbitrators, shall bear in mind the guarantees of competence and impartiality referred to above.

6 of Article 4 of the Protocol, omitting clauses now unnecessary.

The Members of the League undertake that they will carry out in full good faith any judicial sentence or arbitral award that may be rendered and that they will comply, as provided in paragraph ten hereof, with the solutions recommended by the Council. In the event of a Member of the League failing to carry out the above undertakings, the Council shall exert all its influence to secure compliance therewith. If the Council fails therein, it shall propose what steps should be taken to give effect thereto.

Paragraphs nine and ten of Article 15 of the Covenant, and Article 6 of the Protocol.

The Council may in any case under this Article refer the dispute to the Assembly. The dispute shall be so referred at the request of either party to the dispute, provided that such request be made within fourteen days after the submission of the dispute to the Council.

In any case referred to the Assembly, all the provisions of this Article and of Article 12 relating to the action and powers of the Council shall apply to the action and powers of the Assembly, provided that a report made by the Assembly, if concurred in by the Representatives of those Members of the League represented on the Council and of a majority of the other Members of the League, exclusive in each case of the Representatives of the parties to the dispute, shall have the same force as a report by the Council concurred in by all the Members thereof, other than the Representatives of any of the parties to the dispute; and provided further, that in any case referred to the Assembly, the powers of the Council under paragraphs five, six, seven and fourteen hereof, shall continue.

7 of Article 4 of the Protocol. The provisions of this article do not apply to the settlement of disputes which arise as the result of measures of war taken by one or more Members of the League in agreement with the Council or the Assembly.

Article 15a.

From Article 5 of the Protocol. If in the course of an arbitration, such as is contemplated in Article 15, one of the parties claims that the dispute, or part thereof, arises out of a matter which by international law is solely within the domestic jurisdiction of that party, the arbitrators shall on this point take the advice of the Permanent Court of International Justice through the medium of the Council. The opinion of the Court shall be binding upon the arbitrators, who, if the opinion is affirmative, shall confine themselves to so declaring in their award.

If the question is held by the Court or by the Council to be a matter solely within the domestic jurisdiction of the State, this decision shall not prevent consideration of the situation by the Council or by the Assembly under Article 11.

Article 15b.

Articles 8 and 7 of the Protocol, slightly changed. The Members of the League undertake to abstain from any act which might constitute a threat of aggression against another State.

If a Member of the League is of opinion that another State is making preparations for war, it shall have the right to bring the matter to the notice of the Council.

In the event of a dispute arising between two or more Members of the League, they agree that they will not, either before the dispute is submitted to proceedings for pacific settlement or during such proceedings, make any increase of their armaments or effectives which might modify the position established by any agreement in force, nor will they take any measure of military, naval, air, industrial or economic mobilisation, nor, in general, any action of a nature likely to extend the dispute or render it more acute.

It shall be the duty of the Council, in accordance with the provisions of Article 11, to take under consideration any complaint as to infraction of the above undertakings which is made to it by one or more of the parties to the dispute. Should the Council be of opinion that the complaint requires investigation, it shall, if it deems it expedient, arrange for inquiries and investigations in one or more of the countries concerned. Such inquiries and investigations shall be carried out with the utmost possible dispatch and the Members of the League undertake to afford every facility for carrying them out.

The sole object of measures taken by the Council as above provided is to facilitate the pacific settlement of disputes and they shall in no way prejudge the actual settlement.

If the result of such inquiries and investigations is to establish an infraction of the above undertakings, it shall be the duty of the Council to summon the Member or Members of the League guilty of the infraction to put an end thereto. Should any Member of the League in question fail to comply with such summons, the Council shall declare it to be guilty of a violation of the Covenant, and shall recommend measures to be taken with a view to end as soon as possible a situation of a nature to threaten the peace of the world.

For the purposes of this Article decisions of the Council may be taken by a two-thirds majority.

Article 15c.

Article 9 of the Protocol, slightly changed.

The existence of demilitarised zones being calculated to prevent aggression and to facilitate a definite finding of the nature provided for in Article 15d, the establishment of such zones between States mutually consenting thereto is to recommend as a means of preserving peace.

The demilitarised zones already existing under the terms of certain treaties or conventions, or which may be established in future between States mutually consenting thereto, may at the request and at the expense of one or more of the conterminous States, be placed under a temporary or permanent system of supervision to be organised by the Council.

Article 15d.

Article 10 of the Protocol, with verbal changes.

Any Member of the League which resorts to war in violation of the undertakings contained in the Covenant is an aggressor. Violation of the rules laid down for a demilitarised zone shall be held equivalent to resort to war.

In the event of hostilities having broken out, any Member of the League shall be presumed to be an aggressor (unless a decision of the Council, which must be taken unanimously, shall otherwise declare) which

(a) has refused to submit the dispute to the procedure of pacific settlement provided by the Covenant, or

(b) has refused to comply with a judicial sentence or arbitral award or with a unanimous recommendation of the Council, or

(c) has disregarded a unanimous report of the Council, a judicial sentence or an arbitral award recognizing that the dispute between it and the other belligerent arises out of a matter which by international law is solely within the domestic jurisdiction of the latter State, and has not previously submitted the question to the Council or the Assembly, in accordance with Article 11, or

(d) has violated provisional measures enjoined by the Council for the period while the proceedings are in progress as contemplated by Article 15b.

Apart from the cases dealt with in sub-heads a, b, c and d of this Article, if the Council does not at once, by unanimous vote, succeed in determining the aggressor, it shall be bound to enjoin upon the belligerents an armistice, and shall fix the terms, acting, if need be, by a two-thirds majority and shall supervise its execution.

Any belligerent which refuses to accept the armistice or violates its terms shall be deemed an aggressor.

The Council shall call upon the Members of the League to apply forthwith against the aggressor the sanctions provided by the Covenant, and any Member of the League thus called upon shall thereupon be entitled to exercise the rights of a belligerent.

Article 14 of the Protocol. The Council shall alone be competent to declare that the application of sanctions shall cease and normal conditions be reestablished.

Article 16.

This combines Article 16 of the Covenant and Article 11 of the Protocol. It omits much of the pending amendments to Article 16 of the Covenant as superfluous. Should any Member of the League resort to war, in disregard of its covenants, it shall *ipso facto* be deemed to have committed an act of war against all other Members of the League, which hereby undertake immediately to subject it to the severance of all trade or financial relations and to prohibit all intercourse, at least between persons resident within their territories and persons resident within the territory of the covenant-breaking State, and, if they deem it expedient, also between their nationals and the nationals of the covenant-breaking State, and to prevent all financial, commercial or personal intercourse at least between persons resident within the territory of that State and persons resident within the territory of every other State, and, if they deem it expedient, also between the nationals of that State and the nationals of every other State.

It shall be the duty of the Council in such case to recommend to the several Governments concerned what effective military, naval or air force the Members of the League shall severally contribute to the armed forces to be used to protect the Covenants of the League.

As soon as the Council has called upon the Members of the League to apply sanctions, as provided in Article 15d, the obligations of the Members of the League in regard to the sanctions mentioned in paragraphs one and two of this Article will immediately become operative in order that such sanctions may forthwith be employed against the aggressor.

Those obligations shall be interpreted as obliging each Member of the League to co-operate loyally and effectively in support of the Covenant, and in resistance to any act of aggression, in the degree which its geographical position and its particular situation as regards armaments allow.

The Members of the League agree, further, that they will mutually support one another in the financial and economic measures which are taken under this Article, in order to minimise the loss and inconvenience resulting from the above measures, and that they will mutually support one another in resisting any special measures aimed at one of their number by the covenant-breaking State, and that they will take the necessary steps to afford passage through their territory to the forces of any of the Members of the League which are co-operating to protect the covenants of the League.

The Members of the League jointly and severally undertake to come to the assistance of the State attacked or threatened, and to give each other mutual support by means of facilities and reciprocal exchanges as regards the provision of raw materials and supplies of every kind, openings of credits, transport and transit, and for this purpose to take all measures in their power to preserve the safety of communications by land and by sea of the attacked or threatened State.

If both parties to the dispute when so invited refuse to accept of Article 15d, the economic and financial sanctions shall be applied to both of them.

Any Member of the League which has violated any covenant of the League may be declared to be no longer a Member of the League by a vote of the Council concurred in by the Representatives of all the other Members of the League represented thereon.

Article 16a.

Article 12 of the Protocol, with slight changes.

In view of the complexity of the conditions in which the Council may be called upon to exercise the functions mentioned in Article 16 concerning economic and financial sanctions, and in order to determine more exactly the guarantees afforded to the Members of the League, the Council shall from time to time invite the economic and financial organizations of the League to consider and report as to the nature of the steps to be taken to give effect to the financial and economic sanctions and measures of co-operation contemplated in Article 16.

From time to time, the Council shall draw up through its competent organs:

1. Plans of action for the application of the economic and financial sanctions against an aggressor State;

2. Plans of economic and financial co-operation between a State attacked and the different States assisting it;

and shall communicate these plans to the Members of the League.

Article 16b.

Article 13 of the Protocol, with slight changes.

In view of the contingent military, naval and air sanctions provided for by Article 16, the Council shall be entitled to receive undertakings from Members of the League determining in advance the military, naval and air forces which they would be able to bring into action immediately to ensure the fulfilment of the obligations in regard to sanctions which result from the Covenant.

Furthermore, as soon as the Council has called upon the Members of the League to apply sanctions, as provided in Article 15d, the said Members of the League may, in accordance with any agreements which they may previously have concluded, bring to the assistance of a particular State, which is the victim of aggression, their military, naval and air forces.

The agreements mentioned in the preceding paragraph shall be registered and published by the Secretariat. They shall remain open to all Members of the League which may desire to accede thereto.

Article 17.

Article 17 of the Covenant, with verbal changes.

In the event of a dispute between a Member of the League and a State which is not a Member of the League, or between States not Members of the League, the State or States not Members of the League shall be invited to accept the obligations of membership in the League for the purposes of such dispute, upon such conditions as the Council may deem just. If such invitation is accepted, the provisions of the Covenant shall be applied with such modifications as may be deemed necessary by the Council.

Upon such invitation being given, the Council shall immediately institute an inquiry into the circumstances of the dispute and recommend such action as may seem best and most effectual in the circumstances.

If a State so invited shall refuse to accept the obligations of membership in the League for the purposes of such dispute and shall resort to war against a Member of the League, the provisions of Article 16 shall be applicable as against the State taking such action.

If both parties to the dispute when so invited refuse to accept the obligations of membership in the League for the purposes of such dispute, the Council may take such measures and make such recommendations as will prevent hostilities and will result in the settlement of the dispute.

Article 17a.

Article 15 of the Protocol, with verbal changes.

The Members of the League agree that the whole cost of any military, naval or air operations undertaken for the repression of an aggression under the terms of the Covenant, and reparation for all losses suffered by individuals, whether civilians or combatants, and for all material damage caused by the operations of both sides, shall be borne by the aggressor State up to the extreme limit of its capacity.

Nevertheless, in view of Article 10, neither the territorial integrity nor the political independence of the aggressor State shall in any case be affected as the result of the applications of the sanctions of the Covenant.

Articles 18 to 26, Inclusive.
Unchanged.